Not my time to die

Titanic and the Swedes on board

Lilly Setterdahl

NORDSTJERNAN

New York, New York

The title is derived from a letter written by survivor Anna Nysten.
Olga Lundin expressed the same sentiment.

Not my time to die
Titanic and the Swedes on board

ISBN 13: 978-0-9672176-7-3
ISBN 10: 0-9672176-8-7

Nordstjernan Förlag, New York 2012
www.nordstjernan.com
1.800.827.9333
Not My Time to Die – Titanic and the Swedes onboard

Cover Design: Daniel D Berubé-Arbello
Cover photo: Anders Peter Amsnaes / Iceberg in the famous ice fjord beside the city of Ilulissat in Greenland.
isbn-13: 978-0-9672176-7-3
isbn-10: 0-9672176-8-7
First English edition. Printed in the usa.
Nordstjernan Förlag
Swedish News, Inc.
Book Services
P.O. Box 1710
New Canaan CT 06840

Preface

There are three compelling reasons for writing this book:

1. Swedes made up the third largest ethnic group on the *Titanic* after the American and the British; yet, no book has been published about them outside of Sweden.[1]

2. Among the 705 survivors of the *Titanic* only 69 were third-class males—14 of them Swedish. Several of these young, strong, and healthy men fought for their lives in the 28-degree water.

3. The survivor stories that were published in 1912 were almost exclusively told or written down by the rich and famous or members of the crew. Later books have only touched on the experiences of the third-class survivors. This book tells the first-hand stories of some twenty Swedish survivors, one traveling in first class, two in second, and the rest in third class. (Unless otherwise noted, the *Titanic* passengers in this book traveled in third class.) Letters written by Swedish survivors on board the *Carpathia* describe how they were rescued and convey the agony they felt when discovering that loved ones and dear friends had died. Once the survivors arrived in America, they were interviewed by newspaper reporters. Most of these accounts were in the Swedish language. Now, one hundred years later, I am happy to present translations of these first impressions and to follow up with information on their lives after the *Titanic*.

---

[1] I would like to commend Claes-Göran Wetterholm of Stockholm, Sweden, for

APPENDIX:
Summary of Passengers and Survivors from the Senate subcommittee's final report

Including the crew, the *Titanic* sailed with 2,223 persons aboard, of whom 1,517 were lost and 706 were saved. It will be noted in this connection that 60 per cent of the first-class passengers were saved, 42 per cent of the second-class passengers were saved, 25 per cent of the third-class passengers were saved, and 24 per cent of the crew were saved.

	On board.			Saved.			Lost.			
	Women and children.	Men.	Total.	Women and children.	Men.	Total.	Women and children.	Men.	Total.	Per cent saved.
Passengers:										
First class	156	173	329	145	54	199	11	119	130	60
Second class	128	157	285	104	15	119	24	142	166	42
Third class	224	486	710	105	69	174	119	417	536	25
Total passengers.	508	816	1,324	354	138	492	154	678	832	....
Crew	23	876	899	20	194	214	3	682	685	24
Total.............	531	1,692	2,223	374	332	706	157	1,360	1,517	32

Table showing how the passengers were divided on saved and lost men and women and the crew. From The Titanic Disaster Hearings, p. 558. The number of saved was later adjusted to 705 persons.

My research about the survivors and victims alike began by reading both Swedish-American and American newspapers published after the sinking. I also contacted descendants of some of the survivors and obtained copies of more interviews and letters to relatives in Sweden written shortly after the rescue. This book presents the 34 survivors and the 89 victims in separate sections. I have used multiple and varied sources:

A. Swedish Church records in Sweden, mostly birth records, researched by expert Swedish genealogists. This time-consuming work has given all the Swedish passengers their correct birth places listed as parishes and counties, and the same for their parents, which makes it possible to do further research. All Swedish household records are based on the old parish and county division.[2]

B. Swedish-American newspapers on microfilm. By utilizing this source, I have been able to include a considerable amount of new information by and about the Swedish passengers.[3]

---

[2] The local Lutheran Church of the Swedish State Church kept records of all the parish inhabitants until in the 1950s. These records included censuses, births, deaths, relocations, confirmations and funerals.

[3] See *Swedish-American Newspapers.* A guide to the microfilms held by Swenson Swedish Immigration Research Center, Augustana College, Rock Island, Illinois, compiled by Lilly Setterdahl. Augustana Library Publications Number 35. Rock Island, IL 1981.

C. Swedish-American Church records on microfilm. This source was useful in tracing passengers who had previously lived in the U.S. Only a few new immigrant survivors were found to have joined churches founded by their countrymen.[4]

D. The *Calypso* Manifest listing passengers departing from Gothenburg (Göteborg) for Hull, England, April 5, 1912, with *Titanic*-bound passengers.

E. Swedish embarkation records: *Emigranten Populär*, a database on CD Rom listing passengers embarking from the Swedish ports of Göteborg and Malmö produced by the Emigrant Institute, Växjö, Sweden.

F. Microfilmed copies of *The New York Times* from April 1912 and a few other American newspapers published at the time.

G. The website www.ancestry.com and other internet sources gave me the means to search for the survivors in census schedules and other records online.

H. The website www.encyclopedia-titanica.org was helpful, especially to identify the compensation paid out to the victims' families. Contributor C. G. Wetterholm.

I. Literature. The most important books that I have read, researched, and gone back to time and again are listed in the bibliography.

As the author of this book, I do not claim to have provided error-free information; but I have done my best to truthfully translate and present the information available to me. I encourage my readers to compare the various accounts. The excerpts which I have translated are the eye-witnesses' recollections of their experience and the reporters' take on the stories. I have refrained from stating my own opinion or castigating witnesses as not being truthful. Although I have strived to remain objective, I point out discrepancies within brackets or in the footnotes.

It is not always possible to establish in which lifeboat the survivors were rescued. No records of who was in each boat were made when they arrived at the rescue ship. Some were moved from one lifeboat to another at sea. The lists were made up later.

The approximately 1,343 passengers on board the *Titanic* represented about forty-two countries from six continents. The Irish tied the Swedes with 123 passengers, but Ireland at that time belonged to Great Britain, as did Canada. Among the Scandinavian, the Swedes topped the list.[5]

---

[4] Oscar Leander Johansson (Palmquist) joined Bethesda Lutheran Church in New Haven, Conn. Olga Lundin joined Augustana Lutheran Church in Meriden, Conn. Anna Nysten Gustafson joined First Lutheran Church in Des Moines, Iowa.

[5] The Swedes include one Finland Swede, married to a Swede. For more information on the Irish, see *The Irish Aboard the Titanic* by Senan Molony, 2000. *Titanic:* For information on the Canadians, see *The Canadian Story* by Alan Hustak, 1998, which

Comparison with passengers from other Scandinavian countries:

Finland, 63 (43 victims and 20 saved). Norway, 31 (21 victims, 10 saved), Denmark, 14 (12 victims, 2 saved).

To avoid having to list the variety of spellings of names that occur in other sources, I chose to use the original Swedish spelling of personal names as the main identification. Other names used and women's married names are cross-referenced at the end of the book.

Unless otherwise noted, the translations are by the author.

---

includes immigrants heading for Canada, thus duplicating passengers that are listed under the country of origin in other sources.

Acknowledgments

First of all, I like to thank the researchers and genealogists who have searched Swedish records, mainly, Björn-Åke Petersson of Kallinge, Sweden, for his skillful research of church records to identify the passenger's birthplaces. Bo Björklund of Kista, Sweden and Judy Baouab of Chicago assisted in a few cases.

I thank the courteous staff—especially Jill Seaholm—of the Swenson Swedish Immigration Research Center at Augustana College in Rock Island, Illinois, where I researched Swedish-American newspapers on microfilm and other material.

One survivor in particular proved to be especially difficult to trace in the United States, namely, Karl Johnson of Killeberg, Skåne. Researchers on a popular, but now defunct website in Sweden came up with many useful leads. Volunteers for *Hembygdsföreningen* (the local historical society) in Killeberg, researched household records and Landsarkivet in Lund (district archives) provided me with copies of important documents.

After I had gone through thousands of Karl/Carl/Charles Johnson on www.ancestry.com and followed many false leads, I knew I needed help to research records that were not online.

I am indebted to many dedicated staff members and volunteers for answering my letters. Thank you to the "Genclass" in Cowlitz County, Washington, the genealogical societies in Washington County, Oregon, Douglas County, Oregon, Clatsop County, Oregon, the Astoria Library, Oregon, the Washington State Historical Society, the Spokane Library, Spokane, Washington, and Oregon Genealogical Society. In Junction City, Oregon, I was in touch with the Scandinavian Festival Society and the Historical Society. I will mention just a few helpful researchers by first name, Barbara, Becky, Linda, Judy, Jennifer, Elenora, Stephanie, Erin, Amanda, Linda V., and Chester.

Many thanks go to my friend and fellow *Titanic* enthusiast Rick Sundin, who has studied the *Titanic* much longer than I have and has collected a large private library about its history. He lent me many informative books and magazines about the *Titanic* and also assisted with the reading of parts of my manuscript.

Professor Ulf Beijbom of Växjö, Sweden, lent his expertise in reading the "Introduction." Dean Easterlund of Davenport, Iowa, was immensely helpful in editing my entire manuscript. Margaretha and Brian Magnusson, and my writing colleague Dr. Trisha Nelson assisted with proofreading. I take responsibility for any remaining errors that I caused while making the last revisions.

Thanks to Dick Stahl for the poem, "The 2012 Anniversary."

Robert Bracken of the Titanic International Society shared some of his research about the Swedes with me. He also endorsed my book, as did Mr. Edward Kamuda of the Titanic Historical Society. Thanks to both.

Most importantly, I thank Ulf Mårtensson of *Nordstjernan* for publishing this book and for his support and encouragement.

Illustrations:

Günter Bäbler, Switzerland, Mike Pearson, Gerald Wennerstrom, the Swedish Emigrant Institute, Ulf Mårtensson, Robert Bracken, Andrew Aldridge of Henry Aldridge & Sons, the author's photo collection, and public sources with no known restrictions.

Table of Contents

PREFACE....................V

ACKNOWLEDGMENTS....................IX

INTRODUCTION....................17

THE DEPARTURE FROM SWEDEN....................18
WHO WERE THE SWEDES ON THE TITANIC?....................19
SWEDEN IN 1912....................21
WHY DID THEY LEAVE?....................23
MAPS OF SWEDEN SHOWING COUNTIES AND PROVINCES....................25

RMS TITANIC—A BRIEF HISTORY....................27

THE WHITE STAR LINE BUILDS THE TITANIC....................27
CAPTAIN SMITH....................32
THE MOST PROMINENT PASSENGERS....................35
THE CARGO....................36
THE ILL-FATED VOYAGE....................37
THE COLLISION WITH THE ICEBERG....................41
THE SEARCH FOR BODIES....................49
THE INQUIRES....................52
THE DISCOVERY OF THE WRECK....................55
TITANIC'S TIME LINE....................57
TITANIC MEMORIAL IN WASHINGTON, DC....................58

TITANIC NEWS IN THE AMERICAN PRESS....................59

THE NEW YORK AMERICAN, NEW YORK....................59
THE NEW YORK TIMES, NEW YORK....................61
CHICAGO DAILY NEWS, CHICAGO, ILLINOIS....................64

The Chicago Daily Tribune, Chicago, Illinois 66
Moline Daily Dispatch, Moline, Illinois 69
Olympia Daily Recorder, Olympia, Washington 70
Spokane Daily Chronicle, Washington 73

Titanic News in the Swedish Press 77

Dagens Nyheter, Stockholm 77
Kristianstadbladet, Kristianstad 78
Kalmar, published in Kalmar 81

Titanic News in the Swedish-American Press 83

Nordstjernan, New York 83
Hemlandet, Chicago and Galesburg 91
Svenska Amerikanaren, Chicago, Illinois 92
Svenska Tribunen Nyheter, Chicago, Illinois 96
Moline Tribun, Moline, Illinois 97
Iowa Posten, Des Moines, Iowa 99
Kvinnan och Hemmet, Cedar Rapids, Iowa 100
Omaha-Posten, Omaha, Nebraska 100

The Swedish Survivors 101

"We can go back to bed" 104
"Why couldn't we be together until the end?" 106
The 3-year-old boy was in his mother's arms 111
"My clothes had gotten very dirty and wet" 111
"For a moment I felt a cold shiver up my back" 114
"Life no longer has any value for me" 118
New Yorker crossed the Atlantic many times 121
Newly-wed lost her husband 123
Immigrant recruiter waded in water up to his armpits 125
"We were in the lifeboat for six hours" 131
"We clung to that door for hours" 134
Was he murdered or not? 140
Skipper's son was shipwrecked twice 142
Her husband fainted when he heard the good news 144
His mother screamed, "Save my boy." 146
The infant girl had no memory of the Titanic 147
Railroad man repelled on a rope to the water below 147
"The ship has run aground" 153

"I GAVE MY MONEY AND PAPERS TO CAPTAIN HOLM" 155
COUNT POSSE'S DAUGHTER TRAVELED IN FIRST CLASS 156
"OH, HOW I MOURN NILS AND THE OTHERS" 156
"THEY LET ME ROW A WHILE AND THAT WAS GOOD" 160
ENGAGED WOMAN LOST HER FIANCÉ 163
JOLIET-BOUND WOMAN SAW TWO LIFEBOATS CAPSIZE 165
"NOT MY TIME TO DIE" 166
CHICAGO-BOUND WOMAN LOOKED AT THE BRIGHT STARS 170
MARRIED MAN FOUGHT FOR HIS LIFE AND SURVIVED 172
"EVERYTHING WAS MAGNIFICENT ON BOARD" 183
FOUR-YEAR-OLD GIRL GREW UP IN SWEDEN 184
INFANT GIRL HAD NO MEMORY OF THE TITANIC 184
BOY TURNED AWAY FROM LIFEBOATS TWICE 185
"THE LIFEBOATS WERE ALL GONE" 191
SEAMAN ADVANCED TO CAPTAIN IN WW II 195
CONTROVERSIAL EDITOR WROTE ABOUT THE DISASTER 197

THE SWEDISH VICTIMS 207

THE CARPENTER'S WATCH HAD STOPPED AT 2:34 A.M. 210
MARRIED WOMAN ON HER WAY HOME TO MINNESOTA 211
THEY DECIDED TO DIE TOGETHER 212
FARM WIFE DREAMED OF CANADA 214
ELEVEN-YEAR-OLD GIRL LOST TO THE SEA 215
NINE-YEAR-OLD GIRL LOST AT SEA 215
SIX-YEAR-OLD GIRL LOST TO THE SEA 215
FOUR-YEAR-OLD BOY LOST TO THE SEA 215
TWO-YEAR OLD GIRL LOST TO THE SEA 216
TWO MEN WAITED FOR HER IN MICHIGAN 216
HARTFORD SWEDE WAS ON HIS WAY HOME 217
BLACKSMITH AND HIS FRIENDS WERE LIKE SIBLINGS 217
RELATIVE IN JOLIET AWAITED THE YOUNG MAN 218
BODY OF HUSBAND AND FATHER FOUND 219
THIRTEEN-YEAR-OLD BOY LOST TO THE SEA 222
NINE-YEAR-OLD BOY LOST TO THE SEA 222
FIVE-YEAR-OLD BOY LOST TO THE SEA 222
THE FRIENDS STOOD TOGETHER AND PRAYED 222
SAWMILL WORKER WISHED TO SETTLE IN MOLINE, ILLINOIS 223
MAN FROM STOCKHOLM WAS PROMISED WORK IN NEW YORK 224
THE YOUNG MISS FROZE WITH FEAR ON THE BOAT DECK 225
BUTLER GOING BACK TO WORCESTER 226
TOURIST MIGHT HAVE STAYED IN THE U.S. 227
MARRIED MAN LEFT HIS FAMILY IN SWEDEN 228

Coachman bought a Danish waistcoat 229
Sea Captain traveled in first class 229
Chicago-bound woman struggled in the water 230
Immigrant recruiter buried in Stanton, Iowa 231
Wife and mother lost at sea 233
Four-month-old boy was the youngest in the group 234
Swedish American kissed his wife goodbye 234
Farmer's son headed for Joliet, Illinois 235
16-year old was on his way to Arizona 235
South Dakota Swede brought his elderly father 236
Man from Göteborg traveled as tourist 238
18-year old borrowed money for his ticket 239
Widow's son headed for South Dakota 240
Maid from Stockholm buried in Halifax 240
Sea captain hoped to earn good money in New York 241
Smålänning's body buried at sea 242
Future farmer buried in Halifax 242
Stucco worker's fiancée safe at home 243
Give my regards to Father and Mother" 244
Minnesota Swede carried his money in his socks 246
Farmer bought his ticket in Copenhagen 247
Inventor planned to register his patents in the U.S. 247
Single man planned to settle in Massachusetts 249
Los Angeles dressmaker had visited Gotland 249
Young man emigrated with his infant niece 250
The infant girl was 18-months old 251
Engineer buried in Halifax 251
Locksmith on his way to Stamford 252
Hartford-bound man had saved for years for his ticket 253
Montana Swede heading for home 254
New York woman's brother refused to come with her 254
Spinster went to her cabin and locked the door 256
Business man wished to save his estate from creditors 257
Emigrant's hair turned gray in a matter of minutes 258
Newly-wed's ring found in a lifeboat 260
Spokane Swede returned to his cabin to die 261
Educated young man was on his way to Chicago 262
Farmer's son bid sad farewells 263
Man from Skåne wished to settle in St. Paul 264
Uncle in Peoria paid for the farm inspector's ticket 265
Engaged woman perished after entering a lifeboat 265
Blacksmith bought his ticket in Copenhagen 266
16-year old wished to support his parents 266
Mother of four identified and buried in Halifax 267

EIGHT-YEAR-OLD GIRL LOST TO THE SEA 270
SIX-YEAR-OLD BOY LOST TO THE SEA 270
THREE-YEAR-OLD GIRL LOST TO THE SEA 270
TWO-YEAR-OLD BOY LOST TO THE SEA 270
YOUNG WOMAN HEADED FOR MINING TOWN 271
EMIGRANT TRAVELED WITH HIS MINNESOTA SISTER 271
HORTICULTURE STUDENT ON HIS WAY TO RED WING 272
MINING ENGINEER'S CAREER ENDED ABRUPTLY 273
MACHINIST AND HIS ENTIRE FAMILY LOST TO THE SEA 274
MOTHER OF FOUR LOST TO THE SEA 275
ELEVEN-YEAR-OLD BOY LOST TO THE SEA 276
NINE-YEAR-OLD GIRL LOST TO THE SEA 276
FIVE-YEAR-OLD-BOY LOST TO THE SEA 276
TWO-YEAR-OLD GIRL LOST TO THE SEA 276
HUSBAND WAITED FOR HER IN INDIANA HARBOR 277
TWO-YEAR-OLD GIRL LOST TO THE SEA 278
ELDERLY MAN DID NOT WANT TO GO TO AMERICA 278
A SONG WAS WRITTEN ABOUT THIS EMIGRANT 279
GRAVE IN THE ATLANTIC REPLACED LIFE IN ST. PAUL 280
14-YEAR-OLD GIRL'S FATHER LIVED IN AMERICA 280
SAILOR HAD HIS HOME ON LONG ISLAND 281

A FEW CAVEATS 283

THE 2012 ANNIVERSARY 285

BBLIOGRAPHY 287

ABOUT THE AUTHOR 291

CROSS REFERENCES 292

NAME INDEX FOR SWEDISH PASSENGERS 293

Introduction

While *Titanic's* sister ship, the near identical *Olympic,* sailed the seas in war and peace for some 24 years, the slightly larger *Titanic* sank on its maiden voyage. The tragic, sensational news event was memorialized at the 50th anniversary of the sinking, and again after the wreck was located in 1985. One hundred years after the sinking, we still remember.

From the time of the launching of the *Titanic* on May 31, 1911, to its foundering on April 15, 1912, the life of the ship spanned less than a year. Yet, more people recall the name of the *Titanic* than that of the *Olympic.* What is it that makes the *Titanic* so memorable? Simply stated, it was the largest, supposedly safest, most costly, and most luxurious ship built at the time, and despite its much heralded watertight compartments, it was no match for an object formed by nature, an iceberg.

A century later, we still ponder why it sank so fast and why so many people lost their lives. The passengers and crew, whether saved or killed, were all victims of the disaster. The survivors struggled to overcome the loss of loved ones, their own near-death experience, and the memory of the horrible screams coming from the people still on board when the ship sank and in the water.

There was no therapy to help the survivors cope. Many of the passengers were emigrants, who had saved for years for a future in a new land. The survivors lost everything they owned, and struggled to start anew with two empty hands.

Although there was financial help available for the dependents of the victims, the survivors received no retribution, only limited travel funds. Charities in New York housed them for a few days and supplied them with small amounts of cash and odd items of clothing.

Those who had fought for their lives in the ice-cold water were physically weakened and suffered from frostbite. American Colonel Archibald Gracie, a first-class passenger, lived eight months after the sinking, or as long as it took him to write a book about the tragedy. When the shouts, "Women and children first to the lifeboats," were heard, for the men it meant, "Every man for himself," except crewmen needed to man the lifeboats. There were not enough boats for everyone.

The passengers and crew on board the *Titanic* will never be forgotten. Researchers are still trying to properly identify many of them. *Titanic* enthusiasts all over the world post comments every day on various websites. Despite the passage of time, new material continues to surface.

The departure from Sweden

On April 5, 1912, a group of about 58 *Titanic*-bound Swedes boarded the Wilson Line steamer, *Calypso,* in Gothenburg (Göteborg), Sweden's largest western port. The *Calypso* crossed the often stormy North Sea and disembarked her passengers at Hull, England. From Hull, they traveled by train to Southampton. The *Calypso* passengers arrived in Southampton four days before the *Titanic* sailed on April 10th and were put up at a second-rate hotel.[6]

They came as families, large and small, as groups of neighbors and friends, some with one friend only, and some alone. Most had arrived by train to Göteborg days before. They waited in low-priced hotels built for passenger convenience many years ago along the streets near the harbor. Some came from Stockholm on the opposite coast, or from points north, but most came from the emigration belt that stretched from the west coast to the east coast.

The cost of lodging was included in the contract the passengers purchased from the White Star Line agent. The contract usually included their travels to their final destination in the United States or Canada.[7]

The emigrants on board the *Calypso* could not have imagined what awaited them, although one Swede harbored premonitions of something bad happening. They had heard of this new ship, the *Titanic*, described as a luxury hotel. Some were leery of the fact that it had never crossed the Atlantic, but they placed their faith in the slogan that it was "practically unsinkable."

---

[6] See Svensson, Johan Cervin, who changed his name to John C. Johnson.

[7] The *Calypso* passenger list was researched at the Swenson Swedish Immigration Research Center, Augustana College, Rock Island, Ill., courtesy of Jill Seaholm. The source is *Poliskammarens* (the Police Department's) in Göteborg microfilmed registers that have been computerized by SVAR, Ramsele, Sweden. The cost for a third-class ticket was about $40.00. A second-class ticket cost about $60.00.

They worried about not knowing English and thumbed through small booklets that had Swedish words and phrases translated to English. They had heard of Ellis Island from other emigrants and were afraid they would be sick at arrival and retained on the island, or even worse, be sent back home. America wanted healthy, stalwart settlers who could pull their own weight and contribute to the progress of the nation. To make certain that they would not be a burden to the American government, new arrivals had to provide the name of a sponsor, usually a relative or friend, who would receive them once they were at their destination and be responsible for them.

The Calypso leaving the harbor in Göteborg

Farewell to the homeland and on toward the land of dreams.

About 11 Swedes departed from the southern port of Malmö and at least two from the nearby port of Helsingborg. About 40 departed Scandinavia from Denmark. Two first-class-male passengers and one third-class male had not traveled from Sweden at all: They were Swedish-born officers on American ships, who were repatriated from England to the United States. One Swedish first-class woman boarded the *Titanic* in Cherbourg, France.

Who were the Swedes on the Titanic?

Of the 123 Swedes on board, men were in the majority, but an equal number of men and women were saved. Of the 66 adult men, 14 were saved (21 percent). Of the 32 adult women, 14 were saved (44 percent).

Of the 25 children, six were saved (24 percent). Of the 89 Swedish victims, 52 were men, 18 women, and 19 children.

About 32 of the Swedes were Swedish-Americans, one Swedish-Canadian, and one Finland-Swede (residing in the U.S and married to a Swede); 16 were born in the U.S to Swedish parents and part of family groups on the *Titanic*. (14 children and two adults); and the rest were new emigrants. At least three of the Swedish-Americans had moved back to Sweden, but still listed their residence as America when they departed.[8]

The four Swedes sailing in first class were Mauritz Hokan Björnström-Steffanson, a wealthy Swedish-American businessman (survived); Frans Olof Carlson, sea captain (perished); Erik Gustaf (Edward) Lindeberg-Lind, estate owner in Sweden and a former officer in the U.S. Navy (perished); and Sigrid Lindstrom, nee Posse, tourist (survived).

The seven Swedes sailing in second class were Dagmar Bryhl [Lustig], tourist (survived); her brother Kurt Bryhl [Lustig], tourist (perished); Ingvar Enander, tourist (perished); Johan Henrik Kvillner, engineer on a government scholarship (perished); Karolina Byström, Swedish-American, living in New York (survived); Ernst Adolf Sjöstedt, Swedish-Canadian engineer (perished); Olga Lundin, Swedish-American, moved from third-class (survived).

Among the Swedes in third class about 25 were children, 17 laborers, 15 domestics, 12 homemakers, 5 farmer's sons, 4 farmers, 4 sailors, 3 carpenters, 3 factory workers, 2 immigrant recruiters, 2 blacksmiths, and one each of the following occupations: sawmill worker, painter, coachman, farm worker, merchant, machinist, manager, railroad brakeman, inventor, locksmith, cook, missionary, store clerk, chauffeur, gardener, miner, retired farmer, and farm inspector.[9]

Among the married people we find the Asplund family of seven (the mother and two children survived while the father and three sons perished), the Andersson family of seven (all perished); the Skoog family of six (all perished), Mrs. Pålsson with four children (all perished), and the Danbom couple with one child (perished); Mrs. Alice Johnson with two children (survived); Mrs. Agnes Sandström with two children (survived).

Young single individuals dominated the emigration from Sweden at the time, and the same was true for the Swedish passengers on the *Titanic*. Of the adult survivors, 9 were married and 19 single. The difference was much greater among those who perished. While 21 were married, 118 were single, and one widowed.

---

[8] Approximate numbers.
[9] Calculations with reservation for error.

Sweden in 1912

Before World War I, more than half of all Swedes lived in the countryside. Agriculture was important, but Sweden's most vital natural resources came from iron ore, vast forests, and hydro-electrical power. The nation's growing network of railroads and canals greatly aided the transportation of steel and wood products, especially pulp, within the country and for export, as did shipping on the many lakes and rivers, the Baltic Sea to the east, and the North Sea to the west. Manufacturing lagged behind the industrialized countries of Europe, especially Great Britain. Well-paid jobs were scarce. Although many Swedish inventors had laid the groundwork for an industrial expansion, it was not until the 1920s when Swedish industry made a breakthrough thanks to the innovative work of Alfred Nobel (dynamite), Gustaf de Laval (cream separator), Gustaf Dahlén (Aga automatic light-house), Sven Wingquist, ball bearings), L. M. Ericsson (telephones), Jonas Wenstrom (three-phase system for alternating current), and Baltzar von Platen (absorption method refrigeration).

The country had not been at war for nearly one hundred years. (The last time was in the Napoleonic Wars that ended in 1814.) During the subsequent peace time, the invention of vaccines, and a better diet resulted in a growing population, which led to a higher emigration.

By 1912, about one million Swedes lived in America, while 5.5 million remained in Sweden. During the previous year, 1911, close to 20,000 Swedes had left Sweden, the majority of them to settle in the United States.

The Swedes had established a tradition of sailing to America in search better opportunities. The first wave of emigration occurred in the late 1860s and early 1870s, the second and largest wave in the 1880s and 1890s, the third in the early 1900s, and the last peak in the 1920s. During the period, 1891-1900, an average of about eight individuals per 1,000 Swedes emigrated annually. The number was higher for areas with high emigration in the south and lower in the north. About 20 percent of the Swedish emigrants returned to Sweden. Nearly 4,500 returned in 1911 alone. The emigration from Sweden was but a small part of the 31 million Europeans who settled in North America.

When the Swedish central labor union, L.O., was organized in 1898, the socialist movement with impulses from Denmark gained momentum. The workers' central organization could negotiate with the employers' central union, and this worked quite well until a recession occurred in 1908-1909. The unionized workers were disappointed when the labor union became less effective after a general strike in 1909. L.O. lost half of its members and was still struggling to make a comeback in 1914.

A few of the Swedish men on the *Titanic* were socialists. One of them had expressed his extremely critical view of the Swedish king and the church.

In 1901, a new law extended the obligatory military training for young men from 90 to 240 days. This required all able men from the age of 21 to 33 to be enrolled as active recruits. During that time, they could not emigrate legally without special permission. At age 33, men transferred to the reserve.[10]

The mandatory military service resulted in a demand for equal voting rights, *e.g.*, one gun equals one vote. Participation in local elections was still limited to those above certain income levels and to property owners.[11]

The 1911 election in Sweden established a parliamentary government, resulting in a conservative majority in the first chamber and a liberal majority in the second.[12] The leader of the liberal party (*Liberala Samlingspartiet*), Karl Staaff, formed the government.

Staaff had campaigned for disarmament. In this regard, he was opposed by the monarch, King Gustav V (1907-1950), and the conservatives, who warned of the risk of war and the need to strengthen the country's defense.

Although the farmers favored a strong defense, they were dissatisfied by their disproportioned tax burden. Many farmers' sons were at a disadvantage because of inheritance traditions favoring the eldest son. The younger brothers would not inherit the family farm and had to fend for themselves. Their opportunities were often limited to working for other farmers. By 1912, their chances of owning farms in America had also diminished. Instead they looked forward to higher wages in American factories. The goal for some of these emigrants was to save enough money to enable them to return to Sweden and buy a farm.

The work opportunities for single Swedish women, not living with their parents, were largely limited to serving as maids in the cities or on the farms. Young women knew that they could find less labor-intensive work in American homes, and usually worked as domestics until they married.

According to a long-standing tradition, every newborn Swedish child automatically became a member of the Swedish Lutheran Church. America, on the other hand, offered freedom of religion and equality.

Letters from Swedish Americans often emphasized the concept of freedom with comments like, "You don't have to bow to anyone, whether president or priest, and you can use the familiar pronoun *du* (you) when you talk to them." Titles were still important in Sweden and elsewhere in Europe, while in the U.S., all men were referred to as Mr. and women as Mrs., Miss or Madam.

---

[10] Ann-Sofie Kälvemark, "Flykten från exercisen, värnplikten som utvandringsorsak" in *Utvandring/Den Svenska emigrationen till Amerika i historiskt perspektive,* Uppsala University, Uppsala, Sweden, 1973, pp 133-150.

[11] A law in 1918 gave all men and women equal rights to vote.

[12] *Liberala Samlingspartiet*, a coalition of broadminded parties.

Why did they leave?

The lack of opportunities for the growing population, dissatisfaction with the prevailing conditions in Sweden, and a wish to escape the mandatory military service for men were the primary reasons for the emigration at the time. One of the *Titanic* Swedes, documented in these pages, was in danger of losing his large estate (*herrgård*) and hoped to make enough money in the United States to prevent this from happening.

Many young Swedish men emigrated rather than serving 240 days in the military or reporting for repetition training. An emigration certificate from the State Lutheran Church was required to leave the country legally, but many men of military age circumvented the law by escaping to Denmark. One Swedish study concludes that a significant number of the emigrants departing from Copenhagen in the years 1901-1904 were Swedish recruits.[13]

The strengthening of Sweden's defense, fear of the Russians, armament in Germany, and the seemingly inevitable extension of the obligatory military service became added incentives for young men to emigrate.[14]

In my study of the Swedish male passengers on the *Titanic*, I found that 77 percent (aged 21-32), were not recorded in the Swedish embarkation records. This is strong evidence that they had sailed to Copenhagen, where they could buy a new waistcoat with their ticket and necessary papers to enter the United States tucked in one of the pockets.[15]

The draft dodgers who survived the *Titanic* later admitted that they had taken advantage of the Danish assistance and even described their traveling route. One of the victims had bought his ticket in England.[16]

Another reason for buying the America ticket in Copenhagen could have been that it was cheaper. Younger men, aged 18-20, as well as women, some of whom traveled with the draft-dodgers, also bought their tickets in Copenhagen.

Once the young men were in America, and the United States had declared war on the Axis countries in 1917, they were required to register for

---

[13] *Ibid.*, p. 150. Kälvemark used only statistics for her study and did not research any specific emigrant groups. Although she is vague in her conclusion, she states that much speaks for that a large part of the (Swedish) emigration, 1901-1904, consisted of men at the age of conscription, or younger.

[14] The extension of the service was not implemented until war broke out in Europe in 1914 (WWI).

[15] I arrived at these figures by excluding all men in this age group that were Swedish Americans or tourists, and one man on a government scholarship.

[16] Those who bought their tickets in Copenhagen were from Southern Sweden, which made it natural for them to leave from Denmark. There are no records online for those who departed from Copenhagen in 1912, and there is a small margin for error in the embarkation records for Malmö, located across the strait. More research would be required to establish a trend of draft-dodging.

the U.S. draft while Sweden stayed out of the conflict. Many Swedish men ended up serving in the United States military forces, including a few who had survived the sinking of the *Titanic.*[17]

Like other Swedish emigrants, most of the Swedes on the *Titanic* had relatives in the United States who might have helped them with pre-paid tickets. The relatives also assisted the new arrivals in finding employment. One draw-back to the emigration was that the strong family bonds were broken. When the emigrants left, they knew that they may never see their parents again, although it was not unusual that they sent money back home to help with their support. As we will see in the profiles, this was what many parents expected.

I am proud to make my contribution to the 100th Anniversary of the sinking of the *Titanic* with the release of this volume, detailing new findings about the 123 Swedish passengers on board the doomed ship.

More information about how ordinary Swedes fared in America, can be found in my books, *Swedes in Moline, Illinois, 1847-2002* (published in 2003), and *Chicago Swedes: They spoke from the heart* (published in 2010), both available on www.amazon.com as long as the supply lasts.

---

[17] Gunnar Tenglin, Einar Karlsson, John Asplund, and Carl Olof Johnson. There may have been others.

Maps of Sweden showing counties and provinces

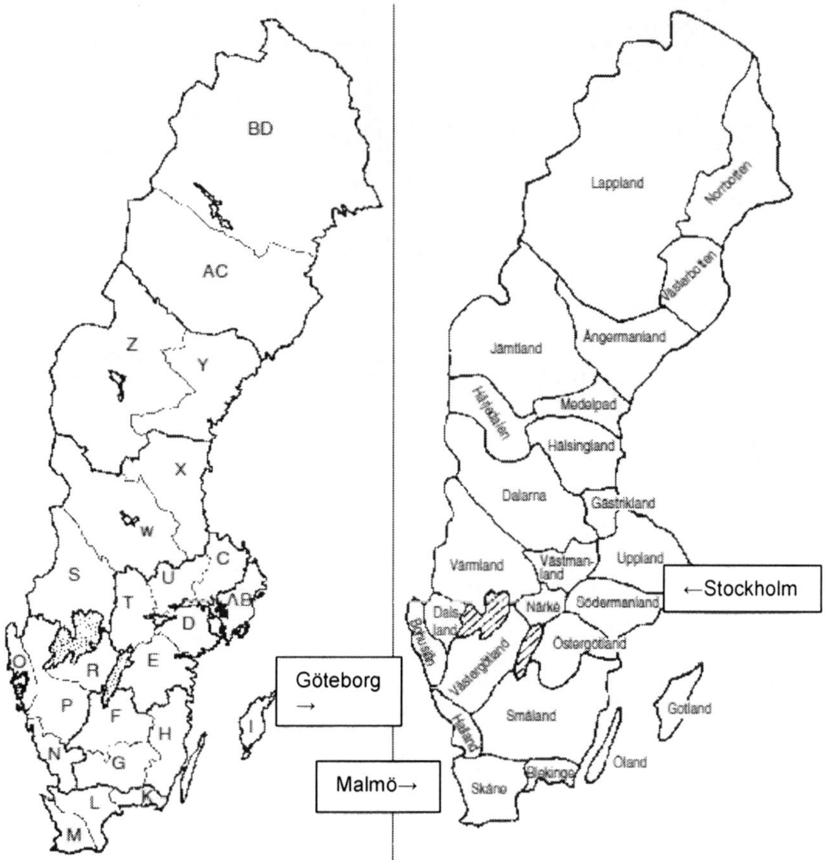

The counties (*län*) as they were before 1991. The provinces (*landskap*).

Maps, courtesy Elisabet Thorsell, editor of Swedish American Genealogist, Augustana College, Rock Island, Ill. Modified by marking the location of the three largest cities.

Explanation of codes on the previous page:[18]

M) Malmöhus län
(L) Kristianstad's län
(K) Blekinge län
(N) Halland's län
(G) Kronoberg's län
(F) Jönköping's län
(H) Kalmar län, including Öland
(I) Gotland's län
(O) Göteborg's och Bohus län
(E) Östergötland's län
(R) Skaraborg's län
(P) Älvsborg's län
(D) Södermanland's län
(S) Värmland's län
(T) Örebro län
(U) Västmanland's län
(AC) Stockholm's län
(W) Kopparberg's län
(X) Gävleborg's län
(Z) Jämtland's län
(Y) Västernorrland's län
(AC) Västerbotten's län
(BD) Norrbotten's län

[18] Malmöhus län is the county closest to Copenhagen. Counties with no representation in this group were Älvsborg's län, Jämtland's län, and Norrbotten län. Skaraborg's län and Östergötland län had the highest representation. In 1991, some of the counties were combined, as for instance, Malmöhus and Kristianstad län became Skåne län. The three counties of Älvsborg's län, Skaraborg's län, and Göteborg and Bohus län became Västra Götaland län. The old church records are based on the pre-1991 counties.

RMS Titanic—a brief history

The White Star Line builds the Titanic

In 1907, the White Star Line decided to build three large liners. Each ship would be 50 percent larger than the Cunard Line's 30,000 ton *Lusitania.*[19] The ships were to be so huge that no ship yard had a dry dock large enough to accommodate them. The goal was to make the crossing from England to New York in one week's time, thereby improving the mail service between Europe and America. To attract wealthy vacationing travelers, the ships would be the most luxurious ships ever built.

Ever since the White Star Line was founded in 1869 it had competed with the Cunard Line for the lucrative Atlantic immigrant traffic. In the 1890s, when the Germans entered the race, the competition became even greater. The shipbuilding firm of Harland and Wolff in Belfast, Ireland, began converting three berths to two and construct a 220-foot-high gantry to make room for the giant ships. It also became necessary to build a larger pier in New York. In December of 1908, the construction of the first ship, the *Olympic*, began, and in March of 1909, the ship yard laid the first keel plate for the *Titanic*. In 1914, a third ship, the *Britannic*, was launched. The designer of the *Olympic* and the *Titanic* was Thomas Andrews, managing director of Harland and Wolff.[20]

---

[19] Carrying passengers from New York to Liverpool, the *Lusitania* was torpedoed on April 7, 1915 outside Queenstown, Ireland, with a loss of 1,200 people. It sank in 18 minutes. The fact that it had enough life boats for all on board did not help when the ship listed so severely that few boats could be launched during the short time it remained afloat. The *Mauretania* in service until 1935 was a troop carrier during WWI in the Gallipoli campaign. For 22 years she was the fastest liner in the world. On her maiden voyage in 1907, she became enveloped in fog, but survived. Many Swedish immigrants recalled sailing on the *Mauretania*. Toward the end of her life, she served as a cruise ship.

[20] *Titanic: An Illustrated History*. Text by Don Lynch- Paintings by Ken Marschall. Introduction by Robert D. Ballard. A Hyperion/Madison Press Book, New York, NY 1992, pp. 16-25. The managing director for the British White Star Line was J. Bruce Ismay, and its principal owner was J. Pierpoint Morgan, a New York financier. Andrews and Ismay sailed on the *Titanic*'s maiden voyage. Ismay entered a lifeboat and survived while Andrews went down with the ship. The *Britannic* was launched Jan. 16, 1914. Having become a hospital ship during WWI she was sunk (apparently torpedoed) Nov. 21, 1916 near Kea Island in the Mediterranean Sea. Thirty people on the *Britanic* died, all aboard a lifeboat drawn into the propellers. The *Olympic* had

The newly launched Titanic

An estimated one-hundred-thousand spectators witnessed the launching of the *Titanic* in Belfast May 31, 1911, one of them being the factual owner J. P. Morgan of New York.[21] About 22,000 tons of lubrication greased the slipway as the *Titanic* slid into the water in 62 seconds. The White Star Line and Harland and Wolff followed their practice of not christening the *Titanic*. For the next 10 months, the ship was fitted with four funnels, machinery, and interiors. It then became necessary to place it in dry dock to attach the three anchors. The center anchor weighed 15.5 ton and required twenty draft horses to pull it to the dock. Equipped with sixteen watertight compartments, extending upward to F deck, the *Titanic* was deemed "practically unsinkable" although the White Star Line never made this claim.

---

a long life in both commercial and war service. She survived four submarine attacks. In 1934, the White Star Line merged with the Cunard Line. The Old Reliable made her final voyage in 1935 before being scrapped.

[21] American financier J. Pierpont Morgan had formed the consortium International Mercantile Marine (IMM) to which he added the White Star Line in 1902. Bruce Ismay became the chairman and managing director of IMM while he remained as the director of the White Star Line.

Twenty draft horses were needed to pull the 15.5 ton center anchor.

Titanic loading cargo

Second-class lounge, where Dagmar Bryhl, Kurt Bryhl, Ingvar Enander, Karolina Byström, and Johan Kvillner may have socialized. Veranda Café below.

First-class grand staircase

Bulkhead

It cost 7.5 million dollars to build the 109-foot high and 882-foot long ship. Her gross tonnage was 46,328 metric tons. Being designed for a maximum speed of about 23 to 24 knots, the *Titanic* carried twenty lifeboats, which exceeded the British regulation, but the lifeboats could only hold a total of 1,178 people. The total capacity of the ship was 3,547 passengers and crew, although it carried much less, or about 2,228 people.[22]

The vessel was insured for five million dollars. Underwriters covered the remainder.[23]

Had the *Titanic* survived its maiden voyage, it would not have remained the world's largest passenger liner for long. Already on May 23, 1912 the Hamburg America Line launched its *Imperator*, which was 919 feet long and had a displacement weight of 70,000 tons. It had added search lights, a fourth class, and could carry 4,000 passengers and a crew of 1,000. It was equipped with 12 transverse bulkheads to a height of 50 feet, well above the waterline. The ship was surrendered to the United States in 1919, and in 1921, it was purchased by the Cunard Line and renamed *Berengaria*.

Captain Smith

The *Titanic* was commanded by Edward J. Smith, a well-liked captain with the White Star Line for more than twenty-five years. He was a married man and father.

---

[22] The precise number of people on board will never be known. When a later law required that there be enough lifeboats on the ships to accommodate all on board, the ship owners protested it would make the vessel so top heavy that it would topple over. They also argued that in case of an emergency there would never be enough time to load and launch all the lifeboats. This could theoretically have been true for the *Titanic* and the *Lusitania*. When the inland cruiser *Eastland* overturned and sank in the Chicago River at Chicago July 24, 1915, drowning more than 800 people, it was partly blamed on the top heaviness caused by the 37 life rafts on board, each weighing 1,100 pounds. Other factors also played a role. The *Eastland* rolled over on her side so quickly that not one of the life rafts was launched. Chris Kohl, *Titanic: The Great Lakes Connection*, Seawolf Communications, Inc. West Chicago, Ill., 2000, pp. 238.

[23] Paul Louden Brown, Edward Kamuda and Karen Kamuda, "Titanic Myths," Titanic Historical Society.

Prior to being transferred to the *Titanic*, he had commanded its sister ship, the *Olympic,* on its first nine voyages. On Smith's ninth *Olympic* voyage, he had the misfortune of colliding with a British warship, the *Hawke,* while sailing near the Isle of Wight. The smaller ship punctured *Olympic's* side above and below the water line. Despite the damage, both ships managed to get to port on their own. The 62-year-old Smith was then transferred to the *Titanic* to take the new liner on its maiden voyage. He went down with the ship [24]

Capten Edward J. Smith

While others have said that Captain Smith had been lucky up to the time of the *Titanic*, John Martin, steward on the White Star Line passenger liner the *Baltic* under Smith, disagreed. "Captain Smith was the most careful man I ever sailed with, he said, "but he was also the most unlucky." On one occasion, the *Baltic,* fully loaded with cotton in its hold, caught fire as it neared Liverpool. If not for the quick action of its firemen, the ship could have been destroyed. In the summer of 1906, the *Baltic* under Captain Smith came close to being wrecked with almost 1,000 passengers on board when it nearly hit Daunt's Rock near Queenstown.

The vessel had been enveloped in heavy fog that suddenly lifted averting the collision. Captain Smith always assembled the crew on deck at 10:30 a.m. for a fire drill and he held lifeboat drills while in port, Mr. Martin said.[25] Drills were not mandatory, and Captain Smith gave no orders for drills on the *Titanic*.

New York Times reported on April 19th that fireman Harry Senior on Collapsible B had seen Captain Smith jump into the sea with an infant clutched in his arms. He was dragged onto the upturned boat, where the child was taken from him. Then he took off his life preserver, tossed the life buoy on the inky waters, and slipped into the water again with the words, "I will follow the ship."[26]

George A. Braden told a different story of how he saw Captain Smith meet his death.

---

[24] Some sources say that Captain Smith planned to retire after Titanic's maiden voyage, but this has not been confirmed.

[25] Kohl, Cris, Titanic: *The Great Lakes Connections*, p. 207-208.

[26] There is no record of an infant on Collapsible B.

"I saw Capt. Smith while in the water. He was standing on the deck all alone. He was swept down by the water, but got to his feet. Then as the boat sank, he was again swept from his feet and this time he drowned."[27]

In a famous quote, Captain Smith once said:

"I cannot imagine any condition which would cause a ship to founder. I cannot conceive of any vital disaster happening to this vessel. Modern shipbuilding has gone beyond that . . ." (On the maiden voyage of the *Adriatic* in New York, 1907).[28]

The wealthiest and most prominent passengers were Colonel John Jacob Astor, American businessman, real-estate builder, inventor, science-fiction writer, and builder of the Waldorf-Astoria Hotel; Mr. Isidor Straus, co-owner of the Macy's Department stores, and Mrs. Ida Straus; Benjamin Guggenheim, who had accumulated his wealth in the smelting industry; Bruce Ismay, the managing director of the White Star Line; Major Archibald Butt, a military aide to President Taft; Arthur Newell, president of First National Bank of Boston; Engelhart Ostby, the owner of the world's largest gold ring company; John Reuchlin, the director of the Holland America Line; Samuel Risen, whose family owned several diamond mines in Africa; Charles M. Hays, president of the Grand Trunk Railway of Canada; John B. Thayer, second vice president of the Pennsylvania Railroad; Hudson J. C. Allison, investment broker from Montreal; Mr. Washington A. Roebling, president of the Roebling Wire Company and nephew of the man who built the Brooklyn Bridge; and Mr. Thomas Andrews, Jr., the designer of the *Titanic*.[29]

---

[27] *New York Times*, April 19, 1912, p. 7.

[28] Displayed at the *Titanic* exhibit at the Putnam Museum in Davenport, Iowa, in 2011.

[29] The owner of the White Star Line, J. P. Morgan of New York, was supposed to be on board, but had cancelled, some say because of sickness, while others say because of his business ventures.

The most prominent passengers

John Jacob Astor, Isidor Straus, and Benjamin Guggenheim

Except for Bruce Ismay, all these prominent men went down with the ship and perished. Those accompanied by their wives led them to the lifeboats and said goodbye. An exception was Mrs. Ida Straus, who insisted that if her husband could not be saved, she would stay with him. Both went down with the ship. Mr. Guggenheim traveled with a mistress while his wife was safe at home in New York with their children. The wealthy Colonel Archibald Gracie of Washington, D.C., traveled alone and survived.[30]

Mrs. Molly Brown (Margaret)

Among the strong, prominent women in the lifeboats was the "unsinkable Molly Brown" (Margaret), the wife of a wealthy Denver mine owner who did not accompany her. She manned the oars in Lifeboat 6 and encouraged the occupants to persevere while Quarter Master Robert Hichens stood by the tiller predicting that they would all die.

[30] Gracie's ancestors had built the Gracie Mansion, which was the home of the mayor of New York. His father was a famous Confederate Civil War general.

Fashion designer Lady Lucille Duff Gordon, with salons in London, Paris, and New York, and her husband, Olympic athlete Sir Cosmo Duff Gordon of London both survived, but it was Lady Gordon who captured the readers with her dramatic account of the sinking of the luxury steamer. *New York American* published an interview with her four days after the disaster. Her story was also published in newspapers in Sweden.

Another prominent woman who did her share of work that night was the Countess of Rothes (Noel Lucy Martha Dyer-Edwards). She stood by the tiller in Lifeboat 8.[31] One man paid a tribute to her in *New York Times*, April 20, saying, "I was in command, but I had to row and I wanted someone at the tiller. And I saw the way she was carrying herself, and I heard the quiet, determined way she spoke to the others and I knew she was more of a man than any we had on board. And I put her in command. I put her at the tiller, and she was at the tiller when the Carpathia came along five hours later."[32]

Also on board were two famous authors, one of them being Jacques Futrelle, novelist and author of the *Thinking Machine* and former reporter for the *Atlanta Journal* and *New York Herald.* He traveled with his wife, Lily May Futrelle. The other famous author and journalist on board was William Stead, who had written the novel, *From the Old World to the New*, about an accident involving a ship colliding with an iceberg.[33]

Also on board were a silent movie star, a theater and traveling entertainment manager, a former football and hockey player, a tennis player, a Canadian sculptor, and a fencer.

The cargo

The cargo of the *Titanic* declared lost included one Renault automobile, one oil painting by Blondel, owned by Swedish-American Hokan Björnström-Steffanson, seven parcels of parchment of the Torah, three crates of ancient models for the Denver Museum, five grand pianos, a jeweled copy of The Rubaiyat by Omar Khayyam (with illustrations by Eliku Vedder), and 1,500 precious stones set in gold, 3,364 bags of mail, and 700-800 parcels.[34]

The ships provisions included 75,000 lbs of fresh meat, 11,000 lbs of fresh fish, 4,000 lbs of salted and dried fish, 7,500 lbs of bacon and ham, 40,000 fresh eggs, 40 tons of potatoes, 2,200 lbs of coffee, 10,000 lbs of

---

[31] Lee W. Merideth, *Titanic Names: A Complete List of the Passengers and Crew.* Rochlin Press, Sunnyvale, Cal., 2002, p. 19.
[32] The man who praised her was not identified other than as an able bodied seaman.
[33] Another author who wrote about the same scenario was Morgan Robertson in *Futility*. In his book, he called the ship, *The Titan.*
[34] "Jim's Titanic website, Titanic: Facts & Figures by Jim Sadur.

...die

s... and on with crockery,
... ns.[35]
... Nature, *Cliquot* Dry, *Mumm's*
... Dry. [36]

...starboard side of the *Titanic* that collided with the iceberg

On...
Olympic, He...
Wilde, came on board ...
the *Titanic*, he bumped down chief officer William Murdoch and first officer Charles H. Lightoller to first and second officers respectively.

On April 10, as the *Titanic* slowly left the harbor in Southampton, its displacement weight of about 60,000 tons created such a strong suction that it snapped the moorings of the *S. S. New York* docked in the harbor. The tug *Vulcan* quickly attached a line to the *New York* while the *Titanic* reversed its propellers, thus barely avoiding a collision.[38]

The *Titanic* proceeded to Cherbourg, France, where it boarded passengers from two tenders as the harbor was too shallow for the large steamer.

---

[35] *Ibid.*

[36] John P. Eaton, Titanic International Society Historian, "High living on the high seas aboard *Titanic*," *Voyage* 34, The Official Journal of the Titanic International Society, Freehold, NJ, Autumn, 2000.

[37] Some of the Swedes mentioned that they had been scheduled to sail on other ships. Ernst Persson had the documents to prove it.

[38] *Titanic: An Illustrated History* with text by Don Lynch. See also Lawrence Beasley, "From Southampton to the Night of the Collision" in *The Story of the Titanic as told by its survivors.* Dover Publications, Inc., New York, 1960, p. 15. Compare p. 279.

On its last stop, Queenstown, Ireland, tenders delivered and loaded mail, cargo, and passengers.

The *Titanic* carried an estimated 2,228 people as it left Queenstown, Ireland, on April 11. There were at least six honeymoon couples on board. The price for a first-class stateroom was around £260.00 (about $1,300) with the exception of the two parlor suites, which were priced higher. A first-class berth could be obtained for $150.00; Second-class tickets averaged $60.00, while a third-class ticket typically cost about $40.00. (In today's money it would about $640.00.)[39]

From noon April 11 to noon April 12, the *Titanic* covered 484 miles in good weather, besting the record of the *Olympic* on its first day. The miles were posted daily, and the passengers began to bet on the next day's numbers. Colonel Gracie wrote that the ship covered more miles with every passing day and during the last recorded 24 hours, it covered 546 miles.[40]

Second officer Charles H. Lightoller

Before Second Officer Charles Lightoller could retire for the night, he had to make the rounds. In a ship of that size it meant a mile or more of deck, not including a few hundred feet of ladders and staircases. It took him days before he could confidently find the shortest route around the large ship.

For the first three days, the passengers enjoyed the facilities and the calm weather, but when the temperature plummeted on the fourth day, they gathered in smoking rooms and reading rooms. First-class passengers enjoyed the Verandah Café, the Café Parisien, the Gymnasium, or the Turkish bath with its swimming pool. Second-class passengers enjoyed accommodations that were equal to first class on other liners. The third-class fascilities included a smoking room and

---

[39] The price in first class varied a great deal depending on the accommodations. Mr. Ismay occupied the most expensive suite, the parlor suite, but his ticket was complimentary. Mr. Astor paid £248 for the suite occupied by him and his wife ($1,200.00). The website www.encyclopedia-titanica.org has posted a conversion rate of about 4.87 USD (with reservation for error) to the British pound in 1912. Most of the third-class tickets cost between 7 and 9 pounds (close to $40.00 or 150 Swedish crowns), while the second-class tickets generally cost about £13 ($65 or 244 Swedish crowns). The Swedes Björnström Steffanson and Lindstrom paid £28 ($136) each for their first-class tickets. Captain Frans Olof Carlson paid only £5.00, while Karolina Bystrom paid £13.27 ($65) for her second-class ticket. Colonel Gracie paid only £28 ($136.00) for a state room in first class, a very special price.

[40] Gracie in *The Story of the Titanic as told by its survivors.* Jack Winocour, ed. Dover Publications, New York, 1960, p. 118. Permission to quote granted by Dover Publications, Feb. 10, 2012.

a general room, which served as a lounge. The dining room extended the width of the ship, but was divided in two by a watertight bulkhead amidships on F-deck. No doubt, many third-class passengers had better accommodations on the *Titanic* than they had been accustomed to at home.

A series of unfortunate circumstances led to the unexpected collision with the iceberg. Surviving first-class passenger Archibald Gracie wrote that the captain had no way of knowing that a great mass of ice and icebergs had floated so far south. This had not happened in 50 years. Gracie also stated that the chance of colliding with an iceberg was one in a million.[41]

First-class state room like the one occupied by Colonel Gracie and other prominent passengers.

Colonel Archibald Gracie served in the Spanish-American War.

Second officer Lightoller was on the bridge between 6:00 and 10:00 p.m. on April 14 when the temperature was one degree above freezing, but the sea was "flat." Lightoller recalled:

The third-class general room

Wireless reports were coming in through the day from various ships of ice being sighted in different positions. Nor was that anything unusual at this time of the year, and none of the reports indicated the extent of the ice seen....

---

[41] Gracie in *The Story of the Titanic*, p.118.

Later on in the day we did get reports of ice sighted in larger quantities, and also two reports of field ice, but they were in positions that did not affect us. The one vital report that came through, but which never reached the bridge, was received at 9:40 p.m. from the Mesaba stating, "Ice report in Latitude.... Saw much heavy pack ice, and great number large icebergs. Also field ice. Weather good, clear." The position this ship gave was right ahead and not many miles distant. The wireless operator was not to know how close we were to this position, and therefore the extreme urgency of the message. That he received the message is known, and it was read by the other operator in his bunk. The operator who received it was busy at the time, working wireless messages to and from Cape Race, also with his accounts....[42]

The Titanic had a well-equipped barber shop.

[42] Lightoller in *The Story of the Titanic*, pp. 280-281.

Officer Lightoller explained why it was difficult to spot the iceberg even though the sea was calm.

The side of an iceberg that has calved or broken away from the parent glacier will usually be black where the fresh ice is showing, and is consequently more difficult to see at night. After considerable exposure, this side turns white like the rest. ... It was pitch dark and cold. Not a cloud in the sky, and the sea like glass. The very smoothness of the sea was, again, another unfortunate circumstance.... If there had been either wind or swell, the outline of the berg would have been rendered visible though the water breaking at the base.[43]

Lightoller was not the only one who said that the iceberg was black. Hugh Woolner, a first-class passenger said that about 150 foot astern he made out a mountain of ice standing black against the starlit sky.[44]

The collision with the iceberg

At 10:00 p.m., Lightoller turned over the command on the bridge to First officer Murdoch. A few minutes after 11:30, Lookout Frederick Fleet without the benefit of binoculars sighted the iceberg. He immediately rang the bell and then picked up the telephone to contact the wheelhouse.[45] Sixth Officer Moody answered and relayed the message to Murdoch, who had already seen the berg. He ordered the man at the wheel, Quartermaster Robert Hichens, to put the helm at starboard which would cause the ship to turn to the left of the iceberg. The bow of the ship slowly began to turn, but the iceberg scraped the starboard bow. Quartermaster Hichens later testified that he was never given an order to countermand the 'hard a' starboard' position of the ship's wheel.[46]

---

[43] Lightoller in *The Story of the Titanic,* p. 282.

[44] Walter Lord, *A Night to Remember*, Henry Holt and Company, LLC, New York, N.Y., p. 6.

[45] Officer David Blair had been assigned to another ship, and when he cleared out his belongings he may have accidentally removed the key to the place where the binoculars were kept, and after that no one could find them.

[46] John P. Eaton and Charles A. Haas. *Titanic: A Journey Through Time*. W. W. Norton & Company, Inc. New York, NY, 1999, p. 60.

The iceberg that was probably rammed by the Titanic. The photographer said he observed a red streak on the berg in the morning of April 15. Photo by Stephan Rehorek, who died in 1935. The copyright has expired and the image is under public domain. This file has been identified as being free of known restrictions under copyright law, including all related and neighboring rights.

Captain Smith was not present on the bridge until after the collision. [47] Why did the water come in so fast? Again, Lightoller explained:

She struck the berg well forward of the foremast, and evidently there had been a slight shelf protruding below the water. This pierced her bow as she threw her whole weight on the ice, some actually falling on her fore deck. The impact flung her bow off, but only by the whip or spring of the ship. Again, she struck, this time a little further aft.[48]

---

[47] *Titanic: An Illustrated History*, pp. 85, 89. Neither Captain Smith nor Murdoch survived. Steward J. Maynard said he accepted a baby from Captain Smith's arm. (Eaton and Haas, p. 79). Surviving second officer Lightoller said he had seen Murdoch being washed away by a big wave as the *Titanic* sank. His body was never found. At least two of the Swedish survivors recalled seeing an officer shoot himself. Quartermaster Hichens and Lookout Frederick Fleet survived.

[48] Lightoller in *The Story of the Titanic*, p. 286

According toLightoller, the *Titanic* bumped along the berg, "holing her each time till she was making water in no less than six compartments, though unfortunately, we were not to know this until later."[49]

The *Titanic* was so constructed and divided into watertight compartments that she would float with any two forward compartments full, and possibly even with three or four compartments full.[50]

"She could not remain afloat when she was holed in the forward stoke-hold as well," Lightoller said. "That made her fifth compartment [flood], counting from forward that was smashed in by the iceberg, and this finally sealed her fate."[51]

"A smaller ship would have withstood the collision," he said. At the U.S. Senate Hearing, he testified that the speed was about 21 ½ or 22 knots. The alarm was not sounding when he came up on the bridge two to three minutes after the ship had struck ice.

The surviving junior wireless operator, Harold S. Bride, was not on duty at the time of the collision. But he was awake in his bunk and aware of the fact that the captain came into the cabin announcing that they had struck an iceberg and that he had ordered an inspection. They were not to send a call for assistance until they were told to do so. When the captain returned and gave the order, Jack Phillips, the senior wireless operator, began to send the standard C.Q.D, but soon changed it to the new S.O.S. Bride delivered messages for Phillips and retrieved their belongings and lifejackets.

Many ships heard the message either directly or through other ships. A few changed their course to come to the aid of the *Titanic*, but only the *Carpathia* of the Cunard Line arrived in time to rescue the people in the lifeboats after the *Titanic* had gone to the bottom of the sea. The *Carpathia* was 58 miles away when it turned around and increased its speed to 17 ½ knots to arrive at about 4.00 a.m.[52]

---

[49] *Ibid.* Later findings say that the iceberg excerted pressure on the hull and caused the plates to buckle and rivets to pop. *Titanic: An Illustrated History*, p. 93.

[50] "The British "Report on the Loss of the Titanic," dated July 30, 1912, stated, "In the preparation of the design of this vessel it was arranged that the bulkheads and divisions should be so placed that the ship would remain afloat in the event of any two adjoining compartments being flooded, and that they should be so built and strengthened that the ship would remain afloat under this condition."

[51] Lightoller in *The Story of the Titanic*, p. 287. It is possible that a sixth compartment also flooded.

[52] John P. Eaton and Charles A. Haas, p. 79.

The rescue ship S. S. Carpathia of the Cunard Line

The *Californian* of the Leyland Line, which was much closer, made no effort to come to the rescue. In the 1912 Senate Investigation, Bride said that the *Californian* had called him with an ice report, but that he was 'rather busy just for the minute' and did not take it. "She did not call again. She transmitted the ice report to the *Baltic*, and as she was transmitting it to the *Baltic,* I took it down. I took it to the captain, but it was not official, because it was not intended for me afterwards."[53]

Bride said that Phillips continued to send messages even after the captain had released all the crew with the words, "Every man for himself."[54]

Colonel Gracie stated that at 12 o'clock the steamer *Californian* bound from London to Boston was only 4 or 5 miles away and could easily have reached the *Titanic* and rescued all its passengers.[55]

---

[53] *The Titanic Disaster Hearings: The Official Transcriptions of the 1912 Senate Investigation.* Tom Kuntz, ed. Pocket Books, New York, N.Y., 1998, p. 78-79.
[54] Harold S. Bride in *The Story of the Titanic*, pp. 313-14.
[55] The distance between the two ships has not been confirmed. Captain Lord testified that it was between 19 ½ and 20 miles, but passengers and crewmen reported clearly having seen a ship at a much closer distance. *The Titanic Disaster Hearings,* pp. 321, 546.

Gracie went on to declare that Captain Stanley Lord stood on the *Californian's* deck and saw a ship in distress and failed to do anything about it.[56]

New Yorkers learn the horrible news about the Titanic

For more information about the exchange of wireless messages, see "Who talked to Titanic?" ET Research by Senan Malony published online March 11, 2010.[57]

The *Californian* wireless operator said they did not receive the horrid news about the *Titanic* until 5:30 in the morning, which prompted her to steam toward the place of the sinking. They finally arrived at 7:50 a.m. to assist in the search for survivors, but found neither survivors nor bodies.[58]

Both the American and British inquiries criticized Captain Lord for his failure to come to the rescue of the *Titanic,* but Lord maintained that the ship he had seen had been too small to be the *Titanic.*

---

[56] Gracie in *The Story of the Titanic*, p. 127
[57] www.encycyclopedia-titanica.org/who-talked-to-titanic.html.
[58] *Titanic: An Illustrated History*, p. 157, 191. *The Californian* had only one wireless operator and he was not required to work at night.

Lifeboat Collapsible D with canvas sides. This lifeboat carried, among others, Håkan Björnström Steffanson, Velin Öhman, and Hilda Hellström.

Later research based on the *Titanic*'s wreck site suggests that the *Californian* and the *Titanic* could have been 4 to 20 miles apart. Defenders of Captain Lord say that a third ship may have been present between the *Californian* and the *Titanic*. The debate continues about whether it could have been the Norwegian schooner, *Samson*.

A newspaper in Trondheim, Norway, wrote that Henrik Naess, an officer on the *Samson* at the time, had said in an interview that both he and the captain on the *Samson* had seen the *Titanic* rockets, but at the time they thought they were flares exchanged between American patrol boats.[59]

These recollections were revealed in a documentary by the Norwegian Broadcasting System in connection with the 50th anniversary of the sinking in April 1962. The information created shock waves among *Titanic* enthusiasts round the world. Captain Lord passed away in January of 1962, three months before this documentary was broadcasted.[60]

The debate also continues whether the *Samson* could have been in the vicinity of the *Titanic* when it supposedly was at Isafjördur, Iceland, for repair

---

[59] The schooner Samson was built in Norway in 1885 and was said to have been sealing [seal hunting] illegally in international waters. She had no wireless. Her biggest claim to fame was allegedly being the mystery boat seen by survivors of the *Titanic,* but whether this is true or not has not been confirmed. American patrol boats did not patrol the waters until 1913 after the *Titanic* disaster.

[60] Per Kristian Sebak, *Titanic: 31 Norwegian Destinies,* Genesis, Oslo, Norway, 1998, p. 171. Referenced to *Arbeideravisen*, Trondheim, Norway.

on both April 6 and April 20. However, in Naess's account, there is no evidence of the *Samson* being at Isafjördur until May 1912.[61]

The inexperience of *Californian*'s chief officer Herbert Stone has been mentioned as one reason why Captain Lord did not act. It is alleged that Stone had never seen a distress signal. The flares, to him, did not match the requirements.[62]

Second officer Stone wrote to Captain Lord on April 18, 1912, saying that at 2:00 a.m. on April 15, he had seen eight white rockets before the steamer went out of sight to the SW and the *Californian* headed WSW. He testified that he had seen the last rocket at about 1:40.[63]

Why weren't all the lifeboats full when they were launched? One reason given was that some women were more afraid of entering the boats than staying on the ship. A few officers knew that the ship was sinking and time did not allow them to wait for more women. Half of the lifeboats had been tested in Southampton carrying weights but not fully loaded with people. Officer Lightoller lowered the boats half-empty so that they could be filled from the gangway doors on the lower decks. He sent six men down to do so, but they did not make it. When the loading from the lower decks did not materialize, he began to fill the boats. He loaded the even-numbered boats on the port side with women and children, but stopped any men from entering the boats, while Officer Murdoch, who supervised the loading of the odd-numbered boats on the starboard side, allowed men to enter when no women or children stepped forward.

A small number of Swedish men were saved by Murdoch without getting wet. Crew members were sent down to bring third-class women and children upstairs, and they were partly successful. Lightoller still stopped men from entering the boats except crew members needed to man the boats, and also denied young boys entrance.[64]

---

[61] Sebak, p. 171. If the *Samson* indeed was in the vicinity of the *Titanic*, it still does not explain why Captain Lord failed to act when he saw the rockets. Lightoller severely criticized Captain Lord in his autobiography.

[62] Charles Chaffee, "The Californian debate: Inexperience or cowardice?" *Voyage*, The official Journal of the Titanic International Society, Freehold, NJ Autumn 2000.

[63] "Rockets, Lifeboats, and Time Changes: ET Research (2010)" by Samuel Halpern.

[64] Lightoller in *The Story of the Titanic*, p. 288. Lightoller seems to have interpreted the captain's order as "Women and Children only," while Murdoch heard it as "Women and Children First."

Colonel Gracie described the wait for the rescue ship while hanging onto Collapsible B that floated upside down. This lifeboat also carried the Swede Ernst Persson and probably also Oscar W. Johansson, and Carl Olof Jansson.

Gracie wrote:

Finally dawn appeared and there on the port side of our upset boat where we had been looking with anxious eyes, glory be to God, we saw the steamer Carpathia about four or five miles away, with other Titanic lifeboats rowing towards her. But on our starboard side, much to our surprise, for we had seen no lights on that quarter, were four of the Titanic's lifeboats strung together in line. These were respectively Numbers 14, 10, 12 and 4, according to testimony submitted. Meantime, the water had grown rougher, and, as previously described, was washing over the keel and we had to make shift to preserve the equilibrium. Right glad were all of us on our upturned boat when in that awful hour the break of day brought this glorious sight to our eyes. Lightoller put his whistle to his cold lips and blew a shrill blast, attracting the attention of the boats about half a mile away. "Come over and take us off," he cried. "Aye, aye, sir," was the ready response as two of the boats cast off from the others and rowed directly towards us.

Just before the bows of the two boats reached us, Lightoller ordered us not to scramble, but each to take his turn, so that the transfer might be made in safety. When my turn came, in order not to endanger the lives of the others, or plunge them into the sea, I went carefully, hands first, into the rescuing lifeboat....

... In the lifeboat to which we were transferred were said to be sixty-five or seventy of us. [No. 12] *The number was beyond the limit of safety. The boat sank low in the water, and the sea now became rougher.... For a short time another Titanic lifeboat was towed by ours....*

My research, particularly the testimony taken before the Senate Committee, establishes the identity of the Titanic lifeboats to which, at day, dawn, we of the upset boat were transferred. These were Boats No. 12 and No.4.[65]

[65] Gracie in *The Story of the Titanic, pp. 167-168.* Having taken on passengers from other boats, Lifeboat No. 12, floated close to the waterline according to other survivors. The Collapsible boats, A, B. C. D, were not poor, but different in that they had canvas sides for easier storage.

The Welin davit that lowered the lifeboats was invented by the Swede Axel Welin (Also spelled Velin), and made in Trollhättan, Sweden.

The search for bodies

First on the scene to pick up bodies was *Mackay-Bennett* out of Halifax, hired by the White Star Line. It recovered 306 bodies, buried 116 at sea, and brought 190 to Halifax. The *Minia* recovered 17 bodies, buried two at sea and brought 16 to Halifax. Two other ships recovered five bodies, buried one each at sea, and took three to Halifax.

Out of some 1,500 victims, only 337 bodies were found.[66] The best preserved victims were taken to Halifax to be buried in cemeteries. The bodies of the most prominent men were easily recognized as they were well dressed, some in black-tail tuxedos.[67]

---

[66] Eaton and Haas, p. 123.

[67] The so-called embalming consisted of "injecting large quantities of a formaldehyde-based solution into the stomach cavities of the bodies...and packing them in ice." Debbie Beavis: *Who Sailed on the Titanic?,* Ian Allan Publishing Ltd, Hersham, Surrey, England, p. 80.

Some of the lifeboats gathered together after the rescue operation

Only a few Swedish victims were taken to Halifax and buried in the Fairview Lawn Cemetery, one of them being Mrs. Alma Cornelia Pålsson of Bjuv, Skåne. The inscription on her tombstone spells her surname, "Paulson," which was the way her husband residing in Chicago spelled his surname. She traveled with her children, Gösta, Paul Folke, Stina Viola, and Torborg Danita, all of whom perished and were not recovered. Her husband, Nils Paulson had lived in the United States since 1910, saving money to bring his wife and children to Chicago.

Buried near Alma was the body of a small child, who for a long time was thought to be her youngest son, two-year-old Gösta. Later DNA testing—established with 98 percent accuracy that the child was 19-month-old Sidney Leslie Goodwin from England. His tombstone reads, "Unknown child of the Titanic." Mackay Bennett had paid for the funeral and the tombstone because the crew had found the little body floating on the water without a life jacket. Most of the tombstones do not have names, only a number and the date of death.[68]

[68] The DNA was based on three teeth and a fragment of a bone, which was all that was left of the body. www.encyclopedia-titanica.org April 28, 2011.

View of Fairview Lawn Cemetery, Halifax, Canada

Why did the water come in so fast? Again, Lightoller explained:

The people floating in lifejackets in the water died from hypothermia. Despite the recovery efforts, about one thousand bodies were never recovered.

Professor Robert W. Wood of John Hopkins University said, "The Titanic's victims who were not carried down with the ship followed until the very bottom of the sea was reached.... At a depth of two miles the pressure of the water is something like 6,000 pounds to the square inch, which is far too great to be overcome...."[69]

[69] *The Rock Island Argus*, Rock Island, Ill., Apr. 18, 1912, p. 1. Also seen in other newspapers.

The Inquires

When the Carpathia arrived in New York, J. Bruce Ismay, managing director of the White Star Line, remained on board a broken man. He had hoped that he and the crew of the *Titanic* could return to England immediately, but it was not to be.

U. S. Senators William Alden Smith of Michigan and Francis G. Newlands of Nevada stepped on board and presented a subpoena to Ismay to testify at a formal inquiry. Senator Smith opened the investigation the following morning at the Waldorf Astoria and called Mr. Ismay as the first witness.

Other important witnesses were *Carpathia*'s captain, Arthur Henry Rostron, *Californian's* captain, Stanley Lord, and the following from the *Titanic*: Second officer Charles Herbert Lightoller, Third officer Herbert John Pitman, Fourth officer Joseph G. Boxhall, and Fifth officer, Harold G. Lowe (by affidavit and statement), the *Titanic* junior wireless operator, Harold Bride, and *Carpathia's* wireless operator, Harold Thomas Cottam, members of the crew, as well as passengers from first, second, and third class.

The third-class was represented by three passengers, Norwegian-American Olaus Abelseth, Berk Pickard, born in Russia, and Daniel Buckley, an Irish immigrant. Abelseth testified that he had jumped off the ship when the deck was only five feet above the waterline. He told about a shut gate, but an officer ordered it opened when a couple of ladies could not get through. Earlier, a group of men had climbed out on a crane and over the railing to get around the gate.

Mr. Buckley had jumped into a lifeboat. When he and some other men were told to get out, a woman threw a shawl over him and told him to stay.

Third-class steward John Edward Hart did not testify, but he later recalled his struggles to get the steerage passengers into lifejackets while assuring them there was no danger. "Interpreter Muller did the best he could with the scores of Finns and Swedes, but it was slow going." Hart said it was hopeless to expect them to find their way alone through the maze of passages normally sealed off to them, so he decided to escort them up in small groups.[70]

Senator Smith's American inquiry raised many questions: Should Mr. Ismay and Captain Edward Smith be held responsible for the accident because the ship sailed too fast for the conditions? Was the *Titanic* a safe ship? Were third-class passengers prevented from reaching the lifeboats? Had the *Californian* ignored the *Titanic's* distress signals?[71]

---

[70] Walter Lord, *A Night To Remember*, p. 55.
[71] Titanic an Illustrated History, pp. 169-173, 182.
[71] Titanic an Illustrated History, pp. 169-173, 182.

Edward John Buley, able seaman and a British Royal Navy veteran from Itchen, England, said he had seen a stationary ship that he judged was three miles away.[72] Other passengers testified that they had seen the masthead of a ship about four miles away.

In regard to the *Californian*, the U.S. Senate hearing concluded:

The committee is forced to the inevitable conclusion that the Californian … was nearer the Titanic than the 19 miles reported by her captain, and that her officers and crew saw the distress signals of the Titanic and failed to respond to them in accordance with the dictates of humanity, international usage, and the requirements of law. The only reply to the distress signals was a counter signal from a large white light which was flashed for nearly two hours from the mast of the Californian. In our opinion such conduct, whether arising from indifference or gross carelessness, is most reprehensible, and places upon the commander of the Californian a grave responsibility….[73]

Colonel Gracie stated that at 12 o'clock the steamer *Californian* bound from London to Boston was only four or five miles away and could easily have reached the *Titanic* and rescued all its passengers.[74]

Gracie went on to declare that Captain Stanley Lord stood on the *Californian's* deck and saw a ship in distress and failed to do anything about it.[75]

---

[72] *Ibid*, p. 270.
[73] *The Titanic Disaster hearings*, p. 547.
[74] The distance between the two ships has not been confirmed. Captain Lord testified that it was between 19 ½ and 20 miles, but passengers and crewmen reported clearly having seen a ship at a much closer distance. *The Titanic Disaster Hearings*, pp. 321, 546.
[75] Gracie in *The Story of the Titanic*, p. 127

Carpathia's captain, Arthur Henry Rostron, was praised by the committee. As soon as he had received the distress message from *Titanic*, he ordered his ship turned around and accommodations made ready for the rescue. He gave orders to the chief steward, "Have coffee, tea, soup, etc., in each saloon, blankets in saloons, at the gangways and some for the boats.

"To see all rescued cared for and immediate wants attended to.

"My cabin and all officials' cabins to be given up. Smoke rooms, library, etc., dining rooms would be utilized to accommodate the survivors.

Arthur Henry Rostron, Carpathia's captain

"All spare berths in steerage to be utilized for *Titanic* passengers, and get all our own steerage passengers grouped together."

These were only some of the orders he issued. Captain Rostron said he was 58 miles away from the *Titanic* and that it took him 3 ½ hours to get there. Once there, he saw only the lifeboats and began rescuing the passengers.[76]

The committee deemed the course followed by Captain Rostron of the *Carpathia* as deserving of the highest praise and worthy of especial recognition.[77]

The White Star Line was found responsible for the shipwreck in a New York Court on April 21, 1912. The case went to the U. S. Supreme Court that decided to limit the amount that the White Star Line would have to pay to $664,000.[78]

The British inquiry conducted by the British Board of Trade lasted 36 days. The final report stated:

---

[76] *The Titanic Disaster Hearings*, p. 27.
[77] *Ibid*, p. 551.
[78] Per Kristian Sebak, p. 141, 144-146. The White Star Line was willing to grant compensation of $664,000 with the condition that the amount would include all the lawsuits which were filed both in USA and Britain, and that the company would no longer be sued for compensation from the *Titanic* disaster.

Captain Arthur Henry Rostron next to the silver loving cup presented to him in May 1912 by survivors of the Titanic in recognition of his heroism in their rescue. (Source: Flickr Commons project, 2008, 2010) Forms part of: George Grantham Bain Collection (Library of Congress). No known restrictions.

"The Court, having carefully inquired into the circumstances of the above mentioned shipping casualty, finds, for the reasons appearing in the annex hereto, that the loss of the said ship was due to collision with an iceberg, brought about by the excessive speed at which the ship was being navigated."[79]

With the benefit of hindsight, current commentators have blamed Captain Smith for failing his passengers and crew by not heeding ice warnings, not slowing his ship, and allowing lifeboats to leave the sinking ship partially filled.[80]

The discovery of the wreck

Years later, having determined the location of the wreck in 1985, Dr. Robert Ballard and his team from the Woods Hole Oceanographic Institution sighted the bow of the *Titanic* on the bottom of the north Atlantic Sea on July 14, 1986. The discovery was made while scanning the area in a tiny sub

---

[79] *Report on the Loss of the "Titanic" (S.S.):* "Report of the Court", dated July 1912, p. 1. Also "British Wreck Commissioner's Inquiry Report, dated July 30, 1912. www.titanicinquiry.org

[80] Paul Louden-Brown, Edward Kamuda and Karen Kamuda in "Titanic Myths."

named Alvin. The sub came to rest on the former wooden deck of the ship, close to where lookout Frederick Fleet had initially spotted the iceberg.

The bow was relatively intact, but where was the rest of the ship? Explorers had hoped that they would find the *Titanic* in one piece although many rescued passengers had said that they had seen the ship break apart. As it turned out, the badly damaged stern lies nearly 2,000 feet away from the bow.[81]

The bow as it rests on the bottom of the sea.

George Frederick Crowe, stewart from Southampton testified that he saw the *Titanic* "break clean into two, probably two-thirds of the length of the ship.... She broke and then the after part floated back." He continued, "Yes, sir; then there was an explosion, and the aft part turned on end and sank."[82]

Mr. Lightoller testified, "Certainly, I think it was the boilers [that] exploded. There was a terrific blast of air and water, and I was blown out clear."[83]

Mr. A. H. Weikman, barber on the *Titanic*, who was washed overboard, testified: "I was about 15 feet away from the ship when I heard a second explosion.... I think the boilers blew up about in the middle of the ship. The explosion blew me along with a wall of water toward the dark object I was swimming to, which proved to be a bundle of deck chairs, which I managed to climb on."[84]

The United States Congress attempted to prevent the wreck from being looted, but an expedition in 1987 brought up thousands of items from the sea bottom. The United States Senate then forbade the sale or display of any salvage for profit in the United States. The expedition determined that the badly rusted and corroded wreck contained no human remains.[85]

A new theory on what sank the *Titanic* was made public in 1998. Two scientists said forensic studies show that the rivets used were made of inferior iron. *The New York Times* wrote, "Many of the rivets studied by the

---

[81] *Titanic: An Illustrated History*, p. 198.
[82] *The Titanic Disaster Hearings*, pp. 277, 278.
[83] *Ibid*. p. 60.
[84] *Ibid*, pp. 483,484.
[85] *Titanic. An Illustrated History*, p. 208.

scientists—recovered over two decades from the *Titanic's* resting place two miles down in the North Atlantic—were found to be riddled with a high concentration of slag, a glassy residue of smelting, which can make rivets brittle and prone to fracture." [86]

John Martin of Toronto, who was quoted earlier, said that the rivets keep loosen during the first six months a ship is in service. He contended that if the *Titanic* had been in service for 12 months, "none of her plate rivets would have been loose and she would not have been damaged so greatly by the iceberg.[87]

Titanic's time line

(Approximate *Titanic* time)

April 14, 1912, 11.40 p.m. Ship hits the iceberg.
April 15, 1912, 12.05 a.m. Lifeboats uncovered on deck.
12:10. First distress signal sent.
12:25. "Women and Children First" in lifeboats.
12:45. First lifeboat lowered, No. 7.
12:55. First rocket signal fired in the night sky.
1:40. Last rocket fired.
1.45. Last message sent to *Carpathia*.

---

[86] *The New York Times*, New York, Apr. 15, 1998. The name of the book that the article refers to is *What Really Sank the Titanic: New Forensic Discoveries* by Jennifer Hooper McCarty and Timothy Foeck.
[87] Chris Kohl, p. 209. Original source: *Port Huron* (MI) *Times-Herald*, April 18, 1912.

Titanic Memorial in Washington, DC

"TO THE BRAVE MEN WHO PERISHED IN THE WRECK OF THE TITANIC APRIL 15, 1912 THEY GAVE THEIR LIVES THAT WOMEN AND CHILDREN MIGHT BE SAVED ERECTED BY THE WOMEN OF AMERICA"

Originally dedicated on May 26, 1931, at the foot of New Hampshire Ave. in Rock Creek Park along the Potomac River, the monument was removed in 1966 to accommodate the John F. Kennedy Center for the Performing Arts. The memorial was re-erected without ceremony in 1968 on the south Washington waterfront outside Fort McNair in Washington Channel Park at Fourth and P Streets, SW.

Titanic News in the American press

As can be seen in the headlines of the newspapers around the world, there was much speculation about what had happened. At first, the wireless reported that the *Titanic* was being towed to Halifax and that all passengers and crew had been taken aboard other steamers. As the news became more serious, relatives of the passengers gathered at White Star Line offices demanding to find out if their loved ones had survived. The lists of survivors and victims that were published were incorrect and incomplete.

The *New York Herald* followed the progress of the *Titanic's* maiden voyage beginning April 10. Already on April 15, it reported that the ship was in trouble:

"The New Titanic Hit by an Iceberg, Appeals for Aid, Says Wireless Report."

The following day, Tuesday April 16, most newspapers carried the dire news.

The New York American, New York

The *New York American* headlined the sinking in LARGE capital letters across the first page:

J. J. ASTOR LOST ON TITANIC (1" Caps)

1,200 TO 1,500 DEAD (3" Caps)

The price for one copy was 1 cent in Greater New York and Jersey City and 2 cents elsewhere. Inside the paper, there were photographs of prominent passengers, including Colonel Astor and his young, second wife. The article, "ASTORS ON WAY BACK FROM HONEYMOON," on page 3 shows the contrast in life between him and the passengers of the lower classes. But at the time of death he was merely a man, who stood aside to let women and children enter the lifeboats. The fortune of Mr. Astor, a New York real-estate mogul, was estimated to between 150 and 450 million dollars. The article said: "He obtained his military title originally by serving on the staff of

Governor Levi P. Morton, as colonel. At the outbreak of the war with Spain, Colonel Astor bought and equipped a mountain battery at an expense of $100,000, which he presented to the United States and which was used in the Puerto Rican campaign."

Unsettled Tuesday. Wednesday fair and cooler; moderate southerly winds, becoming variable.

New York American

EDITION FOR GREATER NEW YORK.

No. 10,499. TUESDAY, APRIL 16, 1912.—24 PAGES PRICE O

J. J. ASTOR LOST ON TI

1,200 TO 1,500 D

Part of first page of New York American for April 16, 1912

On November 9, 1909, he had obtained a divorce from his first wife in a settlement that cost him 10 million dollars. The couple had two children, the eldest, Vincent, was a student at Harvard University. Their ten-year-old daughter lived with her mother in London. According to the divorce decree, Colonel Astor was not allowed to marry in the state of New York. The 47-year-old Astor married the 18-year old Madeleine T. Force in Newport, Rhode Island, and the couple went abroad for their honeymoon. The pregnant Mrs. Astor was saved. The article says that Mr. Astor was well liked and popular with all classes, but his divorce and remarriage to a woman, young enough to be his daughter, created a society scandal.[88]

---

[88] Wikipedia, the free encyclopedia described John Jacob Astor IV as a billionaire and the richest passenger aboard the Titanic.
New York Times, April 22, p. 9, reported how Mr. Astor had stepped into the lifeboat with his wife, believing that she needed his protection. When an officer informed him that the lifeboat was for women and children only, he stepped aside. Mr. and Mrs. Astor, who had honeymooned in Egypt and Paris, traveled with a man servant, a maid, a nurse, and a family pet. The man servant did not survive. Neither did the dog. Mr. Astor paid £247 for their state room on the *Titanic.* Mrs. Astor gave birth to a son in August 1912. She inherited the income from a 5-million-dollar trust, the home on Fifth Avenue and another in Newport, as long as she did not remarry. She remarried twice, but both marriages ended in divorce. She died at the age of 47, the same age as John Jacob Astor was when he died on the *Titanic.*

Another article, headlined, "Prevalence of Icebergs Due to Severity of Last Winter," p. 5, said:

Never in this history of Newfoundland has there been a winter so disastrous to steam and sailing vessels. Since November no fewer than twenty sailing crafts from 100 to 200 tons burden have gone to the bottom, seven of them carrying their whole crews down, some sixty-three souls altogether. The crews of the remaining thirteen were rescued from the sinking hulls in the nick of time.

Two steamers also perished with all hands. The first was the steamer Kampfiord, coal-laden from Sydney, which, it is believed, was crushed by ice in the February ... off Cape Race and with her eighteen men. The second was the Erna, a 3,000-ton liner, purchased in England and remodeled .... She is now forty-eight days out from Glasgow with fifty-one persons aboard and all hope of her survival is abandoned.

The New York Times, New York

The New York Times reported extensively about the disaster April 16-28. On April 19, 1912, it devoted a whole page to "Survivors" with the subtitle, "Tales From the Titanic," which included a story by steerage passenger Carl Johnson. It does not identify him as a Swede, but through the process of elimination, it appears to be Carl Olof Jansson (Johnson from Örebro).[89]

It is well known that there were people who were willing to interpret survivor stories to reporters. It is also known that the *New York Times* paid for *Titanic* survivor stories.

In the story that follows, the contributor states that "Carl Johnson" floated with his companion for two hours.

---

[89] Most likely, it was Carl Olof Johnson, because Karl Johnson of Killeberg told the paper *Hemlandet* that he had repelled on a rope, while Carl Olof said in one account that he had "toppled overboard." Also, Carl-Olof Johnson later told reporters that he was rescued by Collapsible B. The Swedish-American newspaper, *Nordstjernan*, in New York identified Carl-Olof from Örebro as Karl Janson. To add to the confusion, Merideth lists a Carl Jonsson, 32, as a survivor from Huntley, Illinois, headed for Huntley, but he did not survive.

[90] See *Olympia Daily Recorder*. Anna and Carl Olof parted ways in St. Paul, Minn.

"All the News That's Fit to Print."

The New York Times.

NEW YORK, TUESDAY, APRIL 16, 1912.—TWENTY-FOUR PAGES,

TITANIC SINKS FOUR HOURS AFTER HITTING IC
866 RESCUED BY CARPATHIA, PROBABLY 1250
ISMAY SAFE, MRS. ASTOR MAYBE, NOTED NAME

Col. Astor and Bride, Isidor Straus and Wife, and Maj. Butt Aboard.

"RULE OF SEA" FOLLOWED

Women and Children Put Over in Lifeboats and Are Supposed to be Safe on Carpathia.

PICKED UP AFTER 8 HOURS

Part of first page of New York Times, April 16, 1912

Survivor story:

Carl Johnson, a steerage passenger, was asleep in his berth when the collision with the iceberg took place.

There was only a slight jar and a creaking, which partially awakened me. There was no excitement in the steerage, and I paid no attention to the occurrence. I was asleep again when two of the ship's officers passed through the steerage, awakening the passengers. They told us to dress and come on deck—that there had been an accident, but that there was no danger.

When I started to dress I noticed that there was water creeping up about my feet. At first it came very slowly, but after a time it was around my ankles. In the compartment where I was sleeping the water was at an even depth everywhere, and the boat did not seem to have the slightest pitch to starboard or port, indicating that she was settling slowly and steadily and that the bottom had been ripped out. The upper air compartments kept the water from coming in very fast at first and no one seemed to think that she was going to sink.

When I got on deck, I saw the first sign of panic among the passengers. Women were screaming with terror and men were running this way and that. Then I noticed that the boat had begun to settle in the bow where I was standing. All the lights on the vessel were still going, however, and were still lighted when they began to lower the lifeboats. As the second boat swung from the davits the water reached the dynamos in the engine room, and we were suddenly plunged into darkness, save for the cold, clear light of the heavens, for it was a starlit sky.

I could not accustom myself to the change for several minutes. I think I was in a sort of daze and have no clear recollection of what happened afterward. I heard shrieks and cries mid ship, and the sharp reports of several shots. People began to run by me toward the stern of the ship, and as I started to run I realized that the boat was beginning to go down very rapidly, and there was quite a decline noticeable in the deck, showing that her nose was being buried. A wave struck me and I went overboard.

As I rose to the surface I saw a board floating on the top of the water and I seized it. A wave threw me away from the ship, and I began to swim, clutching to the board to keep me afloat. The shock seemed to restore my senses, and I began to see objects in the water quite clearly. The air was rent with screams and curses, and there were a lot of men and women in the water trying to get away from the ship to escape the awful suction when she went down.

There was an overturned lifeboat riding a big wave near me. I was swept toward it and managed to catch hold of its edge. There were seven or eight of its original passengers clinging to its sides. By this time we were almost half a mile from the ship and we could still see it clearly. It was quite low in the bow and was settling rapidly. Suddenly it seemed to give a great lurch forward and the ship plunged head first beneath the waves.

Another *Titanic* survivor, Anna Sjöholm, who traveled west by train with Carl Olof Johnson, said in an interview published by *Olympia Daily Recorder* that Carl Olof was clinging to the overturned lifeboat before being transferred to another lifeboat. When he was hauled aboard the *Carpathia,* his limbs were crusted with ½ inch of ice, and his hair was a mat of solid ice.[90]

For fully a minute as she was going down there was an awful silence everywhere. Not a sound was heard from the lifeboats, which we could now see clustered in a semi-circle a few hundred yards ahead of us, nor was there any sound from the waters behind us, where even then we could see hundreds of dark forms struggling in the water with bits of wreckage and debris.

At the second that the ship took her final dive there was an awful shriek carried to us from the waters behind, as though all of the poor, drowning wretches had joined in a final death cry of agony. I was taken up in the

---

[90] See *Olympia Daily Recorder.* Anna and Carl Olof parted ways in St. Paul, Minn.

lifeboat ahead and by those who were clinging to the overturned boat with me.

My companions and I drifted about for two hours before the overturned boat [Collapsible B] was sighted from another one a quarter of a mile to leeward. The boatswain directed his men to come to our rescue, and we were picked up, although the rescuing boat was already crowded with forty women and ten men. When we were taken in, there was hardly standing room, and the sailors had to stop rowing because they did not have room to move their arms. We drifted about until daylight, when we were sighted and picked up by the Carpathia. When all the survivors had been crowded on board the Carpathia there was a great deal of suffering, especially in the steerage, although every one did their best for us. The first day several died and were buried at sea. I did not witness all of the funerals, being sick and weak from exposure, but I was told about them.[91]

In the same issue, Abraham Hyman, an immigrant from Manchester, England, was quoted as having said, "There were a good many women and children, and they were all well and strong. One of them was a poor Swedish boy named Swenson, traveling alone to some friends in South Dakota. We all made a pet of him, and I am glad to see that he got away in one of the boats and was saved.[92]

Chicago Daily News, Chicago, Illinois

April 24, 1912[93]

TITANIC RESCUED HERE

"Five Left of Party of Ten from Sweden Arrive on Way to Pacific Coast.

---

[91] *The New York Times* April 19, 1912, p. 4, from microfilm at the Augustana College Library, Rock Island, Ill. Compare to Carl Olof Johnson's letter to his parents and what he told other reporters. When Carl Olof came to St. Paul, Minnesota, he repeated that there was no excitement in steerage. See below under "The Swedish Survivors." Many survivors said that they could see the lights from the *Titanic* until it disappeared. The overcrowded lifeboat was No. 12. William H. Lyon, able-bodied seaman died on board the *Carpathia* and was buried at sea, along with two bodies that had been brought to the *Carpathia* from the lifeboats. A Service of Remembrance was held.

[92] The Swedish boy was Johan Svensson, 14. He was on his way to join his father and a sister in South Dakota. (See The Swedish Survivors).

[93] Posted on www.encyclopedia-titanica.org by Thomas E. Golembiewski on Wednesday, January 26, 2011.

"Tells of their Escapes.

"Companions Lost After Entering Lifeboat--Man, Two Women and Two Children Saved."

Interviews with survivors

Edwin Lundstrom, 32 years old, who left Sweden in charge of a party of ten bound for California, and embarked on the Titanic, arrived in Chicago over the Erie today with just half of the original party. They were met at the Polk street station at 7:54 a.m. by officials from the local office of the White Star line and took an early train for Los Angeles.

Besides Lundstrom, the party was composed of Mrs. Agnes Sandstrom with her two daughters, Marguerite and Beatrice, 4 and 2 years; and Karin Abelseth, a 16 year old Norwegian girl. Lundstrom told a stirring story of his escape. He guided his party from the third cabin to the second and watched them placed in lifeboats. Mrs. Sandstrom and her children were placed in the thirteenth boat. The other members of the party, Mrs. Hulda Classen, Albin Classen, Gertrude Classen, Elida Olson and Hulda Verstrom [Vestrom], *got into the next boat.*

They were never seen again and Lundstrom is of the opinion that the boat in which they started did not have its plugs in or else was overturned. [The people mentioned above all perished.]

Lundstrom's story is related below under "The Swedish Survivors."

The following was reported about Agnes Sundstrom:

"Mother Tells of Escape from Death." Mrs. Agnes Sandstrom and her two little daughters were exhausted with their long trip. She told of their escape from the sinking ship. "We were placed in the boat and they swung us down into the water," said Mrs. Sandstrom. "We didn't want to leave the ship. They told us before we started that nothing could happen to us. That was why so many people were drowned. They thought the ship could not sink, but they did not trust the lifeboats. After we got in the water the men rowed and rowed and rowed. That's all I know. I was scared for my babies."

"Seek News of Nephew"

There was one pathetic incident connected with the arrival of the five survivors today. Anton Nelson, 5256 Laflin street, the uncle of Oliver Myhrman, 18 years old, who was lost in the shipwreck, was there to meet the train with his wife. Each carried a picture of the boy and when the fortunate arrived they hovered about them, anxiously striving to hear some word of the lost one." Did you know this boy?" asked Nelson of Lundstrom. "He was on that ship and he's dead now. Did you know him? Here's a picture that looks just like him." "I saw him lots of times," said Lundstrom, examining the photography. "He was a fine boy. We all liked him. He was there on the deck when I jumped."

"Gets Word of Lost Sister"

Helga Dahlberg, 1830 Calumet Avenue, sister of Gerda Dahlberg, who was lost, was also at the station seeking information. She had not heard a word except that her sister sailed, but did not reach the Carpathia. Here she found her sister's friends. Many tears fell as she listened to their stories. While they were talking suddenly a station employee forced his way through the group.

They were sitting at a table in the lunchroom. Nelson still fingered the picture of his nephew and gazed wistfully at the people who saw him last. "Clear out!" cried the station man. "Quit bothering these people. We can't have it. Get out, get out!" "I hope I'm not bothering you," said Nelson earnestly to his new found friend. "Not at all," said Lundstrom, heartily. "I know how you feel. I've seen a lot of this since I landed."

"Driven Out by Station Employee"

In spite of the remonstration of both, the station man forced Nelson and his wife from the lunchroom and they remained outside on the train platform to hear more when the survivors came out again. Mrs. Sandstrom will be met in San Francisco by her husband, who has been out there a year making a home for his family. Lundstrom and Karin Abelseth are bound for Los Angeles.[94] .

The Chicago Daily Tribune, Chicago, Illinois

This Chicago paper reported about the tragedy on April 15, 1912:[95]

EXTRA. EXTRA. EXTRA. TITANIC, BIGGEST SHIP AFLOAT, SINKING; HUNDREDS OF PASSENGERS MAY BE LOST

"Cape Race, N. F., April 15, 1 a.m.—at 10:25 last night [Central time] the steamship Titanic called "C.Q.D" and reported having struck an iceberg.

---

[94] *Chicago Daily News*, Wednesday, April 24, 1912, p. 4, c. 2, posted by Thomas E. Golembiewsky on www.encyclopedia-titanica.org.

[95] Microfilm, Glen Ellyn Historical Society, Glen Ellyn, Ill.

"The steamer said that immediate assistance was required.

"Half an hour afterwards another message came reporting that they were sinking by the head and that women were being put off in the lifeboats.

"Including the crew, there are more than 2,000 souls aboard the doomed vessel.

"The weather was calm and clear the Titanic's wireless operator reported and gave the position of the vessel 41:46 north latitude and 50:14 west longitudes.

"Signals Suddenly Stop.

"The last signals from the Titanic were heard by the Virginian at 12:27 a.m. The wireless operator on the Virginian says these signals were blurred and ended abruptly.

"The Marconi station at Cape Race notified the Allen liner Virginian, the captain of which immediately advised that he was proceeding for the scene of the disaster.

"The Virginian at midnight was about 170 miles distant from the Titanic and expected to reach that vessel about 10:00 a.m. Monday.

"The Olympian [Olympic] at an early hour Monday morning was in latitude 40:32 north and longitude 61:18 West. It was in direct communication with the Titanic and is now making all haste toward it.

"The steamship Baltic also reported itself as about 200 miles east of the Titanic and was making all possible speed toward her.][96]

The bulletin continued with the listing of some of the passengers on the ship.

On April 16, the paper reported:

*Boston, April 16 (2 a.m.) A wireless message picked up late tonight relayed from the Olympic says that the Carpathia is on her way to New York with 866 passengers [*later revised] *from the steamer Titanic aboard. They are mostly women and children, the message said, and concluded: "Grave fears are felt for the safety of the balance of the passengers and crew.*

The paper also reported on the prominent people on the Titanic.

It then published the following:

FEAR FOR TITANIC FORETOLD BY NAVIGATOR OF SWEDEN

"Capt. Roden Alarmed by Tendency to Luxury in Modern Steamships—Safety Sacrificed for Ease."

"Washington, D. C, April 16 [Special]

---

[96] The *Olympic* and the *Baltic* were too far away and their rescue missions were aborted.

In discussing the loss of life in the sinking of the Titanic, officers of the navy recall an article published in The Navy, a service magazine, by Capt. E. K. Roden, a well known Swedish navigator, who contended that the present day tendency in shipbuilding was to sacrifice safety for luxury.

Roden mentioned the Titanic by name, and, with foresight that now seems almost prophetic, portrayed some of the dangers into which the modern tendency of shipbuilding for luxury is leading. He pointed out that the new steamships would be the finest vessels afloat, no expense having been spared to attain every conceivable comfort that a man or woman of means can possibly ask for—staterooms with private shower baths, a swimming pool large enough to permit diving, a ballroom comprising an entire upper deck, a gymnasium, a café so arranged as to render the [illegible] of a café at seaside resort as realistic as possible, a sun deck representing a flower garden, and other luxuries and novelties.

The reading of these reports," says Roden, "is fascinating to the average man who takes it for granted that side by side with the luxurious comforts are combined the elements that make up the factor of safety that a well equipped passenger ship should possess. As a general rule the traveling public pays slight attention to the measurers taken for its safety. It prefers to assume that the steamship company has done everything to insure the safety of passengers in case of ship wreck, and that all regulations stipulated by law to safeguard life have been complied with.

April 17, 1912, "Saved From the Wreck: Men 79; Women 233; Children 16. Steerage Women and Children, 400; Seamen, 140."

The report said that 740 passengers had traveled in third class. The paper published names of passengers saved from first and second cabin, but the list was incomplete. (Compare with table in Preface.)

Also on April 17, 1912, "See No checks on Sea Travel; Titanic Disaster Appears to have Little Effect on Bookings of Outgoing Steamships."

On April 18, 1912, the paper asked: *If you were in a shipwreck, and you had an opportunity to be saved, but ... if you would have to leave your husband, what would you do? If your children were with you, would you go and take them, or would you send your husband, who is the money maker, with them, and stay behind to die?*

Mrs. John Bass, secretary of the fashionable north side suffrage organization and of the new Cook County federation declared:

"When I found the boat was in danger I would seek out the person on the boat in whom I felt the most confidence. It probably would be somebody whom I had just met during the voyage; maybe a maid, or some kindly wholesome woman who had inspired me with confidence. I should say to her, 'Take my child and get into the boat in my place. Please take the best care of my child that you possibly can.' Then I should stay behind with my husband."

On April 19, one of the headlines read, "Twelve of the Victims Worth $191,000.000."

The same day the paper reported that the *Carpathia* had arrived in New York.

"Carpathia In With Rescued From the Sea; Lands 745 Survivors of the Titanic in New York. Anxious Crowd at Pier. Only One Person Taken From the Wreck Dies on the Way. Victims Tells of Tragedy. Thirty-Nine Women Widowed."

Moline Daily Dispatch, Moline, Illinois

In addition to the usual headlines about the *Titanic*, this paper reported on the sermons delivered on the Sunday after the sinking by two pastors in Moline, Illinois.

The Rev. A. F. Bergstrom of the Swedish Lutheran Church [now First Lutheran] preached on the text John 10:11-16:

In alluding to the Titanic horror, [he] dwelt on the present-day mania for speed and amusement, compared with which human life seemingly is held very cheap. The great steamship, the largest ever built by man, to the speaker appeared as a result and embodiment of the accomplishments, the ideals and desires of civilization as it is today. The spirit of the day demands pleasure and amusement and the public is intoxicated with an unquenchable desire for these things.

The spirit of the times also would defy the Almighty, as is shown in the arrogant boast that this greatest product of man "could not sink," and so there was no need for lifeboats. Even to the last the doomed victims could not realize that this great ship would actually go down. In the final moments, however, as death was at hand, thoughts were turned to the last refuge….

The Rev. A. M. Johanson, pastor of the Swedish Mission Tabernacle Church preached to a congregation of 700 people at the Sunday evening service at his church.

He likened the working of God's hand in the destruction of the Titanic to the scene of tower building and confusion at Babel as it was manifest in Old Testament times. The pastor declared the catastrophe was a warning that none could discountenance. Better government regulation for insuring of safety of the ocean traveler must come at once.

The minister urged special prayers for the comfort of loved ones who have been made widows and orphans....[97]

Olympia Daily Recorder, Olympia, Washington

On April 30, 1912, the paper published a survival story told by18-year-old Anna Sjöblom of Finland. It was also published in *Tacoma Ledger.*

The story is included here because of its validity as an eyewitness account and because Anna was a Finland Swede, who traveled with Swedes, and spoke Swedish. She was from Mansala, Finland, and headed for Olympia, where her father, Gabriel Gustafson, as well as her uncle, Daniel, worked for Simpson Timber Company. Another article in *Minnesota History*, Fall of 2007, lists her as a Swede, traveling through St. Paul with Oscar Hedman, Paul Johnson [Carl-Olof] and Bertha Nilsson. Anna's boarding pass on the *Titanic* was valued at six million on the auction circuit, causing a major custody battle in the 1990s.

Anna's 18th birthday fell on the tragic day of April 14, 1912, when the *Titanic* hit the iceberg. She and another Finnish girl lost their way when they tried to find the boat deck and ended up on second-deck promenade deck, A deck. This probably saved her as she was able to enter lifeboat 16. Her Finnish traveling companions perished.[98]

Interview with survivor Anna Sjöblom

I woke up when the boat struck the iceberg" she said last night speaking in the Swedish language to Mrs. Matilda Nelson, who translated her sentences. "Everyone became excited at once. I got up and put on some clothes so that I could go outside. When outside, I had no time to go back again. My railroad ticket to Tacoma and a small amount of money was sewed in a little bag and hung around my neck, so that I could not lose it.

Water began coming up where I was in a short time, and I fought my way to get above it. I went up the stairs to the deck above and then tried to climb clear to the top. I climbed as far as a window, where I hung by my fingers. I couldn't go farther and I couldn't go back again. I waited there some minutes.

---

[97] "Wonders of Deep Revealed" in *Moline Evening Dispatch*, April 22, 1912, p. 7. Similar sermons were held at Moline's Second Congregational Church and United Presbyterian Church.

[98] *Olympia Daily Recorder*, Apr. 30, 1912. Anna Sjöblom settled in Tacoma, where she married Gordon Kinkaid and lived in Olympia. She died Nov. 3, 1975.

I was awfully afraid that I would fall and kill myself. Then an officer of the ship saw me and dragged me to the next deck.

Everywhere everybody was confused. I tried to get into a lifeboat and was pushed back. The boats kept filling up and going over the side, and it seemed as though I would go down with the ship.

I remember watching a little boy about 13 years old, whose parents had gone off in one of the lifeboats. He slipped into a boat and was thrown back up on the deck by a sailor. He crept into another boat and again they threw him back to the deck. The third time… he slipped into a boat and was saved. I talked with him afterwards.

The boat that I got into finally was the next to the last boat launched. There must have been 50 people in it. It was so crowded that we sat on each other's laps, three deep. While the boat was being lowered, a man jumped into it from the deck above. He came down feet first on my head and nearly broke my neck. He splayed over the people in the lifeboat and nearly fell overboard. I was in intense pain for hours after he had jumped on me. [Anna is listed as being rescued in lifeboat 16.]

The lifeboat was so crowded that I sat on a man's knee and had a woman on my lap. Several others did the same. There wasn't room for another person in the boat. When we rowed away from the Titanic my face was towards the sinking steamer, and the things I saw I never will forget.

I saw an officer shoot himself through the temple with a revolver on the bridge when the collision occurred. I saw passengers throw themselves overboard, shrieking for help. I saw men in the water floating on lifebelts, who were crusted with ice so thick that you could hardly make out their faces. I saw dead bodies floating about, covered with ice. Oh, it was too terrible to talk about.

I watched the big steamer every second of the last few minutes she was afloat. The reports were wrong when they say the boilers exploded. The ship just gradually sank in front, the bow went down out of sight, the lights, the low ones first and then the higher around the side of the hull, blinked out, one after the other. The steamer without a sound, except the shrieks of the people still on board, stood right up on end. It stood there several moments; then slid straight down into the water.

The sounds as the ship sank were the most awful sounds I ever heard. I never expect to hear worse. When the boat first began to sink, the people on board began to shriek and wail and moan. As it went down farther and farther the shrieks arose louder and louder and more awful. Then, as the boat began to tip up on end, the sound of cries was like something terrible. I still hear it," the girl shuddered as she tried to explain.

A terrible thing occurred right in our own lifeboat. A young couple, well dressed and refined, were in the boat when it was lowered. The young woman fell overboard. She struggled about and finally the men in the boat pulled her aboard.

Her husband, a fine looking young man with black hair and beautiful features, sat in a seat in the middle of the boat, and helped to make her comfortable Then, a few minutes after she had been pulled aboard, she collapsed, fell forward and died. She lay on the bottom of the boat, her face upward. We were all of us powerless to move, so crowded was the boat."

The young man just sat there and stared at her. He sat there without moving for an entire hour. At the end of that hour his hair, which had been very black before, had turned to all white. He was about 30 years old. At the end of an hour he looked like he was 70. He never spoke or moved after his wife died. The woman's dead body remained in the boat with us until we were rescued. After we had been taken on board the Carpathia, and the young man had been taken aboard, he collapsed on the deck of the rescue ship, fell over, and died. I never learned who he was. His hair had become white just like snow, and I doubt if any of his relatives or friends would know his body."

Miss Sjoblom reached New York on the steamer Carpathia, April 18, and remained there in the Swedish immigrant mission until last Tuesday, when she left for Tacoma. With her on the trip West were Paul Johnson [Carl-Olof], *and Oscar Hedman, countrymen* [Swedes] *who left the train at St. Paul, and Bertha Neilson* [Nilsson], *a countrywoman* [Swedish woman] *who came as far west as Montana. They were the first survivors of the wreck to come as far west and were objects of great interest on the train.*

Paul Johnson [Carl Olof] *one of her companions on the train, had remained in the ice-cold water, supported by a lifebelt, for six and one-half hours. He was of a powerful physique, or he could never have withstood the strain.* [Reported to be over six feet tall, he was rescued in one of the collapsible boats floating below the waterline.] *When he was hauled aboard the Carpathia, there was a half-inch crust of ice on his limbs and his hair was a mat of solid ice. He collapsed and was in bed for two days, but recovered quickly and was able to leave the ship unassisted when she arrived in New York.*[99]

Miss Sjoblom said that the waters about the wrecked steamer were literally covered in bodies after the Titanic sank. She saw a missionary, a large man in clerical clothing, floating about on a lifebelt. The bodies drifted about him so closely that he was forced to push them away from him with his hands. She said that other people in the water swam to the missionary, and tried to grasp his clothing for support. In order to save himself, he had to knock them roughly away. The missionary, she said was later saved.[100]

[99] 6 ½ hours is probably exaggerated although he was out of the cold water.
[100] *Olympia Daily Recorder*, Apr. 30, 1912. The underlining is mine.The missionary may have been Edvin Lundstrom, although he was not known to have worn clerical

Look for more stories from the American Press in the chapter, "The Swedish Survivors."

Spokane Daily Chronicle, Washington

April 15, 1912[101]

"Passengers of Titanic Saved, but the Ship is Sinking."

HUNDREDS TAKEN IN SAFETY FROM DISABLED VESSEL.

"Squadron of Liners Gather to Rescue of Disabled Ocean Monster.

"Leviathan of the Sea Badly Damaged on Maiden Trip [Caption for picture of the ship].

April 16, 1912

OVER THIRTEEN HUNDRED DROWNED IN SINKING OF THE STEAMER TITANIC-- WRECK SPREADS HORROR IN MANY CITIES OF THE WORLD

"Loss of Leviathan of the Sea Greatest Maritime Disaster in History—Men Gave Lives to Save Women and Children.

"Carpathia Almost too Late; Found only the Crumpled Wreckage and boats bobbing in Waves." [Page 2]

April 17, 1912

CARPATHIA CONFIRMS TALE OF HORROR ENDING HOPE THAT MORE ARE LIVING; Hope to find victim's bodies.

"Finnish Colony Lost.

"Duluth, Minn., April 16—A Colony of Finlanders, coming to settle on land in the vicinity may have perished when the Titanic took her fatal plunge. The colony consisted of 110 persons."

April 18, 1912

WRECK VICTIMS DEAD ON CARPATHIA; LINER SENDS REQUST FOR COFFINS

---

clothing. The 13-year-old boy was probably Johan Cervin Svensson, who was actually 14. The article was also published in the *Tacoma Ledger*. There were rumors that First Officer Murdoch, who was on the bridge when the collision occurred shot himself, but witnesses had seen him in the water. His body was never found. See other footnotes.

[101] *Spokane Daily Chronicle* for April 1912 scanned by Google and available online. I searched in vain for something about the Swede John Svensson Lundahl, who had lived on East Carlisle Avenue in Spokane, and was one of the *Titanic* victims.

Cunard Liner bearing only living of Titanic's human freight groups through fog to port—Senate Committee prepares for immediate investigation; Will demand presence of Ismay and Ship's officers—Naval official amazed that Titanic did not slow up when warned of icebergs—British House of Commons prepares for inquiry—International Marine conference on new shipping rules proposed.

April 19, 1912
SPLENDID HEROISM MARKED CONDUCT OF MARTYRS AT GREAT SEA TRAGEDY
"'Be British, my men' called Captain Smith to stalwart seamen who guarded boats and calmed passengers in face of doom. Millionaire and pauper alike stood aside to let weakest pass to safety.
"Capt. Smith Saves Drowning Baby and then Swims to Ship. [Page 2]
"Mrs. Futrelle Tells of her Husband's Brave Death."

April 20, 1912
"Sick, Distraught, Penniless Titanic Survivors Cared for: Ismay Calls Senate Disaster Inquiry 'Brutally Unfair.'"
MRS. ASTOR TELLS OF HER EXPEREINCE....

April 20, 1912
EXACT TOLL OF LIFE IN MONMOUTH DISASTER WILL NEVER BE KNOWN

April 22, 1912
TITANIC LOOKOUT ASLEEP?" [Not true]

April 23, 1912
RAILROAD OFFER LOWER RATES; PASSENGERS PREVENTED MORE RESCUES, SAYS THIRD OFFICER, ONE LONG MOAN AS SHIP SANK—LOOKOUT HAD NO GLASSES
DEATH STRUGGLES OF TITANIC VICTIMS TOLD BY OFFICER PITTMAN

April 24, 1912
OLYMPIC'S CREW DESERT; SAYS THE BOATS ARE UNSAFE

April 25, 1912
OLYMPIC CANNOT FILL HER CREW

April 26, 1912

CALIFORNIAN WITHIN TWENTY MILES OF THE TITANIC; CAPTAIN WOULD NOT AID DOOMED, SWEARS SEAMEN[102]

"Bodies of Astor, Straus, and Hays Found.

"Babies Tossed Across Chasm into Lifeboats."

April 27, 1912 [Page 3]

"Bodies Identified. MacKay Bennett Will Arrive at Halifax Monday, says Wireless Report."

[102] The distance between the *Californian* and the *Titanic* was likely less than 20 miles.

Titanic news in the Swedish Press [103]

DAGENS NYHETER.

Den stora katastrofen på oceanen: Titanic sjunken!
Omkring halftannat tusental människor omkomna

Titanic sjunker, efter att ha hållit sig flytande blott 4 timmar, 50 kilometer från den plats där kollisionen skedde. Ligger nu på ett djup af två kilometer.

Endast 700 människor räddade. Telegrammen uppge att det är de rika re som i främsta rummen köpt sig lifvets räddning på de andras bekostnad!

Dagens Nyheter (Daily News), Stockholm, April 17, 1912

Dagens Nyheter, Stockholm

The headline of *Dagens Nyheter* (Daily News), April 17, 1912, read:

”Den stora katastrofen på oceanen: Titanic sjunken” (The big ocean catastrophe: Titanic sunk)

”Omkring ett halftannat tusen människor omkomna” (About 1,500 people lost.) The paper expressed its ire over the fact that after four days it was still impossible to find out the identity of the Swedes on board and the number of casualties. It also reported that a special fund was established for the benefit of the Swedes who had survived the disaster.

---

[103] *Kristianstadbladet*, microfilm read at Vänersborg’s Bibliotek in 2010, 3 rolls for 1912 on inter-library loan from Landsarkivet in Göteborg, Sweden.

Kristianstadbladet, Kristianstad

Kristianstadbladet reported all passengers saved on April 16, 1912. (As did *Sydsvenska Dagbladet*, Malmö, which added that the ship was being towed to the United States.)

Kristianstadbladet wrote:

According to a wireless message from Halifax to New York, all Titanic's passengers have been saved in the boats. Among the passengers were about 70 Swedes. According to a telegram yesterday from Montreal, the Titanic slowly proceeded on its own in the direction of Halifax. A later telegram added that two other steamers accompanied the Titanic, side by side, and that all the passengers were aboard these steamers. A telegram sent at 4:00 p.m. from the cable steamer Minia, outside Cape Race, reported that the steamers pulling the Titanic tried to get it to shallow water near Cape Race to set it aground. According to a wire received in Halifax, the Titanic was sinking. [Except for the last sentence all of this turned out to be incorrect.]

On April 17, 1912, *Kristianstadbladet* reported a much darker story.

"Only 800 saved. The rest followed the giant steamer to the bottom.

"According to the latest telegrams, which are reported to be wholly believable, 635 passengers and 200 crewmembers were saved. The number of lost thus ought to be about 1500, a number that is considered minimum by the latest American telegrams....

"The *Carpathia* [the rescue ship] was in constant contact with the *Virginian* last night and wired the list of those saved." [Names not printed in this issue.]

The paper offered the opinion that the reason behind the accident seemed to be the race to cross the "big ditch" in the least amount of time and questioned whether the crew was sober.[104]

April 18. "When the Titanic sank" [Still no passenger names]

April 20. "Titanic's foundering

"The Carpathia arrives in New York. 1,635 people lost [Not the final number] Colonel Gracie's report." [Related elsewhere].

A Swede by the name of August Wennerstrom, who is among those saved, has told the following:

As the ship was about to sink, I noticed a collapsible lifeboat behind one of the funnels. Together with three other men I released it, and all four of us jumped overboard with the boat. It overturned four times, but every time we

---

[104] Even if speed played a part, there is no evidence of a race or misconduct by the officers.

managed to get it on the right keel again. While we drifted around, we saw at least 200 people floating on the water. All of them drowned. At last, my friends and I were taken up by the Carpathia.[105]

April 22. *Kristianstadbladet* reported on the *Titanic* inquiry. "Floating icebergs and their victims, and other tragedies."

April 24. "The Ocean graveyard. The ship that did not listen to the warning signals."

April 25. "The Titanic disaster." [Still no reports about the Swedes on board.]

April 26. "Captain Smith

"The White Star Line ordered to pay 12 million in compensation"

April 27. New 25-*öre* book about the horrible Titanic disaster.

"What Lady Duff Gordon witnessed." Her account can be found in the English language elsewhere, but one interesting comment quoted here was: "Several men stood nearby and joked with those going in the lifeboats. They said, 'The ship cannot sink. You will freeze to death among the ice down there.'"

April 29. "Titanic's foundering. The saved crewmembers isolated for questioning."

April 30. "The Insurance Companies' losses."

May 2. "The swimming graveyard as told by the crew and passengers aboard the *Bremen*."

May 4. "The arrival of the recovered bodies in Halifax."

May 6. "The Titanic disaster. The result of the inquiry."

"The Titanic had gone full steam despite the warnings. Only a few of the able-bodied seamen *(matroser)* were competent to manage the lifeboats, and the machinery to the water-tight compartment did not function satisfactorily. Adequate lifesaving material was also lacking."[106]

May 8. Finally the paper published the names of 22 of the 34 Swedish survivors. Here are their names divided on the ports from which they departed:

From Göteborg: Bertha Nilsson, Oskar Johansson, Elisabeth Dyker, Selma Asplund, Lillian Asplund [Felix Asplund omitted], Agnes Charlotta Sandstrom, Margaret Sandstrom, Beatrice Irene Sandstrom [Margaret and

---

105 This is only a small part of Wennerstrom's letter. As far as I know, no one else has reported that Collapsible A overturned more than once.

106 As pointed out earlier, the lifeboats were filled by the experienced first and second officers assisted by other officers. The water-tight compartments functioned the way they were supposed to, but when the ship sank by the bow, water flowed in from the top.

Beatrice were children] , Serwin Svensson [Johan Cervin], Karolina Byström, Dagmar Bryhl.

From Malmö: Olga Elida Lundin, Helmina Josefina Nilsson, Elis [Elisabeth] Johnson, Harold Johnson, Elenora Johnson. [The two latter were children.]

From Copenhagen: Carl Jansson (Karl Johnsson), Gunnar Tenglin, Einar Karlsson, Jan [Thure Edvin] Lundström, Carl [Carl Olof] Jonsson [Jansson], and Aurora Adelia Landergren.[107]

From Helsingborg: No one saved.

On May 29, 1912, the headline read, "800 people sacrificed due to bad discipline."

June 7. "The icebergs in the North Atlantic" [This was the last article about the *Titanic* that I found in *Kristianstadbladet*.]

Many of the young men of military age left Sweden to escape their military service. They went to Copenhagen, where they could buy a waistcoat that included the ticket and the necessary papers.

They were then directed to take a train to Esbjerg on Denmark's west coast and board a ship that took them on a 30-hour sail to Parkeston, England, where they boarded a train to London and on to Southampton. It was not the most convenient way to travel, but the only one that was open to them. Although they could have been labeled as illegal, they got away with it because the United States wanted settlers.[108]

Once in the U.S., they did not escape the U.S. Draft registration in 1917-18. Whether citizens or not, they had to register.[109]

[107] The main purpose for reading *Kristianstadbladet* was to search for information about Karl Johnsson from Killeberg, Kristianstad län, but this was all that I found about him. I already knew that he had departed from Copenhagen.

[108] The law that replaced the previous professional soldier system required 240 days of initial military training for Infantry men and 365 days for specialized forces, plus later repetition training in peace time. All able-bodied men between 18 and 47 could be mobilized in war time. In 1912, there was talk about extending the service, but this did not happen until the outbreak of the war in Europe in 1914 (World War I).

[109] If called to service, the non U.S. citizens had the option of returning to Sweden, in which case they would never again be allowed to enter the U.S.

Kalmar, published in Kalmar

On April 17, 1912, the paper reported about *Titanic's* collision with the iceberg. The ship began to sink ½ hour later. The Virginian had changed course to come to the rescue. Three steamers had heard the distress signals. On the same day, another article said 675 people had been saved and some of them were on board the *Parisian* and the *Virginian* although this had not been verified.

April 19: According to the latest wire, 7 million letters have been lost. The captain of the *Olympic* has reported that *Carpathia* was the only vessel with survivors on board. A few Scandinavian names were listed.

April 22: The Swedish mail carried by the *Titanic* consisted of seven sacks containing letters, 23 sacks with printed material, and 212 certified packages, which had been mailed from Sweden on Good Friday, Easter Eve, and.... In a separate article: 675 passengers have been rescued, but as of 10 o'clock on April 16, there was no news about the steamers *Parisian* and *Virginian*.

April 26: "The human genius had once again created a miracle ship, the *Titanic*. Nature was now definitely conquered by modern technology. Then, with just a slight shaking of mankind's triumphant work it breaks to pieces."

May 18: Relatives of two perished passengers from Halland, Nils Larsson of Falkenberg and Carl Carlsson of Sörby near Falkenberg, have requested compensation.

May 29: The steamer *Oceanic* has brought a sad reminder of the *Titanic* disaster ashore to the White Star Line in New York, a collapsible lifeboat carrying three bodies that had been found 300 nautical miles from the place of the sinking.

July 5: The families of 51 Swedish *Titanic* victims have asked for support from the Lord Mayor Fund in London. On August 14, the number of requests from Swedish families had risen to 72. [110]

---

[110] Translated from the Royal Library's digitalized newspapers, Stockholm.

Titanic news in the Swedish-American Press

As was the case with the American press and the Swedish press, the Swedish-language newspapers published in America contained both accurate and inaccurate accounts of the *Titanic* sinking. Many of the smaller papers reported very little or printed what *Nordstjernan* (the North Star) in New York had already published. Unfortunately, the largest Swedish paper in Worcester, Massachusetts, *Svea*, is not available on microfilm for 1912. The other Swedish-American newspapers reported similar stories and are therefore omitted here. Special interest stories about the Swedes on board have been included in their respective profiles.[111]

Nordstjernan, New York

The paper *Nordstjernan* (The North Star) reported on the sinking April 19, 1912 under the headline, "Titanic's förlisning" (Titanic's foundering).

Shortly after ten o'clock Sunday evening a wireless telegram to the Marconi station at Cape Race, Newfoundland, announced the awful news that the White Star Line's newest giant steamer, Titanic, had crashed into an iceberg and that immediate help was desperately needed.

A short while later came the message that the steamer was sinking. Additional wireless messages indicated that the steamer foundered at 2:20 Monday morning at 41.16 N and 50.14 W, about 1,150 miles east of Sandy Hook.

When the steamer began to sink, women and children were placed in lifeboats that were manned by necessary crew members and lowered into the water which was calm at the time. The first steamer to arrive at the place of the accident was the Cunard liner, Carpathia. The steamer found all the lifeboats that had been launched from the Titanic and everyone in the boats were saved by the Carpathia, which then attempted to search for the shipwrecked at the place of the sinking.

---

[111] *Swedish-American Newspapers: A guide to the microfilms held by Swenson Swedish Immigration Research Center, Augustana College, Rock Island, Illinois,* compiled by Lilly Setterdahl and published by Augustana College Library in 1981, lists 236 titles of the 1,158 Swedish-American newspapers and periodicals published in North America.

Shortly thereafter, several other steamers arrived—the Olympic, the Virginian, the Parisian, the Californian—and continued the search for the shipwrecked, so that Carpathia could steam toward New York. It looks like no others than the ones who were aboard the Carpathia have survived the catastrophe.[112]

Referring to Captain Smith, the paper reported:

Until recently, his career at sea had been remarkably accident free. But then he commanded the Olympic when it collided with the cruiser Hawke on Sep. 20, 1911, outside the Isles of Wight, and last February he commanded the Olympic when the steamer lost a propeller blade and made it difficult for her to reach New York.

With the air saturated with wireless messages from all stations along the coast, it has been difficult to receive reliable telegrams. The ones received have been interrupted with messages from other ships within reach. Also, several private wireless stations have sent out a lot of wireless messages, thus only increasing the confusion.

The custom people had been ordered not to question the survivors. The ship would not be stopped at the quarantine station but was allowed to proceed directly to the pier, where Immigration officers came aboard.

A list of passengers with Scandinavian names was published with the reservation that the names were garbled and that a complete list was not yet available. The paper also reported that President Taft had received telegrams of sympathy from King George V of England.

Nordstjernan's former logo, courtesy Ulf Mårtensson, publisher. The first issue came out on September 21, 1872. Published continously for 140 years, it is now the only Swedish-American newspaper in America.

---

[112] The *Olympic* and the *Virginian* were too far away. The *Californian* arrived in the morning, but found no survivors. *Mount Temple* of the Canadian Pacific Railroad Line, 49 miles away when notified, was also on the scene searching for bodies. The *Parisian* was not at the scene.

TITANIC-KATASTROFEN

Nordstjernan, New York, page 7, April 23, 1912. Courtesy Ulf Mårtensson, publisher. The photo on the bottom left was taken at the Swedish Immigrant Home in New York. The man to the left is almost certainly the tall Karl Johnsson. The man in the back standing one step up is Pastor Lilja, the director of the home, and the boy to the right is 14-year-old Johan Cervin Svensson. He is also shown standing alone in the middle of the page.The women are Olga Lundin, Adelia Landergren, Hilda Hellstrom, Anna Sjöblom, and Berta Nilsson. The text about the survivors has been translated and included in various parts of this book. The flag-wrapped memorial, top center, says, "Jag går mot döden vart jag går." (I go toward death wherever I go.)

Interviews with survivors

On April 23, 1912, the *Nordstjernan* reporter, G. G., reported:

In order to hear something about the awful disaster from the survivors themselves, we looked up a few of the rescued Swedes last Friday. We found them at the Swedish Lutheran Immigrant Home, the Salvation Army Officer School, and St. Vincent's Hospital. First, we visited the Immigrant Home, where the director had gathered the female survivors Anna Nysten from Kisa, Östergötland, Bertha Nilson from Lysvik, Vermland, Hilda Hellstrom from, Domnarfvet, Dalarna, Anna Sjoblom from Finland, Aurora Landergren from Karlshamn, and Olga Lundin from Hällaryd, Blekinge [should be Småland].

All looked healthy and vigorous without the slightest cold despite the fact that they had been exposed to the elements for hours. Neither did the terrible disaster seem to have dampened their spirits. All were calm, collected, and dispassionate. Perhaps it was apathy following their awful and nerve-wrecking experience.

We were aghast to hear them talk about the disaster in this cold manner like it had not affected them at all. Perhaps they could not yet grasp what had happened. At least that's the way it felt. Hilda Hellstrom appeared to be the most talkative of the girls.[113]

Hilda's story is included in the chapter, "The Swedish Survivors."

After the reporter had talked to the women, he continued with the Swedish men at the same Immigrant Home. They were:

Ernst Persson from Stockholm, whose parents resided in Julita, Södermanland; Oscar Johansson [formerly Olsson] from Lunna, Orust on its way to Detroit, Michigan; Oscar Hedman, who had traveled from Ragunda (Jämtland län) and was on his way to Bowen, North Dakota; Karl Janson [Johnsson] from Killeberg, Skåne; and 14-year-old Severin Svensson.

See the stories of Ernst Persson, Oscar W. Johansson, Oscar Hedman, Karl Janson [Johnsson], and Johan Severin Svensson in the section, "The Swedish Survivors."

The reporter then went to St. Vincent Hospital, a Catholic institution, where he found Norwegians, Danes, and Finns, along with the following Swedes:

Mrs. Agnes Sandström from Hultsjö, Småland, with two children, on her way to join her husband in San Francisco; Edw. Lundström from Simrishamn, a former missionary to China, headed for Los Angeles; Miss Velin Öhman from Mariestad, traveling to Chicago; Wm. H. Törnqvist, employed by the American Line; and Selma Asplund from Småland with a son and a daughter. Her husband and three sons had perished at sea.

See the stories of Lundström, Hedman, and Karl Johnsson as reported by *Nordstjernan* in the section, "The Swedish Survivors."

The reporter praised the Women's [Relief] Committee:

The kind sisters and nurses at this hospital give the sick as well as the healthy the most loving care, and nothing was left undone to assure their comfort. During our stay (visit) here, we could observe the admirable work that is carried out by the Lady's Committee and its assistants for the benefit of the rescued. They go from one to the other, taking down their names and addresses, relations and living conditions, place of destination, and so on.

For the rescued, the committee sends telegrams for free to relatives at home, and those who lack cash get both [that] *and tickets. Nothing is spared to help these unlucky people. The ladies work up a sweat laboring day and night, and surely thousands of blessings are bestowed upon them.*

Next, the reporter visited The Salvation Army Cadet School, where he found five Swedes, whom he described as "*raska gossar*" (robust boys). They were Gunnar Tenglin from Stockholm on his way to Burlington, Iowa; Einar Karlson from Oskarshamn, headed for Brooklyn; John Asplund from Oskarshamn, also headed for Brooklyn; Karl [Olof] Jansson from Örebro on his way to Swedeburg, Nebraska; and the newspaperman Aug. E. Wennerström, who wrote and published his own account for the same issue of *Nordstjernan*. See more about these men in the chapter, "The Swedish Survivors."

In summary, G. G. wrote:

All these young men confirmed with one voice what the other Swedes had said, namely, that all the Swedes on board the Titanic had behaved splendidly. The officers did not have to use the pistols on them.

The same could not be said for sydlänningarna [the southerners, referring to passengers from the Mediterranean area]. All five men were healthy and robust, bodily and spiritually, and all expressed their great appreciation to the kind and helpful Salvation Army soldiers, who had cared for them in every way. They had afforded them a large, light, and splendid room and seen to their all-compassing wellbeing.

Nordstjernan's reporter Gunnar Wickman wrote a separate article about his interview with Lt. Haakon Björnström-Steffanson. The reporter expressed his own admiration for him.

"This dashing lieutenant—so typical for a Swedish officer—does not seem affected by the hardships of the last few days. The refreshing, honest coolness of an army officer has stayed with him." See "The Swedish Survivors."

Survivor August Wennerstrom, himself a journalist, wrote his own account of the journey published April 23, 1912. See the stories about these Swedish survivors in translation under their respective names.[114]

On April 26, 1912, *Nordstjernan* wrote about the Dyker couple of New Haven, Connecticut. Mr. Dyker, who stayed on board and perished, was said to have emigrated when he was 18-years old. He worked in New York for one year before coming to New Haven, where he became a popular tram conductor. His elderly mother lived in Sweden. About Mrs. Dyker (the former Elisabeth Anderson), it said that she was ill and recuperating at the home of her parents at 187 Center Street in New Haven. Dr. A. P. Bergman was hopeful about her recovery. Her mother, Mrs. Anderson, and brother, architect Fritz Anderson, were in New York when the *Carpathia* arrived. Mrs. Dyker did not want to leave her husband, and waited as long as she could to get into a lifeboat.[115]

---

[114] *Nordstjernan,* New York. 23 Apr. 1912. Microfilm, SSIRC, Augustana College, Rock Island, Ill. A group picture of the survivors appeared, but Björnström-Steffanson and [Johan] Severin (Cervin) Svensson were pictured separately.
[115] Elisabeth Dyker was rescued in lifeboat 16.

The same issue, April 26, reported from New Haven about "En underbar räddning" (A wonderful rescue) concerning the brother of Andrew Palmquist, Poplar Street. The brother, Oscar L. Johansson, was incorrectly named Axel Johanson, but is identical with Oscar Leander Johansson from Vilstad, Småland.

Buoyed by two life jackets, he floated on a door. A girl in one of the lifeboats tossed him a shawl that he kept until he was rescued by the *Carpathia*. The reporter said it was a miracle that he survived in the ice-cold water.

The April 30th issue of *Nordstjernan* carried information about additional Swedish *Titanic* survivors not accounted for earlier. These survivors had been taken to St. Luke Hospital and St. Hoving Hospital.

Mr. G. Peterson and another ambulance driver by the last name of Erikson had taken Mrs. Alice Johnson and her children, a one-year-old daughter and a four-year-old son, as well as Helmina Nilson to St. Luke Hospital in New York, where they had received the best of care and received new trunks.

Miss Dagmar Bryhl was taken Dr. Hoving's Hospital. Her brother and fiancé had been turned away from the lifeboat despite the fact that no women and children were in sight. The lifeboat was lowered with only six people [?]. It added 50 at sea. Miss Bryhl departed for Rockford, Illinois.[116]

On May, 14, 1912, *Nordstjernan* reported on engineer Axel Welin's well-attended lecture about safety at sea at the American Museum. Mr. Welin said the lifeboats were constructed to carry 65 people, but could carry 100 in a calm sea. He also said that it was of utmost importance that the passengers took part in lifeboat exercises. Mr. Welin illustrated his talk with slides. After the lecture, Engineers Broady and Sivert demonstrated the exhibited davits and the life-saving equipment. [117]

---

[116] Dagmar Bryhl Lustig was rescued in a lifeboat that took on passengers from Collapsible B, either 4 or 12.

[117] The newspaper did not acknowledge that the Swedish engineer was the inventor of the davits used on the *Titanic* to lower the lifeboats.

On May 17, 1912, *Nordstjernan* reported on a talk given in Chicago by August Wennerstrom from Ystad, in which he accused the Swedish Immigrant Home in New York of withholding parts of the funds from the Women's Relief Committee. Instead of giving the survivors $25.00, they had received only $5.00, he said. While Wennerstrom stayed at the Salvation Army, he went to the Swedish Immigrant Home and threatened to report the home to the Red Cross.

To find out what had happened, *Nordstjernan* interviewed the director of the home, Pastor Lilja, who explained the matter.

The funds from the Women's Relief Committee had been forwarded to the Swedish Immigrant Home by Mrs. Signe Stolpe as follows:

Hilda Helstrom, Carl Johnson (of Killeberg), Ernst Person, Oscar Johanson, Berta Nilsson, Aurora Landergren, and Anna Sjoblom received $25.00 each, While Cervin Svenson received $15.00 and Oscar Hedman $10.00. Anna Nysten (who was probably the survivor who was met by relatives), received $25.00 directly from the office of the Women's Relief Committee. The recipients signed the receipts on April 22, 1912.[118]

In addition, on April 23, the survivors at the Immigrant home received money as follows: Anna Nysten, $25.00, Hilda Hellstrom, $25.00, Cervin Svensson, $25.00, Ernst Persson, $50.00, Oscar Johnson [Johanson], $25.00, Berta Nilsson, $25.00, Aurora Landegren (spelling varies), $25.00, Anna Sjoblom, $25.00, Olga Lundin, $25.00. On April 26, Olga Lundin received an additional $50.00.[119]

The five-dollar gifts mentioned by Wennerstrom were not from the Women's Relief Committee, but from the White Star Line as shown in Pastor Lilja's report to his board:[120]

[118] Pastor Lilja met *Carpathia* when she docked in New York. The Department of Immigration released twelve Swedes to him. Of these, one was cared for by relatives. Pastor Lilja was told not to let any of the others leave until "Immigration" had investigated them.

[119] *Nordstjernan*, New York May 21, 1912.

The White Star Line's officer George Edenholm presented a train ticket to each of the survivors to their point of destination. The women received sleeper tickets. Everyone also received a voluntary gift of five or ten dollars in cash, depending on the length of their journey. It was rumored that by accepting these gifts, they forfeited any compensation for lost luggage, but this was completely untrue. Mr. Edenholm visited the Immigrant Home three times before he could meet all the survivors and personally present the funds. Pastor Lilja never had access to these funds. The only funds he handled were special donations from private sources and from the Swedish Lutheran Church in Brooklyn. These donations from private sources were divided into small gifts between the most needy.[121]

In the same issue for May 17, *Nordstjernan* related welcome news from the Stockholm paper *Dagens Nyheter.* More than 2,000 Swedish crowns had been sent to the Swedish Consulate in New York for distribution among the Swedish *Titanic* survivors. The money had been raised at a matinee for which everything was donated.[122]

Hemlandet, Chicago and Galesburg[123]

The April 16 issue carried the paper's first headline about the *Titanic.* *Jätteångare förgås* (Giant steamer founders). "The World's largest ship, Titanic, crashes into an iceberg and sinks after four hours. 600 passengers rescued. Several steamers rush to assist and save Titanic's passengers."

The iceberg was described as huge and the *Titanic* as sinking. "For several hours nothing was heard from the stricken steamer resulting in fears for the same and its 1,470 passengers and 860 crewmembers."

The news that gave false hopes to many included: Passengers were taken on board the *Carpathia* and the rest had been taken on board the *Parisian*, the *Virginian*, and the *Olympic.* The *Titanic* was said to be towed by the *Virginian* and other ships that were trying to get it to shallow water before it sank.

---

[121] *Nordstjernan*, New York, May 17, 1912. Pastor Lilja continued to defend the Immigrant Home against Mr. Wennerstrom's accusations in the *Nordstjernan* issue for May 21, 1912, saying that those who said they had received less money were not telling the truth.
[122] *Nordstjernan*, New York. Microfilm, May 17, 1912.
[123] The actual title in 1912 was *Det Gamla and det Nya Hemlandet* (The Old and the New Homeland). The paper started in Galesburg, Ill., in 1855.

Before *Hemlandet* went to press, a wire was received with the bad news. The *Titanic* had gone down outside the Newfoundland Banks with about 1,500 people on board.

On April 23, the paper wrote: Among her victims were about 150 Scandinavian and Finns. One survivor was quoted as saying, "When the water reached the boilers, three terrific explosions occurred and the steamer split in two."

On page 10, the paper published the first but not definitive list of Scandinavian passengers divided on first, second, and third class.

On April 30: Memorial services to be held in New York, Washington, D.C., and Chicago. On page 8, an article written by August Wennerstrom and first published in *Nordstjernan* was reprinted.

On page 30 of the same issue, a report began entitled, "*De Våra*" (Our Own). The reports continued on May 14, 21, and 30. One subtitle read, "New route announced." West-going steamers should set their course 180 English miles south of their ordinary route outside the Newfoundland fishing banks. The paper also reported on the U.S. Senate Hearings with excerpts from some of the testimonies.[124]

On May 14 and 21, 1912, *Hemlandet* published the names of the Swedes on board the *Titanic*, some of whom were not Swedish:

Svenska Amerikanaren, Chicago, Illinois

Svenska Amerikanaren reported extensively on the sinking. On April 18, 1912, it published a dramatic story headlined, "*Jätteångaren Titanic förliser*" (The Giant steamer Titanic founders). Having recapped the tragedy, the reporter continued about his own reaction to the event.

I ask myself and others how such a tragedy could occur. With the equipment and science available to seafarers it's possible to see icebergs from miles away.... Did they depend too much on Titanic's strength and good luck and therefore [were] *less observant? Titanic was not the only steamer that met an iceberg, but it was the only one that could not avoid it.*

[124] *Hemlandet, various dates.* When I found something substantial about the Swedish passengers, I added it to their profiles.

As the paper went to press, we received a message from Rockford saying that Curt Lustig and his sister from Skara, Västergötland, were on board the Titanic, traveling under the names Carl and Dagmar Bryhl. Among the names of the rescued we find Dagmar Bryhl, and among the victims. Carl [Kurt] *Bryhl, Miss Lustig's brother, and Ingwald* [Ingvar] *Enander was supposedly also on board…* [Enander was Dagmar's fiancé.]

From Aurora, Illinois, with reference to Mrs. Alice Johnson, "Mrs. Johnson, was accompanied by her two sisters, Louise and Marie Anderson. We have reasons to believe that Mrs. Johnson and her two children were rescued…."[125]

In the issue for April 25, *Svenska Amerikanaren* wrote about the arrival of *Carpathia* in New York.

At 9 o'clock in the evening, Carpathia was anchored at the pier. The gangplank came out and with it the shipwrecked. It was a row of mourners, because each one had lost a loved one. Most of them were women and children—widows and orphans, who had lost the most beloved to the grip of the ocean. The 25,000 people on the quay stood breathless. Large tears rolled down the cheeks of a mother when she learned that her son was not among the rescued. And then there was the smile from another eye that had seen a sister…. Captain Rostron was greeted with hurrahs when he stood on the bridge with hat in hand and bid the masses farewell 24 hours later….

The paper continued the report on "How Titanic sank":
…a severe explosion shook the Titanic. The stern rose and the propellers became visible and the bow took a dive…. The explosion was caused by the water hitting the steam engines. The Titanic was doomed. It sank to a depth of two miles.[126]

According to this paper, as well as other sources, the last piece rendered by the band was *Nearer My God to Thee*, but Junior Wireless Operator, Harold Bride, said it was *Autumn*. Some argue that the band would not have played the former because it would have been too scary for the passengers to hear. Lawrence Beesley, a second-class passenger, however, noted that many of the hymns sung dealt with dangers at sea, as for instance, *For*

---

[125] *Svenska Amerikanaren*, Chicago, Apr.18, 1912. Mrs. Johnson was identical with Elisabeth (Alice), married to Oscar W. Johnson, St. Charles, Ill. She was saved along with her two children. The two sisters have not been found on any of the *Titanic* passenger lists.
[126] *Svenska Amerikanaren,* Chicago, April 25, 1912.

Those in Peril on the Sea [correct title, *Oh, God our help in ages past*]. He said it stirred emotions when it was sung in the morning. The article goes on to state that the managing director for the White Stare Line, Mr. Ismay, entered a boat while women were still waiting, something that he denied in his testimony to the Senate.[127]

The article continued: "One would think that everyone on board the Titanic when the steamer sank would have been lost, but this was not the case. Several rescued men jumped into the water… and managed to get hold of floating wreck…."

The following story is attributed to Colonel Gracie, a first-class passenger rescued on Collapsible B, a capsized lifeboat.

[I] *swam toward wreckage that I saw ahead of me. I reached it and saw that it was one of the four poorest boats* [Collapsible B]. *A man took my leg and pulled me into the boat. Soon after came the second officer, Lightoller, swimming. He also managed to reach the boat. There were no oars, so the men lay prostrated in the boat and drove it forward with their hands in the water or pieces of boards that they had found floating in the water. All around us we saw men fighting for their lives. They reached the boat and clambered to the edge. … Several of those taken up in the boat froze to death before Carpathia could come to the rescue.*[128]

The paper went on to report on the Swedish victims and survivors with Chicago as their place of destination and who their relatives in Chicago were:

Passengers with relatives in Chicago:

[127] Mr. Ismay maintained that he saw no women waiting, and said he had helped many women getting into the boats. *The Titanic Disaster Hearings*, pp. 14-15. Newspapers owned by William Randolph Hearst were especially critical of Bruce Ismay.

[128] Gracie's opinion. The collapsible boats were not poor, but different. They had canvas sides for more compact storage. During the U.S. Senate Hearings, Colonel Gracie testified: "The top [of Collapsible B] was irregular, and about 3 ½ feet wide… and it was between about 25 and 30 feet long… We did not stand on it [the bottom] until just before sun up. *The Titanic Disaster Hearings*, pp. 415-416.

Victims

"Gärda Dahlberg from Stockholm, sister of Signe Dahlberg, 1830 Calumet Avenue.

"Oliver Myhrman from Värmland on his way to his uncle (morbror) John Nelson, 6526 Laflin Street.

"Mrs. E. E. West, Eric West, and Kene [?] West. Mrs. West was the sister of Andrew Larsen, 3759 Wabansia Avenue. [The only people named West on the Titanic passenger list were British.]

"The wife and four children of Nels Paulson, 938 Townsend Street. Paulson has been in this country for only a short time. He had sent travel money to his wife and children, the eldest being 8 and the youngest 2. The family came from Hälsingborg [Bjuv], Skåne. Mrs. Alma Paulson was the sister of Olof Berglund, 2305 N. Spring Street, and Axel Berglund, 1725 Kimball Avenue.

"Gustaf Swanson, brother of Isaac Swanson, Norwood Park.

"Olof Nelson, who traveled with Swanson and was on his way to Norwood Park. [No passenger record found of either Gustaf Swanson or Olof Nelson].

"Marie and Louise Anderson, 16 and 18 years old sisters of Mrs. Alice Johnson, St. Charles, Illinois [These two girls are not listed as *Titanic* passengers.]

"Alfred Gustafson from Waukegan, who had been on a visit to his homeland. [Buried at Sea].

"Paul Andreason, brother of Ernst Nelson, 8109 Sherman Avenue, Chicago, and son of Andreas Nilsson, Kalfahult, Hallaryd parish, Kronoberg's län.

"Nels Johanson, travel companion of Andreason, son of Johannes Karlsson, Svaneryd, Hallaryd parish, Kronoberg's län.

"Carl Bryhl [Kurt Lustig] son of Public Prosecutor Lustig, Skara, Västergötland, on his way to his uncle, Oscar Lustig, Rockford."

"Survivors:

"Mrs. [Elisabeth] Alice Johnson, wife of Oscar E. Johnson, St. Charles and their two children were saved, and so was Mrs. Thelma Nelson of St. Charles. [Thelma not found in the records]. They were cared for at a hospital in New York. At the same hospital were Mrs. Selma Asplund and her two small daughters [one daughter and one son].

"Dagmar Bryhl, sister of the earlier mentioned victim, Curt Bryhl, was saved. Their actual surname was Lustig."

The paper also reported on the joy that Alma Anderson, 2728 Hamden Court, Chicago, felt when she found out that her fiancé, Ivar Holmstrom, had not sailed on the *Titanic.*[129]

Svenska Tribunen Nyheter, Chicago, Illinois

(Merged with *Svenska Amerikanaren.)*

In the issue for April 23, 1912, the first-page headline read, "*Atlanten slukar Titanic...*" (The Atlantic swallows up the *Titanic.*" The article named a few Chicagoans who went down with the ship, the same ones listed earlier by *Svenska Amerikanaren.*

The paper also wrote about some non-Swedish passengers: Mr. and Mrs. Allison's nanny had taken their 10-month-old baby and stepped into a lifeboat. When the parents could not find the baby, they began a fruitless search that prevented Mrs. Allison and the other child, 2-year-old Helen Loraine, from entering a lifeboat.[130]

Major Archibald Butt, military aide to U.S. President Taft, was described as having died like a man. He assisted with the loading of the lifeboats and refused to step into any of them.

Jacques Futrelle, the French author, had trouble convincing his wife to part from him. Time and again, she rushed toward him, hugging him, and asking him to come with her in a lifeboat. "For Gods sake," he said..."Go, it's your last chance to be rescued." When a couple of officers came forward, he was finally able to free himself and get her to step into the boat."

About the treatment of third-class passengers, the article stated in error that passengers were shot:

The third-class passengers who managed to leave their cabins were held back by crew members, but the pressure from the masses became too great.... Four men managed to reach a lifeboat but an officer ordered them to leave their places to women, and when they did not obey, he shot them down and threw their bodies overboard.

---

[129] *Svenska Amerikanaren,* Chicago. The list of rescued Swedes is too inaccurate to copy here. I recognized only a few of the names. Errors were frequent in the immediate aftermath of the tragedy. The discrepancies must have caused tremendous anguish.

[130] The baby, Hudson Trevor, was raised by an aunt and uncle. Helen Lorain may have been the only child victim in first-and second class.

No one was shot, although one officer admitted that he used his revolver to scare some men off. He said his weapon was unloaded. Surviving fifth officer Lowe fired some shots in the air to keep the men from entering the boats. The foreigners did not understand the directions given, but they understood what a gun meant.

The story of first-class passenger Björnström-Steffanson was retold. In this account, he admitted that he had jumped into a lifeboat.[131]

Moline Tribun, Moline, Illinois

Moline Tribun published quite a bit about the *Titanic*, but the personal information about survivors and also the photographs appear to have been reprinted from *Nordstjernan.*

On May 15, 1912, the paper published the "Official Statement by Survivors:"

We the undersigned, surviving passengers from the steamship Titanic, in order to forestall any sensational or exaggerated statements, deem it our duty to give to the press a statement of facts which have come to our knowledge and which we believe to be true.

On Sunday April 14, at about 11:40 p.m., on a cold, starlight night, in a smooth sea and with no moon, the ship struck an iceberg which had been reported to the bridge by lookouts, but not early enough to avoid collision.

Steps were taken to ascertain the damage and save passengers and ship. Orders were given to put on life belts and the boats were lowered.

The ship sank at about 2:20 a.m. Monday, and the usual distress signals were sent out by wireless and rockets at Intervals from the ship. Fortunately the wireless message was received by the Cunard's Carpathia at about 12 o'clock midnight, and she arrived on the scene of the disaster about 4 a.m. Monday.

The officers and crew of the steamship Carpathia had been preparing all night for the rescue and comfort of the survivors, and the last mentioned were received on board with most touching care and kindness, every attention being given, irrespective of class. The passengers, officers, and crew gave up gladly their staterooms, clothing, and comforts for our benefit. We all honor them.

---

[131] *Svenska Tribunen Nyheter,* Chicago.

The English board of trade passengers' certificate on board the Titanic showed approximately 3,500. The same certificate called for lifeboat accommodation for approximately 950 in the following boats:

Fourteen large lifeboats, two smaller boats, and four collapsible boats.

Life preservers were accessible and apparently in sufficient number for all on board.

The approximate number of passengers and members of the crew carried at the time of collision was:

First class 330, Second class 220, Third class 750, Officers and crew 940. Total 2,340. [All totals were later revised.]

Of the foregoing about the following were rescued by the steamship Carpathia: First class 210, Second class 125, Third class 200. Total 535 passengers.

Officers 4, Seamen 39, Stewards 96, Firemen 71, Total crew 210.

Total on board, 2,340. Saved 745, Lost 1,595.

The total saved was about 80 percent of the maximum capacity of the lifeboats.

We feel it our duty to call the attention of the public to what we consider the inadequate supply of life saving appliances provided for on modern passenger steamships and recommend that immediate steps be taken to compel passenger steamers to carry sufficient boats to accommodate the maximum number of people carried on board.

The following facts were observed and should be considered in this connection:

The insufficiency of lifeboats, rafts, etc. Lack of trained seamen to man the same (stokers, stewards, etc., are not efficient boat handlers). Not enough officers to carry out emergency orders on the bridge and superintend the launching and control of lifeboats. Absence of search lights.

The board of trade rules allow for entirely too many people in each boat to permit the same to be properly handled. On the Titanic the boat deck was about 75 feet above water and consequently the passengers were required to embark before lowering the boats, thus endangering the operation and preventing the taking on of the maximum number the boats would hold.

Boats at all times should be properly equipped with provisions, water, lamps, compasses, lights, etc. Life-saving boat drills should be more frequent and thoroughly carried out, and officers should be armed at boat drills. Great reduction should be made in speed in fog and ice, as damage, if collision actually occurs, is liable to be less.

In conclusion, we suggest that an international conference be called to recommend the passage of identical laws providing for the safety of all at sea, and we urge the United States government to take the initiative a soon as possible.[132] ˙[No names of signees.]

Iowa Posten, Des Moines, Iowa

Iowa Posten reported on May 3 about the investigation concerning the *Titanic's* demise.

... *No less than two steamers and one sailing vessel were within 20 miles of the Titanic. The steamers were the Californian and Mount Temple. The captains denied it, but the passengers made it clear that they saw Titanic's distress rockets. Three warning signals were received by the Titanic regarding packed ice and icebergs, but they were disregarded.* [Mount Temple was 49 miles away.]

The paper accused the wireless operator on the *Titanic* of being shameless, which was based on the report that he had told the *Californian* operator to shut up.[133]

On May 17, the paper reported on the rescued, the saved, and the lucky ones who had sailed on other ships, but were thought to be on board the *Titanic.* Augusta Bäckström and her two sons from Jönköping had traveled on another steamer. Petrus Persson from Brearyd had sailed on the *Cymrie.* Swedish-American Martin Jonsson with roots in Kristianstad had changed his mind about going on the *Titanic* and gone on another steamer.The paper erroneously reported that two siblings Mauritz and Tekla Karlsson, 19 and 17 years old, and their uncle and foster father, farm owner, Johan Nilsson from Burs, Gotland, had perished on the *Titanic.* The farmer was said to have left a wife at home, who was taking the loss so hard that she was in danger of losing her mind.[134]

---

[132] *Moline Tribun*, Moline, Ill., May 15, 1912, in Swedish, and *Chicago Daily Tribune,* April 19, 1912 in English. Neither paper lists the original source. I compared and adjusted my translation with the English version. Bread and water were stowed under the seats in the lifeboats.

[133] *Iowa Posten,* Des Moines, Iowa, May 3, 1912. If the senior wireless operator Jack Phillip, had known that the *Titanic* was in danger, he had, no doubt, stopped sending hundreds of telegrams to Cape Race paid for by the passengers. Bride later said that the *Californian's* message was so loud that it hurt his ears. The *Californian* became quiet when its operator went to bed at 11:30 p.m. Phillips was on top of the collapsible boat B, but died on board the craft.

[134] *Iowa Posten*, Des Moines, Iowa, May 3 and 17. The last three names could not be found in Merideth's *Titanic Names.* The paper, *Hemlandet*, Chicago, May 21, 1912, also reported in error that the siblings Mauritz and Tekla Karlsson, 16 and 17 years

Kvinnan och Hemmet, Cedar Rapids, Iowa

This monthly magazine for women printed short comments about the *Titanic* tragedy on its editorial page in the May and June issues. In June, it wrote: It is well known that *Carpathia's* Captain Rostron is of Swedish heritage. [She was right. He was born in London to Swedish parents. He had one older brother who was born in Göteborg and two sisters.][135]

Omaha-Posten, Omaha, Nebraska

On the 24th of April, the paper displayed a bold headline on the first page about the disaster and was critical of *Titanic's* junior wireless operator, who was identified as the 20-year-old junior operator, Harold Bride. The reporter assumed that the two young wireless operators on the *Titanic* were hired because they were "cheap labor."[136] One of the victims, the paper reported, was Emil Brandeis, a well-situated Omaha businessman.[137]

A long list of Scandinavian names followed, including one that named survivors, but like other lists published at this time, it was incomplete and/or incorrect. Among the Swedish survivors, I recognized the names of Selma Asplund, Lillian Asplund (misspelled as Astlund), Dagmar Bry(h)l, Karolina Byström, Einar Carlson, Sigrid Lindström, Bertha Nelson, and Ernst Persson.

On May 1: The captain of *Mount Temple* of the Canadian-Pacific Line received messages in the morning of the 15th saying that *Titanic* was in trouble. He hurried toward the site, but 14 miles from the place of the sinking, he encountered so much drift ice that he was unable to continue. The *Californian* was also stopped by the ice. Its captain, Stanley Lord, had seen the rockets, but was unable to move because of the surrounding ice. The accusations continued saying a large part of the *Titanic* crew was not boat wise and therefore unable to launch the lifeboats in an orderly fashion, while it is well known that the boats were loaded mainly by the experienced first- and second officers, assisted by other officers. Foremost, the paper blamed the disaster on the ship's high speed and the lack of lifeboats. A new list of names appeared that included names of persons whose bodies had been recovered.[138]

---

old, had been on board the *Titanic* in the company of their foster father, farm owner, Johan Nilsson, from Burs, and that they perished.

[135] *Kvinnan och Hemmet*, Cedar Rapids, Iowa, June 1912. *Nordstjernan,* New York, reported on his Swedish parentage on April 30, 1912.

[136] The wireless operators were hired by the Marconi Company to send messages paid for by the passengers. Phillips was born Apr. 11, 1887 and had just turned 25.

[137] Emil Brandeis was 48-years old. His body was found and buried in Omaha.

[138] *Omaha-Posten,* Omaha, Neb., Apr. 19, 24, and May 1, 1912. Officer Lightoller stood with one leg in the lifeboat and the other on deck helping the women into the boats. Despite the cold, he sweated profusely wearing only a sweater and pants as

The Swedish Survivors

Titanic survivors in New York, photo courtesy Günter Bäbler, Switzerland (From the left: Olga Lundin, Hilda Hellstrom, Johan Cervin Svensson, Alida Landergren, Ernst Persson, and Berta Nilsson.)

Life after surviving the *Titanic* could be difficult. Some of the men suffered severe frostbite and were affected by the damage for the rest of their lives. Added to their physical injuries were the psychological affects of the disaster. For the victims it was all over on the fateful night of the sinking of the

---

he practically lifted the women by their elbows and lower arms. When he lowered the last boat, the listing of the ship created a large gap and it may have been impossible to lower additional lifeboats.

leviathan, but for many of the survivors the tragedy was too painful to even talk about.

The women and children were rescued in the lifeboats. First officer Murdoch allowed a few men to enter lifeboats when no women were present, but several men survived through any other means available to them. They jumped into a boat or into the water and grasped onto wreckage, or were washed overboard when the last collapsible boats floated off the deck. They survived by pushing others aside and clinging to the collapsible boats, one that was floating upside down and one that was filled with water. Those still alive at dawn were transferred to other boats and brought aboard the steamer *Carpathia*.

The shipwrecked were young, strong men, used to hard work. Carl Olof Johnson and Karl Johnson were described as "huge" and exceptionally strong. Karl Johnson continued to prove his strength later in life as a logger in the American Northwest and Carl Olof fought on the frontlines in World War I.

In Victorian times, men were supposed to protect women and die for them if necessary. They accompanied their women to the lifeboats, kissed them good bye, and prepared to die. They were not supposed to take up space in the lifeboats meant for women and children even though there were spaces left when the boats were launched. The White Star Line manager, J. Bruce Ismay, was judged harshly for the rest of his life.

The surviving men had to fend themselves. Were they cowards or heroes? Naturally, they were sensitive to being judged harshly. As the reader will see in this section, a couple of the men made up stories to save their reputation when interviewed by reporters. Therefore, those who actually survived by fighting the cold Atlantic were unfortunately also suspected of fabricating their stories.

Only a few of the Swedish survivors married, and if they married, they usually did not have children. But there were exceptions. August Wennerstrom married a woman he met at the Salvation Army in Chicago, and they had seven children. Ernst Persson had left his wife and two children in Sweden. After the tragedy he planned to return home because he did not want to expose his family to the voyage. His wife might have thought otherwise, because she and the children arrived in the fall of 1912. Mr. & Mrs. Persson made their home in Indiana and were blessed with two more children.

Two marriages ended in divorce. It also happened that the victims' parents in Sweden were divorced after the tragedy. One male survivor became mentally Ill. Karl Johnson broke his ties with his large family in Sweden.

Hilda Hellstrom married a man 29 years her senior. Alice Johnson had divorced once and was then twice widowed. Olga Lundin lost her fiancé on the *Titanic* and married in the 1930s. Having worked as domestic in the U.S. for many years, she and her husband returned to Sweden. Anna Nysten married and seemed to have lived a happy life, but she, too, experienced sorrow when her firstborn died in infancy. Nine of the 34 survivors returned to Sweden for good and one for a few years.[139]

According to the director of the Swedish Immigrant Home in New York, where some of the survivors recuperated, they received first-class-railroad tickets to their destination from the White Star Line and a small amount of cash. The women also received sleeper tickets. From the Women's Relief Committee they received items of clothing and cash in amounts between $10.00 and $75.00 dollars depending on need.

Note that married women usually kept their maiden names in Sweden at this time in history. If they immigrated to the U.S., they assumed their husband's surnames. Also, note that the patronymic name tradition still prevailed, e.g., the son of Anders Larsson received the last name of Andersson, meaning the son of Anders, while the daughter (dotter) of Anders received the last name of Andersdotter. In the early 1900s, the parents could choose whether the children should continue with that tradition or adopt their fathers' surnames (or in some instances their mother's). Once the name tradition had been altered, it was supposed to continue in the same manner. Surnames not ending in "son" or "dotter," as for instance, Asplund, were usually soldiers' names or names adopted by clergy, burghers, merchants, or tradesmen. Many Swedish immigrants changed their names more than once after they had arrived in America. Therefore, one cannot say that one version is wrong and another correct.

The survivors are listed in alphabetical order except for the children who are listed after their mothers. The passengers who sailed on the Wilson Line's steamer *Calypso* from Sweden to England were found on the *Calypso* Manifest as referenced in the "Preface."

---

[139] Two of the nine were tourists.

"We can go back to bed"

Asplund, Johan Charles

When his cabin mate woke him up and said, "The ship has gone aground," Asplund, the sailor, laughed and said, "Gone aground! Here in the middle of the Atlantic? We can go back to bed."

The 23-year old emigrant carpenter traveled with Einar Karlsson, also from Oskarshamn. The two men, like so many other Swedish men of military age, went to Copenhagen to buy a waistcoat that included the tickets and the necessary papers.

Born January 31, 1889, in Oskarshamn, Kalmar län and baptized John Charles, he was the son of seaman Johan August Asplund (born August 13, 1854 in Mörlunda parish, Kalmar län), and Emilie Augusta Jonsdotter (born April 16, 1864 in Mörlunda). The parents divorced in 1894, and John Charles grew up with his mother and two brothers. All three brothers followed in their father's footsteps and went to sea. John sailed as *jungman* (approx. deckhand) on the brig *Frida* out of Oskarshamn before he emigrated from No 1 b, Oskarshamn on April 2, 1912. He was listed as having died in Oskarshamn, but might have died at St. Gertrud's Mental Hospital in Västervik.[140]

In an undated letter to his mother written from the rescue ship *Carpathia*, John wrote that they left Copenhagen on April 4 and went by train and ferries to Esbjerg, on Denmark's west coast, where on April 6, they boarded a ship that took them to Parkeston, England. From there they went by train to Southampton, where they stayed at the Emigrant Hotel a couple of days.[141]

Asplund and Karlsson were booked on the *Adriatic*, but due to the coal strike they were transferred to the *Titanic*. They were both rescued in Lifeboat 13, but he said that he and Karlsson jumped into the next to last lifeboat. In New York, they stayed at the Salvation Army Cadet School, and while housed there, they had their picture taken with Gunnar Tenglin, August Wennerstrom, and Carl Olof Jansson.

---

[140] Information courtesy Björn-Åke Petersson, Kallinge, Sweden.

[141] Jerker Pettersson, "Titanicmannen-en Oskarshamnares sorgliga öde." Submitted by Britt Maria Ekstrand. *PLF-Nytt*, Oskarshamn, Sweden, April, 2011, Nr. 97. While he praised the *Titanic* and likened it to a hotel, Asplund was critical of the squalor on the *Carpathia* despite of its life-saving role and the fact that it took on about 700 extra passengers.

According to the Ellis Island records, Asplund was going to his brother, Fred (Karl Alfred) Asplund, 110, Washington Avenue, Minneapolis, and also received and used a ticket to Minneapolis, but returned to New York, possibly to Mrs. A. Engstrom, 212 53rd Street, New York City, who may have been his aunt on his mother's side.

John Asplund registered for the WWI draft June 5, 1917 in Kings County, New York while residing at 409 Berglin (?) Street, Brooklyn. He was single and a painter for A. Larson. He had served in the Swedish Navy for ten (?) years and was described as short with blue eyes and brown hair. [142]

Both Asplund and Carlsson served at sea in World War I.

On May 24, Asplund wrote a lengthy letter to his "beloved mother" from Minneapolis.

Johan Asplund's letter

We were asleep when the collision happened. Einar woke me up and said. The ship has gone aground." I laughed and said, "Gone aground here in the middle of the Atlantic! We can go back to bed." After about 15 minutes, a passenger came and knocked on our door saying that we had collided with an iceberg. We got up and dressed, and took our time. We did not believe that the ship would sink because of the watertight compartments....

It was a long walk below. We could not go up on deck amidships to get to the stern. When we came astern ... they opened the gates to first class, and third-class passengers could go up there. We followed the crowd, and when we got up there, the lifeboats were lowered and they said that women should go first. The first boat was lowered, and Einar and I agreed that we would go in the second. I entered, but when Einar was ready to enter, he was boxed on the ear and when I saw that, I jumped back up on deck.... When the next to last boat had been lowered a bit, I decided to jump. Einar agreed. When it was down about 3 meters, we jumped. If we had not, we would not have been saved.[143]

They sat in the lifeboat for six hours, perhaps a little longer, before they were taken up by the *Carpathia*, where they were treated to a sip of coffee, Asplund wrote. They shook from the cold. He had given his coat to a fireman who was dressed only in his underwear. "I thought he needed it better than I," Asplund said.

---

[142] www.ancestry.com. There were three different registrations for the First World War draft. The first one was on June 5, 1917 for men aged 21-31.

[143] Jerker Pettersson, April, 2011, Nr. 97.

On August 14, 1919, The Swedish Consulate in Rouen, France, issued a Swedish passport for Asplund and two other Swedes, and on August 16, Asplund boarded *La Lorraine* in Le Havre as a passenger sailing to New York. The voyage was paid for by his employer. [This was customary for employees who needed to get back to the home port.] He had sailed from New York on June 25 on a French steamer.[144]

Asplund returned to Sweden in 1923 and was admitted to a mental hospital in Västervik. He tried to escape the hospital three times, but was found and brought back.

According to a distant relative, Asplund had snuck onboard a ship in Portland destined for Antwerp in Belgium and was confused and violent when he arrived. The Swedish Consulate in Antwerp sent him to Sweden, where he was admitted to an institution for the destitute in Göteborg on February 5, 1923. Appearing confused, Asplund displayed an aversion to wearing socks and being touched.

In April, 1923, the patient was picked up by his brother but became violent toward him and had to be arrested. He was admitted to the hospital in Västervik. Asplund was confined to bed but was often getting up trying to get out through windows and doors. His earlier experience on the *Titanic* and in the war was not mentioned. After many years in confinement, he died at the mental institution on August 14,1943.[145]

"Why couldn't we be together until the end?"

Asplund, Selma

Mrs. Carl Oscar Asplund, 38, had emigrated in 1893 and was on her way to her former hometown of Worchester, Massachusetts, with her husband and children. [No relation to Asplund above].

Selma was born October 10, 1873 in Alseda parish, Jönköping's län, the daughter of Gustaf Otto Johansson (born 1859 in Alseda) and Johanna Larsdotter (born 1850 in Alseda). The family lived at Pilagården, Vagnhester, Alseda. In 1890, she had three sisters and three brothers.[147]

---

[144] www.titanicmannen.se/ It's not known who his employer was at the time.
[145] www.encyclopedia-titanica.org. See also www.titanicmannen.se.
[146] Jerker Pettersson, see earlier notes.
[147] *Emibas* created by the Swedish Emigrant Institute & the Federation of Swedish Genealogists, 2005. SSIRC. Her siblings were Gustaf Adolf Roderik, born 1872, Anna Serafia, born 1877, Johan Vilhelm, born 1877, Thekla Josefina, born 1880, Carl Eugene, born 1884, and Hanna Elisabeth, born 1886.

Mrs. Asplund did not talk much about the tragedy, but at one time, she reflected on why her husband had not allowed them to die together as a family. Lillian and Felix were removed from her and placed in a lifeboat. The people in the boat demanded that the mother come down also. When the father and three sons remained behind, she turned to her husband and said, "Why did you do that? Why couldn't we be together until the end?"[148]

On May 9, 1896 Selma married Carl Asplund at Gethsemane Lutheran Church in Worcester (now First Lutheran).[149]

Following a visit to Sweden, Selma, her husband, and their first-born son, Oscar Filip, sailed from Göteborg in August 1901, listing their destination as Worcester. They arrived in Boston on the *Ivernia* from Liverpool.[150]

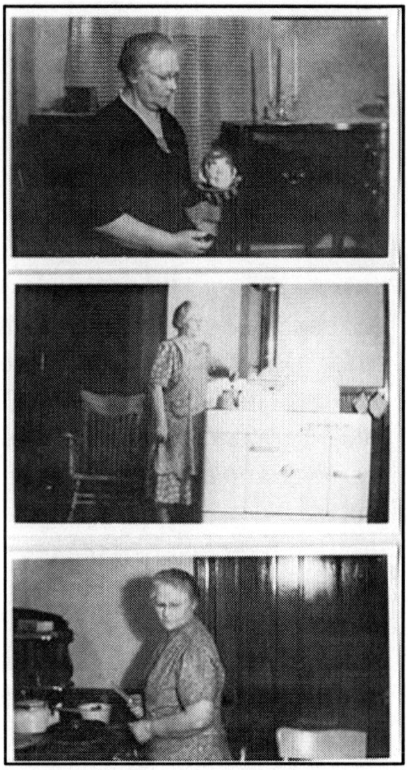

Three photos of Selma taken later in life, courtesy Andrew Aldridge, Henry Aldrige & Sons.

In 1910, the family lived in Alseda, Sweden. The census for Alseda shows that the couple resided at Gustafsgården, Pepperda. Their children, except for the youngest, were all listed as being born in "North America:" Oscar Filip, born December 12, 1898, Clarence Gustaf Hugo, born September 17, 1902, the twins Carl Edgar and Lillian Gertrud, born October 21, 1906. The youngest, Edvin Roy Felix, was born March 13, 1909 in Alseda.[151]

In 1912, the Asplunds decided to return to Worcester where they had lived earlier. Selma boarded the *Calypso* in Göteborg, April 5, 1912 together with her husband, Carl, and their five children. They reported the residence for all of them as America and their destination as Worcester.[152]

---

[148] www.titanicnorden.com
[149] Swedish-American Church Records on microfilm.
[150] *Emigranten Populär.*
[151] *Emibas.*
[152] Four of their children were American citizens and Carl Asplund had his first American papers.

The price of their third-class cabin with four bunks on the *Titanic* was about $105.00.[153]

Selma's husband and three sons, Philip Oscar, 11, Clarence Gustaf Hugo, 9, and Carl Edgar, 5, perished while Selma and two of her children, Lillian (twin sister of Carl) and Felix, 3, were rescued in Lifeboat 15.

With a smile her husband guided her to a lifeboat saying that he would follow with their eldest sons. (See more details about their efforts to be rescued in the profile for her husband in "The Swedish Victims.")

A Swedish-language newspaper, published in Worcester, wrote the following about Selma Asplund and her children:

.... Several relatives of the Asplund family.... were to meet the ship-wrecked at the arrival of the Carpathia last Thursday evening and bring them to Worcester. Mrs. Asplund and her two small children had however been taken to St. Vincent Hospital, where Mr. Charles E. Carlson after much searching found them, and last Saturday, the severely tested family arrived in Worcester and were taken to the home of Mrs. Asplund's brother-in-law and sister, Mr. and Mrs. Olof Ahlquist's, on 151 Vernon St. Many relatives and friends of the Asplunds and others, who had been drawn to the train station, became deeply touched at the sight of the unfortunate wife, pale and drawn, supported on the arm of her brother-in-law.... Among the friends who met Mrs. Asplund when she stepped off the train was Pastor J. A. Eckstrom, who pressed her hand and offered a few words of comfort. Mrs. Asplund's face was distorted by a bruise that she had suffered when a half-crazed man jumped down in the lifeboat. His shoe hit her in the face and his body knocked her so hard on her shoulder that she was almost lame. She was pressed into a corner of the lifeboat. Before she could scream, the man placed his hand over her mouth and ordered her to be quiet. Then he stretched out face down on the bottom of the boat....

Mrs. Asplund recalled how her husband had awakened at the collision with the iceberg, and run up on deck. He soon came back saying that an accident had occurred.... It took a while before she had dressed herself and her four [five] *young children. When they came up on deck, it was very cold. Mr. Asplund put lifebelts on all of them. Mrs. Asplund ran over to the other side of the ship to see about lifeboats there. She stopped by the first and saw how women and children were squeezed in. A sailor took the baby boy from her arms and gave him to a woman who was already in the boat. The mother did not know if she should call out to get her child back or if she should step into the boat, but in the same moment her husband came and hurried to take*

---

[153] www.encyclopedia-titanica.org.

the little girl from her. "We will find room in one of the other boats," he said encouragingly to her.

There were about 40 people in the boat.... When she turned to the ship, she could see her husband and their three boys at his side, waving to her with a handkerchief. This was the last she saw of her husband and her three boys. It was bitingly cold in the open boat and she and her children were thinly dressed. A man took off his coat and swept it around the little boy, who was the only who didn't seem to be freezing. It seemed like it took forever before they were brought on board the Carpathia....

We had gone to bed at the usual time in the evening in our family cabin. It was at this time that my husband had a premonition. Before retiring, he sat down on the edge of the bed and uttered in all seriousness, "The noise is terrible. Ever since we left England they haven't done anything but drink, dance, and play cards. If everything goes well, it's remarkable, and if we make it to land, it will probably be the last time we travel over the Atlantic." (Mr. Asplund had crossed the Atlantic five times.)[154]

On the same page, the following notice appeared:

We have now learned that a benefit concert will be held for Mrs. Asplund at the Worcester Theater Sunday May 5 with a variety of performances presented by local and other talents, which we have reason to believe, shall bring in a considerable sum. A committee of 25 persons is heading this effort.

When *Boston Post* questioned Mrs. Asplund about her ordeal, she said:

I had no clothing on to speak of and the night was bitter cold. A man from steerage took off his coat and wrapped it around little Felix, my baby. Looking up I saw my husband with six-year-old Lillian in his arms. He cried out to a man in the boat with me and dropped Lillian over to him. He caught her and placed her by my side. "Now you come," I cried, "with the boys," but he shook his head. We pulled away. As the water came between us and the Titanic, I still saw him standing there by the rail. I shall always see him as I did in the last few minutes. There at the rail with my three growing boys, hand in hand smiling sweetly at me to the last.[155]

Gethsemane Lutheran Church in Worcester held a memorial service for the victims of the disaster and a collection was taken for the benefit of Mrs. Asplund and her children. The pastor of the church, Reverend Eckstrom, was

---

[154] *Skandinavia*, Worcester, Mass., Wednesday April 24, 1912, p. 20, in Swedish.

[155] *Boston Post*, April 20, 1912, as quoted by Andrew Aldridge in *The Voyage* 64, Summer 2008, p. 18.

the first to welcome Selma as she stepped off the train in Worcester. A local newspaper wrote:

Slowly recovering from the effects of her experience, Mrs. Asplund is today confined to the home of her sister, Mrs. Olof Ahlquist, at 151 Vernon Street, where she was taken upon arriving from New York.

Many relatives and friends called today, but little mention was made of the disaster which tore husband and three loving children from her side. Lillian and Felix are rapidly recovering from the effects of their sad experience. The girl realizes to some extent what had happened, but little babe Felix, three years old, cries for his papa. A gloom is cast over the relatives of the Asplund family and mention of the tragedy is made only in whisper.[156]

In the 1900 Federal Census for Worcester (Ward 2), Charles Asplund was listed as 29-years old, a renter and wire roller. Having arrived in 1893, he had acquired his first papers. Selma's year of immigration was also listed as 1893. Phillip was five months old. One source listed Selma as having lived in Kansas City, Missouri, before coming to Worcester. The same source quoted her as having said upon her arrival in Worcester after the tragedy that the third-class men were as gallant as any in declaring, "Women and children first," and that was the reason why she was widowed.[157]

In the 1920 Census, Ward 6, Worcester, Selma was listed as head of her household, renter, and laundress in her own home. Lillian was 13 and Felix 10. In the 1930 Census, Selma had no occupation and was presumably supported by her children who lived at home. Lillian, 23, was listed as typist, and Felix, 21, as draftsman in a factory.[158]

Selma died April 15, 1964 at the age of 90 in Worcester. She had been cared for by her daughter, Lillian. See more under Asplund, Lillian.

---

[156] *Worcester Evening Gazette*, Apr. 22, 1912.
[157] "The Last American Survivor of the Titanic Disaster: Lillian Gertrud Asplund, October 21, 1906-May 6, 2006," The Editors. *The Titanic Commutator*, Vol. 30, No. 173, 2006.
[158] US Census Schedules, www.ancestry.com.

The 3-year-old boy was in his mother's arms

Asplund, Felix

Lillian and Felix

The 3-year-old Felix was the youngest child of Selma and Carl Oscar Asplund, born March 193, 1909 in Alseda, Jönköping's län and baptized Edvin Rojj Felix.

He was rescued along with his mother and sister in Lifeboat 15. His mother said that a man in the lifeboat took off his coat and wrapped it around the infant. When he boarded the *Calypso* in Göteborg with his family on April 5, his residence was listed as America, the same as the rest of his family. He worked as a draftsman for Coppus Engineering and Engraving in Worcester for 35 years. He died a bachelor at the age of 73 in 1983 in Worcester, Massachusetts.[159]

"My clothes had gotten very dirty and wet"

Asplund, Lillian Gertrud

Lillian lived until she was nearly one hundred years old. She usually shunned reporters. On the frightful morning of April 15, 1912, Lillian lost her father, two older brothers, and her twin brother.

The 5-year-old girl was a U.S. citizen, born October 21, 1906 in Worcester, Massachusetts, the daughter of Selma Asplund and her husband Carl Oscar. Lillian boarded the *Calypso* in Göteborg, April 5, together with her family.

She was rescued along with her mother and a younger brother in Lifeboat 15. Her father and three brothers perished. After the tragedy, the destitute survivors of the Asplund family lived with Lillian's aunt and uncle at 151 Vernon Street.

---

[159] "Felix" Asplund is mentioned only briefly in articles about his mother and sister. The WWII draft registration for his age group is not available online.

Lillian Asplund, photo courtesy Andrew Asplund, Henry Aldridge & Sons

While the lifeboats were loaded, Lillian's mother said she would rather stay with her husband and go down with the ship, but he told her that the children should not be alone. Lillian said, "She had Felix on her lap and she had me between her knees. I think she thought she could keep me a little warmer that way." Lillian later described the sinking ship as looking like a big building going down."[160]

The city of Worcester raised nearly $2,000 for her mother, which was invested and used as needed. Lillian held various secretarial jobs in Worcester, but worked mainly for the State Mutual Life Insurance Company. Upon her passing, the *Boston Globe* reported that 30 people had attended the service at Nordgren Memorial Chapel in Worcester, some of them strangers.

Lillian Asplund never married. Her hobby was growing roses. At one time she related a memory from the rescue ship:

A woman took all my clothes off me. My clothes had gotten very dirty and wet in the lifeboat. My mother was trying to find me. She was saying, 'I have a daughter!' Well, she found me. And eventually my clothes were dry, and I put them back on. They took us, the children, to the place where they take people who are sick. Well, not sick, but people who needed a little more attention. The people on the Carpathia were very good to us.

She remembered that the *Titanic* was very big, and had just been painted. "I remember not liking the smell of fresh paint," she said.

---

[160] www.absoluteastronomy.com/

From the same source, we learned why the family had left their home in Worcester to visit Sweden:

In 1907, Lillian's father had taken his family to Småland, Sweden, to help his widowed mother settle problems with the family farm. By early 1912, the family was ready to return to the United States, and Lillian's father booked passage for all of them aboard the RMS Titanic." Lillian was the last Titanic survivor to remember the actual sinking. At the time of her death, two survivors lived in England, and both were less than a year old at the time of the sinking. [161]

Lillian Asplund

In the spring of her 98th year, Lillian welcomed a member of the Titanic Historical Society into her home for an impromptu visit. Lillian rested on a couch and was pleased to receive flowers. As she spoke of her rose garden, she revealed that she once had a beau, an admirer, who planted 25 rose bushes around her house. She recalled a memory from when she was little, saying that she used to pick dandelions for her mother, who put them in a vase even though they were only weeds.[162]

Lillian Asplund died in her home in Shrewsbury, Massachusetts, on May 6, 2006, at the age of 99 ½ and was buried in All Faiths Cemetery in Worcester alongside her father, mother, and younger brother were buried.[163]

A representative of the Titanic Historical Society wrote that about fifty people attended Lillian's funeral service on a cold spring day in May at Nordgren Memorial Chapel on Lincoln Street. Lillian's plain, white metal casket decorated with pink inlaid roses was closed. Live flowers decorated the room. There were flowers from the Titanic Historical Society. Pastor Newhall opened the service by reading the 23rd Psalm. The simple monument at the cemetery has the family name of Asplund engraved on each side.[164].

After her passing, a shoebox was found containing letters, photos and mementos. It included her father's pocket watch stopped at 2:19 a.m. and a

---

[161] http://wikipedia.org.

[162] Shelley M. Driedzic, TIS Trustee, *Voyage*, 56. The official journal of the Titanic International Society, Summer 2006, Freehold, New Jersey.

[163] http://en.wikipedia.org/wiki/Lillian-asplund/

[164] Paul A. Phaneau, *The Titanic Commutator*, No. 173, 2006.

ticket contract for the *Titanic*, kept dry in his lifejacket pocket until his body was recovered 12 days later.[165]

The 364 items found in Lillian Asplund's shoebox were expected to bring in a combined total of £150,000 (about $300,000). At an auction held in London April 19, 2008, the contract (*Utvandrarkontrakt*) for the tickets purchased from the White Stare Line representative Carl Eriksson in Göteborg sold for £33,000 ($65,772.00) to Stanley Lehrer, an American collector. (The contract shows that Mr. Asplund paid 795 crowns for the tickets, equal to about $212.00 at the time.) Mr. Asplund's pocket watch sold for £31,000 ($61,766.00) to an unnamed leading Swedish collector. The family's "Inland Passage paper" from New York to Worcester sold for £27,000 (about $54,000) to a collector in London.

Andrew Aldridge of the Henry Aldridge and Son Auctioneers said the collection was, "one of the most important of its type in recent years." The article does not state how much Carl and Selma's wedding rings sold for. Neither does it say who the beneficiary of the money was. The White Star Line had returned the items to Mrs. Asplund because it considered them of "small value." A notebook included in the collection revealed that Mr. Asplund at one time contemplated settling in California. One of the items was a letter from Selma Asplund to her mother-in-law in Sweden. She wrote, "My nerves are so weak and my eyes are so poor because I have been crying so much…."[166]

"For a moment I felt a cold shiver up my back"

Björnstrom-Steffanson, Mauritz Håkan

The single 28-year-old Swedish-American, a wealthy businessman traveling in first class, admitted to feeling fear when the call came for "Women and children to the lifeboats." Using the first name of Hokan, he lived at a prestigious address in Manhattan, New York.

Born November 9, 1883 in Gysinge, Österfärnebo parish, Gävleborg's län, he was the son of mill administrator (*bruksförvaltare*) Erik Samuel Steffansson (born 1849 in Sunnemo, Värmland) and Berta Maria Brunström (Björnström?) born in 1852 in Uleåborg, Finland). When Håkan was 5-years old, the family moved to Sofiedal in Valbo. In 1900, the father was the operating manager (*disponent*) at the Mackmyra Sulfite Mill in Valbo parish, Gävleborg's län, and Håkan lived at home. In 1905 and 1906, he lived in

165 *Daily News*, London, Apr. 19, 2008.
166 *Ibid.* See also Andrew Aldridge, *Voyage*, 64, Summer 2008. Courtesy Barb Shuttle, editor, and Rick Sundin, Davenport, Iowa. It was later learned that Lillian's cousins were the beneficiaries.

Stockholm, but in 1906, he had moved back to Österfärnebo. He was listed as lieutenant in the Reserve.[167]

Having matriculated in Falun in 1902 and studied at the University of Uppsala, he began graduate studies at a technical institute in Stockholm. The same year, he became a first lieutenant in the Reserve (Svea Artillery Regiment).

During the years 1903-1909, he was employed at Rydö Sulfite Works. He had a brother in Stockholm, who was also a lieutenant in the Reserve.[168]

Steffanson followed in his father's footsteps and became a chemical engineer. In 1909, he traveled to Washington on a scholarship from the Swedish government to inquire about the possibility of exporting Swedish pulp to the United States. He stayed and established himself as a businessman in New York. After a short visit to Sweden in the spring of 1912, he booked passage in first class on the newly built *Titanic*.[169]

His port of embarkation in Sweden is unknown, but he boarded the *Titanic* at Southampton as a first-class passenger (ticket number 110564). He may have shared Cabin C-52 with the Englishman Hugh Woolner. The two knew nothing of the danger until an officer came and ordered the passengers to get their lifebelts and go to the boat deck. While Steffanson was on deck, he joined Woolner in assisting women, among them Mrs. Edward Candee into Lifeboat No. 6.

Later, Woolner and Steffanson heard pistol shots fired by Purser Herbert McElroy intended as a warning to prevent a rush on Collapsible D, which was fitted into the davits previously occupied by Lifeboat 1. The two men rushed over and helped the officer pull men out of the boat and the loading soon resumed.[170] Woolner and Steffanson then jumped into the same boat, Collapsible D, as it was being lowered.

In the interview published in *Nordstjernan*, Steffanson says, "It was I, Colonel Archibald Gracie, and an English Captain Woolner (a former Cambridge rower)—we sat in the smoking salon playing a game of cards when the collision occurred." They hardly noticed the jar, so they continued to play cards and enjoy a hot drink because the night was bitterly cold.

But before long, the shout, "Life belts on," spread like wildfire though the ship. And when an officer yelled, "Women and children to the life boats," we understood that there was danger ahead. And I have to admit that for a

---

[167] From Swedish Church records courtesy Björn-Åke Petersson, Kallinge, Sweden. The information from Stockholm was excerpted from *Rotemansarkivet.*
[168]*Hemlandet*, Chicago, May 14, 1912.
[169] Ulf Ivar Nilsson, "Titanics hjälte," *Det hände I Gävle*. (2002).
[170] www.encyclopedia-titanica.org. Fifth officer Lowe admitted that he fired shots in the air to scare male passengers from entering the lifeboats.

moment, I felt a cold shiver up my back. But when faced with such danger, one becomes a man and feels a huge responsibility.

However, an unbelievable chaos broke out on the various decks. Never in my life will I forget the terrible sights that I witnessed on that Sunday night. It's not easy to forget. It will leave deep marks for the rest of life. We helped hundreds of women and children into the lifeboats. Many by force.... I thought I had strong nerves, but more than once I had to turn away from the unnerving moments when many dear ones stepped over the line to the unknown, and as big, strong men without fear embraced their chilling deaths. I managed to put a Swedish woman, a countess Posse, into a lifeboat; but it was impossible to hunt the ship for Swedes....

Having talked about other first-class passengers (Mr. Astor, Major Butt, Widener, Guggenheim, and Mr. and Mrs. Strauss), Steffanson was asked what happened to him.

"When the call came, 'Everyone for himself' as the last boat had left the Titanic, we threw ourselves in the water 20 feet below. It was Col. Gracie, Woolner, and I. We managed to grab on to one of the collapsed canvas boats and stayed afloat for about 15 minutes until we were taken up...."[171]

Woolner, the Englishman, on the other hand, testified during the Senate Hearings that he and Steffanson had jumped 9 feet out from A Deck into a collapsible boat that had room left in the bow. Steffanson jumped first, but when Woolner jumped he tumbled off the gunwale, and Steffanson pulled him into the boat.[172]

Lightoller reported that he had seen two men jump into a lifeboat from A Deck. They were the only men he had seen doing that, but he added that he did not blame them.[173]

From about 200 feet the shipwrecked people saw the *Titanic* go under.

"Huge and dark, the enormous giant lay there with its thousands of electric lights casting shimmering reflexes on the bluish-black waters that swallowed it all, living and dead. Then it rose as in a last convulsion of death, and with a horrible thunder the *Titanic* ceased to exist."[174]

---

[171] Gunnar Wickman, *Nordstjernan*, New York. April 12, 1912, p. 12. Col. Archibald Gracie survived and wrote an account about his experiences that was published as a separate book and also as "Struck by an Iceberg" in the *Story of the Titanic as told by its survivors.* On pages 125-126, he wrote that he had met "H. Bjornstrom Steffanson, the young lieutenant of the Swedish Army, who, during the voyage, had told him of his acquaintance with Mrs. Gracie's relatives in Sweden. Gracie was rescued by Collapsible B and Steffanson and Hugh Woolner by Collapsible D.

[172] *Titanic Disaster Hearings*, p. 373.

[173] Lightoller in *The Story of the Titanic*, p. 296-297.

[174] *Nordstjernan,* Interview with Steffanson.

The *Carpathia* manifest shows Steffanson as being in the Diplomatic Service with his last permanent address as Stockholm. His destination was his brother Lt. Bjornstrom, New York City and his latest connection to Sweden as "Ryda" (Ryd), Sweden.[175]

Steffanson registered for the WWI draft as Hokan Mauritz Byernstrom Steffanson of Manhattan living at E 57, a citizen of Sweden and president of Steffanson & Co located on E. 42nd in New York City. His wife was listed as Mary Byernstrom Steffanson. Describing himself as tall and slender with blue eyes and brown hair, he signed the registration on September 12, 1918.[176]

On June 26, 1926, Hokan Steffanson and his wife Mary arrived in New York on the *Aquitania* from Southampton after a visit to "Ruda" (Ryd, Sweden). On November 11, 1930, Hokan B. Steffanson and his wife Mary arrived in New York from Bremen, Germany, after a visit to "Osterfern" (Österfärnebo, Sweden.)[177]

Hokan Bjornstrom Steffanson was naturalized November 11, 1954 in the New York Southern District.[178]

More information about Steffanson is available on the Internet.

While returning to New York on the *Carpathia,* Steffanson and a few other prominent survivors, including Molly Brown, formed a committee to honor Captain Rostron with a silver cup, and his 320 crew members with medals.

Steffanson, who retired in the 1930s, died May 21, 1962. He had amassed a fortune from his investments in pulp and land. His home on 57th Street had also turned out to be a good investment. Steffanson's heirs were his sister, Mrs. J. H. Douglas Webster of London and his nephew, Thord B. Steffanson, New York City.[179]

His long obituary read that Bjornstrom Steffanson of 56 East Fifty-Seventh Street died at the age of 78 at Doctor's Hospital after a long illness. It mentioned that he was a survivor of the sinking of the *Titanic* in the North Atlantic in 1912. His father, Erik Samuel Steffanson, was described as a pioneer in the Swedish wood pulp industry. When Hokan came to New York in 1909, he continued in the pulp business.

The obituary said that he was a graduate of the Stockholm Institute of Technology. He owned a considerable amount of real estate in the Park

---

175 www.Ellis Island.org. The *Carpathia* passenger arrivals in New York, Apr. 18, 1912.

176 www.ancestry.com. Hokan was too old for the first registration, but not for the second. At that time, the registrants were not required to list previous military experience.

177 www.ancestry.com

178 www.ancestry.com. No. 7382320.

179 *New York Times,* New York, May 23, 1962. Obituary posted to www.encyclopedia-titanica.org.

Avenue area. I the1920s he had acquired interests in Canadian paper and pulp industries. In 1917, he had married Miss Mary Pinchot Eno, introduced to him by Mrs. Churchill Candee of Washington, a *Titanic* passenger he had helped to a lifeboat. Mrs. Steffanson died in 1953. They had no children.

In 1960, Mr. Steffanson had established trust funds at Uppsala University in Sweden and at the Swedish-American Foundation in Stockholm. He had established trust funds for Swedish students at Yale University and supported the Swedish Historical Museum in Philadelphia.

He had been bestowed the title of Commander of Sweden's Royal order of Vasa, First Class. He was a Commander of Sweden's Royal Order of Vasa, First Class. His memberships included the Metropolitan Club, the Long Island Country Club, the Travelers Club, and the St. Cloud Country Club of Paris and *Sällskapet* in Stockholm. He owned the Ryd estate outside Kalmar, Sweden. The funeral was announced to be held at St. Bartholomew's Protestant Episcopal Church, Park Avenue at Fifty-First Street at 10 A.M. Friday.[180]

Steffanson was buried in Simsbury, Hartford, Connecticut May 25, 1962. His wife's father had financed and built a large part of the Canadian railroads.[181]

"Life no longer has any value for me"

Bryhl, Dagmar Lustig

The 20-year-old Miss Lustig was a visitor to the U.S. She traveled in second class under her grandmother's surname of Bryhl. While recuperating in New York, she was so distraught that she wished she had been permitted to die on the *Titanic* together with her brother and fiancé.

Born October 2, 1891 in Skara Domkyrkoförsamling (Cathedral parish), Skaraborg's län, she was the daughter of *Statsfiskal* (public prosecutor) Edvard Gottfrid Lustig (born in 1857 Grönahög parish, Älvsborg's län) and Ida Jenny Gustafsson (born in 1859 in Höreda, Jönköping's län).

Dagmar Bryhl

She was accompanied by her brother, Kurt Bryhl (Lustig) and her fiancé, Ingvar Enander. Both men

[180] www.encyclopedia-titanica.org.(1961)
[181] Ulf Ivar Nilsson, see above.

perished. Dagmar boarded the *Calypso* in Göteborg April 5, 1912 together with her brother and fiancé.

She was rescued in Lifeboat 12. On the *Titanic*, all three traveled in second class. The *Carpathia* Manifest listed her height as 4'6" (?) with dark eyes. Her reason for visiting America was to attend a wedding in Red Oak, Iowa, and to visit her uncle Oscar Lustig, 511 Pearl Street, Rockford, Illinois. This is the letter Dagmar wrote to him from New York:

Dear Uncle,

As uncle has, of course, read in the newspaper, the Titanic has gone down. I don't know whether my fiancé and my brother Kurt are saved. Evidently they are not for most of the men went under. I was saved and have been taken in charge by good people. I am at a hospital, but am not sick, although very feeble. I have lost everything. I have no clothes, and so cannot get up, but must lie in bed for present.

I would have been glad if I had been permitted to die, because life no longer has any value for me since I lost my beloved. I feel myself so dreadfully alone in this land. These people are certainly good, but nevertheless do not understand me. Could uncle possibly come here if it would not be too difficult or expensive? Would rather wish uncle to come, because father has spoken so much of you that I feel I know you best. I need someone to help me to rights.

Perhaps uncle thinks I ask too much, but I feel myself so bewildered and lonely. With heartfelt greetings to all relatives,

Uncle's affectionate, Dagmar. [182]

Mr. Lustig went searching for Dagmar in New York, but had a hard time finding her. When he inquired at the White Star Line office, he was met with "icy looks and chilly courtesy." The manager refused to talk to him.[183]

It was not until Oscar received a telegram from home that he learned where Dagmar was staying. Miss Bryhl was described as well educated, speaking French and German fluently, and able to write English and make her self understood in that language.

The Rockford Republic carried an article about Dagmar Bryhl on Thursday April 25, 1912, in which it described Mr. Lustig's difficulties finding his niece in New York. As it turned out, a wealthy Jewish woman had walked her down the gang-plank, placed her in an automobile, and hurried her to a

---

[182] www.encyclopedia-titanica.org/biography/359/.
[183] Cris Kohl, p. 126.

charitable institution supported by Jewish philanthropists, foregoing the registration with the relief committee.

Having arrived in Rockford after a long and tiresome journey, Miss Bryhl required bed rest and would not talk to reporters. Mr. Lustig related what she had told him in bits and pieces.

I was in my berth when the Titanic hit the berg. I noticed the jar and soon I heard Ingvar [her fiancé] *knocking on the door of my cabin, "Get up, Dagmar," he said. "The ship has hit something." I put on a skirt and a coat as quickly as possible and hurried up to the deck. But the officers said, "Go back, there is no danger; you go to your cabins." I turned to my berth and went back to bed. I had not lay there very long before there was more knocking on my door and Ingvar was yelling, "Get up, Dagmar, we are in danger. I don't care what the ship's officers say. I tell you we are in danger of our lives. The boat is sinking."*

Again I flung on my skirt and coat and ran up. Someone said we had hit an iceberg. The screaming and yelling was awful. They were putting women and children into boats and lowered them into the sea. Men and women were kissing each other farewell. Ingvar and Kurt led me to a boat and Ingvar lifted me into it. I seized his hands and wouldn't let go. "Come with me!" I screamed as loud as I could, still holding his hands tight. There was room in the boat. It was only half-filled, but an officer ran forward and clubbed back Ingvar.

This officer tore our hands apart and the lifeboat was let down. As it went down I looked up. There, leaning over the rail, stood Kurt and Ingvar side by side. Screamed to them again, but it was no use. They waved their hands and smiled. That was the last glimpse I had of them.

The men that rowed our boat pushed away from the Titanic. The air was very cold and we all shivered. They rowed us around and we saw the great ship sink. Then more dreadful screams. The water filled with crying people. Some of them climbed in our boat and so saved their lives.

We were out in the life boat from 11 o'clock Sunday night until 6 o'clock Monday morning when the Carpathia came. Seven hours without any clothing thick enough to protect me from the stinging cold benumbed my limbs. Oh, I can't ever tell the thoughts that came to me out there. The sea was so still and clear as a mirror, it seemed, and over us was a clear and cloudless sky.

The newspaper report continued:

Miss Bryhl, according to her uncle, has again and again declared between hysterical sobs, that if she had thought that her brother and her sweetheart would be lost she would never have allowed them to put her in the life boat. She said that she would rather have died with them when the great ship settled into the deeps than to live with the memory of all that took place graven into her mind for all the subsequent days to come.

"Poor father," she has said several times to her uncle, "It is for him I weep! This blow falls heaviest on him over there in Sweden."

Miss Bryhl's father wired his brother in Rockford saying that Dagmar should be sent home immediately. His brother answered that it would not be possible. She would have to remain in Rockford several months. Her mother was alive. She had four sisters, Mrs. Ringman of Göteborg, Lily, Jane, and Alice. She also had four brothers, Ragnar, Arthur, and Gunnar, all living at Skara, and Kurt, who was lost.

Having lost both her brother and fiancé, Dagmar was heartbroken and returned to Sweden in May of 1912 after only a short time in Rockford, Illinois. The White Star Line paid for her ticket on the *Adriatic.* It arrived at Liverpool on May 12.

According to the *Liverpool Post*, Dagmar appeared to have recovered but now and then seemed to fall into a trance brought on by some unpleasant memory."[184]

In Sweden, she later married Eric Holmberg, a teacher, and they made their home in Kungälv, Bohuslän. She died in August of 1969.

New Yorker crossed the Atlantic many times

Bystrom, Karolina

Having visited her parents in Sweden, the 42-year-old Mrs. Bystrom was returning to her home in New York City. Until recently, very little has been known about her, but my research reveals that she was born November 11, 1872 in Östanbyn, Högbo parish, Gävleborg's län Hälsingland, the daughter of Isak Jonsson and Lisa Andersdotter, Östanbyn, Högbo. The mother still lived in Östanbyn in 1930, but died in 1940. Karolina first emigrated May 2, 1893 from Högbo and left Göteborg on May 15 as Karolina Jonsson with the destination listed as New York.[185]

On July 8, 1899, she married Louis Byström in Manhattan, New York. On September 11, 1900, Lewis and "Lina" left Göteborg together for New York. His year of birth was listed as 1870.

The 1910 US Census shows her living with her husband Lewis [spelling varies] Bystrom in Manhattan, Ward 19. Both were listed as 38 years old. No

---

[184] Titanic Biographies-www.encyclopedia-titanica.org.
[185] Information Katarina Sohlberg, Sweden.

children are listed. After a visit to Sweden in 1912, Karolina left Göteborg alone on April 5 sailing on the *Calypso* as Karolina Bystrom. Her residence is marked as America and her destination as New York. She boarded the *Titanic* in Southampton as a second class passenger. She may have been rescued in Lifeboat 10.[186]

Karolina claimed $350.00 from the White Star Line for lost luggage.[187]

In 1913 she moved back to Högbo, Sweden, and stayed there until July 7, 1916 when she once again emigrated from Östanbyn. She left Göteborg as Karolina Jonsson Byström. Upon her arrival at Ellis Island, the record stated that she was widowed, but she may have been divorced, as the 1930 US Census shows Louis Bystrom as remarried. He lived until November 21, 1946. Ellis Island records list Mr. Bystrom's last residence in Sweden as Nälden, located near Östersund, Jämtland.

In 1916, Karolina's destination in New York was her friend Mrs. August Larson, 468 78th Street. In 1923, Karolina Bystrom arrived in New York once again from Östanbyn. She was 50 and a masseuse. Her destination in New York was McNulty, Lexington Avenue.[188]

Karolina crossed the Atlantic many times, but 1923 may have been her last time. That year, she sailed on the *Albania*, the same ship as Per Berggren, whom she later married in Manhattan on July 23, 1924.[189]

Karolina's brother, Anders Johan Jonsson, died July 16, 1957 in Sandviken. His probate court records show that his sister and only heir, Carolina Berggren, lived at 69 Hawthorne Avenue, Floral Park, New York (Nassau County, Long Island). It is the same address as Per Berggren reported in 1948 when he returned from a visit to Sweden.[190]

Berggren was born March 20, 1890 in Växjö, Kronoberg's län, Sweden, and 18 years younger than Karolina. He had emigrated in 1911 and was naturalized in New York City March 14, 1923 as Per Berggren, watchmaker, 160 W. 78, New York City. The intent had been filed in Bridgeport, Connecticut.[191]

---

[186] Manifest filed in June, 1912.

[187] www.encyclopedia-titanica.org.

[188] Research by Margaretha Hedblom, Malung, Sweden, from parish records, *Emigranten*, and Ellis Island records.

[189] Marriage certificate 22316. I would like to acknowledge the valuable assistance by researchers in Sweden via Proveniens.ifokus.se and Lars Hagström, Sandvikens släktförening.

[190] *Bouppteckning* (Probate) obtained from Landsarkivet in Härnösand.

[191] Information provided by various individuals in Sweden. Berggren was *urmakare* (watchmaker). His father Frans Berggren was *överlärare* (school principal) and *riksdagsman* (served in the *parliament).* The naturalization record is from Ancestry.com.

He died before 1955. Karolina then lived alone in the house she owned at 69 Hawthorn Avenue in Floral Park. Having no family, she donated the house to her Norwegian neighbors, who got to read her diary about her *Titanic* experience. She died June 3, 1964. The interment was in a single grave in Evergreen Cemetery in Brooklyn, on June 6, 1964. Her name was recorded as Carola Berggren.[192]

Newly-wed lost her husband

Dyker, Anna Elisabeth Judit

Mrs. Adolf Dyker, 22, was a newlywed U.S citizen. Her parents were born in Sweden. She gave music lessons and studied to become a singer. Following a visit to Sweden together with her husband, Adolf Dyker, she was on her way home. Their address was 468 Washington Street, New Haven, Connecticut. The couple had visited Gnesta, Sweden, because Adolf's father had died and he was to help his mother with the probate. With that accomplished, they left Gnesta and sailed from Göteborg on April 5 on the *Calypso,* listing their residence as America and their destination as New York.

Born November 22, 1889, Elisabeth was the daughter of Carl Anderson and his wife Matilda, nee Johnson, both born in Sweden. She had one brother, Fritz Anderson. She was rescued in Lifeboat 16. Her husband's body was never found.

The Dykers new house in New Haven was almost finished when they left for Sweden. Her husband, whom she called Fred, kissed her goodbye before putting her in the lifeboat. She said that she lost him and everything she owned, including her handbag with two diamond rings, two gold watches, and a sapphire necklace. Wounded and heartbroken, she had a hard time recovering. Unable to work, she depended on her elderly father, who shared his home with her. She received $300.00 from The Women's Relief Committee and sued the White Star Line for $4,000.00 for her lost luggage and $14,000.00 for the loss of her husband.[193]

The editor of *Skandinavia* in Worcester wrote:

"Lizzie saved, Fred Lost."

(So) said the sad telegram that we received last Thursday night at 4 a.m. from New York. At the same time, the father of the saved, Mr. Carl Anderson, and her younger brother, Willie, received a telegram with similar contents. Mrs. Fred Adolf Dyker sailed with her husband to Sweden last December to

---

[192] Research by Robert Bracken. Per Berggren's death record has not been found.
[193] www.encyclopedia-titanica.org.

attend Mr. Dyker's father's funeral. They had received a wire saying that he lay dying in his home in Gnesta. They took the first ship but did not make it in time. The funeral had been held a few days earlier. How they came to board the Titanic is unknown to us because they had said that they would travel via Boston to the parents. The last note was a post card written in Göteborg on the 4th of this month to Mrs. Dyker's cousin, Miss Lilly Svenson, Lyon Street. Nothing was said about that they would sail with the ship that sank. Mrs. Dyker now lies ill in her father's home, 187 W (est) H(aven), under the care of Dr. A. P. Bergman, who has high hopes about her recovery. Her mother, Mrs. Anderson, and the brother, architect Fritz Anderson, and Dr. Bergman were in New York when the Carpathia arrived, because they had an inkling that they were among the saved ….

Mrs. Dyker has a clear memory of the entire tragedy; she did not want to be separated from her husband, and did not step into a lifeboat until the last one was loaded. Several other women had waited as long in the hope of getting their men to go with them. She does not remember how she got on board the rescue ship, but when she came to she was on board and received the best of care… She is hopeful that her husband was saved although she saw him standing on the deck of the sinking ship….[194]

In 1916, Mrs. Dyker married John A. Josephson. The 1930 US Census shows them residing in East Orange, New Jersey. Her husband, 41, had emigrated in 1899, was a naturalized citizen, and a buyer for an electrical company. Their sons, Kenneth, 12, and John W., 10, were born in Connecticut.

Anna Elisabeth died February 9, 1961 at the age of 71 while residing in Haworth, Bergen, New Jersey. Prior to that, she had lived in Fort Lee. The Reverend Joseph L. Helle, Jr. officiated at her funeral, held at the Bethany Methodist Church in Fort Lee. She is survived by her two sons, Kenneth O. of Haworth and John W. of Summit, and three grandchildren. The interment was in Glendale Cemetery in Bloomfield, New Jersey.[195]

---

[194] *Skandinavia*, Worcester, Mass., April 24, 1912, p. 10. Original text in the Swedish language.
[195] "Bergen Record," www.encyclopedia-titanica.org.

Immigrant recruiter waded in water up to his armpits

Hedman, Oscar

One of the more extensive accounts of the tragedy was provided by Oscar Hedman. Although he did not speak of the event to friends and family, multiple versions of his dramatic rescue and his life were published in various newspapers through the years.

Hedman, 27, was a naturalized Swedish American, who had immigrated in 1903. In 1912, he was on his way from Ragunda, Jämtland, where he had visited his sister and her husband, the merchant O. J. Näsvall. Combining pleasure with business, he had also recruited settlers for a land company in St. Paul, Minnesota. Oscar was known as a jovial man with an unpretentious Jimmy Durante look. [196]

His many occupations include mechanic, hotel employee, chauffeur, farmer, settler-recruiter, masseur, chiropractor, and "doctor."

Born July 5, 1884 in Hörnefors, Umeå *landsförsamling* (country parish), Västerbotten län, he was the son of forest ranger Gustaf Hedman (born 1843 in Odensvi, Östergötland) and Sara Sofia Nilsson (born 1845 in Karlskoga, Örebro län).[197] Oscar had at least three older siblings, Karl Gustaf, born in 1874, Jenny Hilda Sofia, born in 1877, and Robert Emanuel, born in 1879.

When he arrived at Ellis Island, on May 1, 1905, on *Hellig Olav* from Christiania, following a visit to Sweden, he was listed as a mechanic of Finnish ethnicity residing in Stockholm. [Both of his parents were born in Sweden.] At that time, he was on his way to Braham, Minnesota.[198]

In 1911, he lived in Bowman, South Dakota, while farming in the area and working at the Carter Hotel. He also worked as a driver for the Western Land Securities Company.

He sailed from Göteborg on April 5, 1912 on the *Calypso*, listing his destination as Sioux Falls, South Dakota. On the *Titanic* manifest he is listed as settler-recruiter. According to the Ellis Island records, he was returning to his employer G. P. Rogers & Company, 1003 Pioneer Press Building, St. Paul, Minnesota. The building had been erected in 1888-89 to house the *St. Paul Pioneer Press* newspaper office. G. P. Rogers was a land company, and as land agent, Hedman had recruited new settlers for the firm.[199]

---

[196] www-titanicnorden.com.
[197] From Swedish Church records, courtesy, Björn-Åke Petersson, Kallinge, Sweden.
[198] www.encyclopedia-titanica.org. He was not found to have arrived in New York in 1903. He may have traveled from Norway to Boston or to Canada.
[199] His group might have included Berta Nilsson, Hilda Hellstrom, and Oskar Leander Johansson.

On the *Titanic*, he shared a cabin with Malcolm Johnson, and possibly also Carl Johnson [Karl Johansson], another Swedish American. Both of these men perished. Hedman related how he was saved, but how he got to the lifeboat is a long story that varies from source to source. Oscar himself may have made it more dramatic each time he told it. Here is one version:

While the *Titanic* was sinking, he waded in water up to his armpits and lost sight of his two cabin mates. He saw how officers pointed guns on the men and ordered them back. The lifeboats were launched, and family members were separated according to gender. He gave his coat to a woman who was half naked.[200]

In another version, Oscar said he jumped overboard with Malkolm. "My friend grabbed on to something that floated and it turned out to be a dead body. He told me to hold on to it. I climbed up [on it] as one [would] a horseback," he said. When they had been in the water for about 30 minutes, Malkolm drowned. Oscar approached a lifeboat, and when one of the four men fell overboard, he asked if they needed someone to row. He lied and said that he was an expert rower and was pulled on board. They rowed away minutes before a boiler exploded. "At 2 a.m. *Titanic's* deck fell apart and people fell through the opening and into the sea," Oscar said. The sight was too awful to describe, and he likened it to how the grain was sucked up by the feeder on his farm. [201]

In a letter to Sweden, he apparently told the truth about his rescue:

I slept in a cabin located in the bow of the ship. At midnight, I awoke from a jolt and noticed right away that the ship had stopped. I dressed hastily and went up on deck, where I heard that the steamer had hit an iceberg, but I was told that there was no danger. Twenty minutes later, I went back to my cabin to get my life jacket. The cabin was filled with water. I went up and talked to my buddies—a few good friends from Göteborg. We realized that the steamer was slowly sinking. The lifeboats were finally put in place, and women and children were loaded first.

We knew that there were nearly 3,000 people on board and only 18 lifeboats [20], *so I did not see any way of rescue. The night was calm. The stars glittered. I went up on the stern* [poop] *deck by myself. Many hundreds had already jumped to their graves. I looked toward heaven and asked God*

---

[200] www.titanicnorden.com.

[201] *Ibid.* Other witnesses testified that they had heard explosions, and some said they thought it came from the boilers. A. H. Weikman, barber on the *Titanic* reported in an affidavit to the Senate Hearings that, "I was about 15 feet away from the ship when I heard a second explosion. I think the boilers blew up about in the middle of the ship." *The Titanic Disaster Hearings*, p. 483.

to take my soul. Calmed down, I faced death. But oh, how much moaning and prayer for salvation from hundreds of people! When I searched for my friends, they had disappeared.

I stood alone and saw how the last lifeboat was lowered. An officer stood there with a pistol in his hand to stop frantic people from rushing the boats. The boats were filled with women. I sprang forward to see if I could find someone to bring a last farewell. A woman jumped toward the boat, but fell down into the deep. The lifeboat was lowered. At that moment, I thought, perhaps I should try to jump. If I get shot, I'll die faster. I jumped and came down in the lifeboat. At once it was lowered, and I got hold of an oar and began to row with all my might out to sea.

The large steamer was then about to sink. All the lights went out. A crash and horrible screams were heard before the stern rose toward the sky. It stood there for about two minutes and then disappeared into the sea. Right then, I heard the most awful cries. Thousands of people lay in the water screaming for help, but got no help. Eventually, the calls ceased.

The sea was rather calm. The stars glittered in the dreadful night. No one seemed to know the direction of our rowing and no steamer was in sight. This will be more painful than going down with the steamer, I thought. We rowed round for several hours until daylight slowly appeared. Then we saw a steamer far away. At this time, the wind picked up, but it blew us toward the steamer. At about 5.30 in the morning we reached the steamer that brought us to New York. It took 8 days [3 days. The *Carpathia* arrived in New York, on the 18th of April.]) *Several died on the way and were thrown overboard, and many pitiful women stood on deck with children on their arm, looking at the ocean that had taken their husbands to their graves.*

At the end of his letter, Hedman says that the steamer was afloat for two hours after the collision with the iceberg. The lifeboat in which he was rescued was No. 10 [?]. It was occupied by 50 women and two men, he said.[202]

In New York, he recuperated at the Swedish Immigrant Home, where he received a railroad ticket to his destination, plus a small amount of cash from a representative of the White Star Line. He also received about $10.00 from the Women's Relief Committee.[203]

After an interview with Hedman, a reporter for *Nordstjernan,* a newspaper in New York, wrote:

---

202 Letter in Swedish published in *Jämtlands-kuriren,* May 7, 1912. *www.titanicnorden.com.*

203 *Nordstjernan, New York,* May 17, 1912.

"Oscar Hedman got in the next to last lifeboat launched from the Titanic. But before it was rowed away, he had jumped into the water and was taken on board. It was only a few minutes before the steamer sank. Hedman had only words of praise for the crew that, according to him, carried on as it behooves men in that situation."

The *Nordstjernan* reporter commented that the survivors, whether men or women, showed no emotions as they related their experiences. "It seemed like their nerves were made of steel, no, as if they had no nerves at all, because even if they were made of steel they would have been touched by something so horrible."[204]

Another Swedish-American paper also wrote how Hedman jumped into the sea when the *Titanic* foundered and was lucky to be picked up by the next to last lifeboat.[205]

In 1918, Hedman registered for the draft in Sentinel, Butte, North Dakota, as a farmer of average height, with blue eyes and blond hair, partly bald.[206]

When the U.S. Census was taken in 1920, Hedman lived in Wanagan, Golden Valley, North Dakota. He was 35 and a farmer at the time. His wife Tillie, 37, was born in South Dakota, and so were her parents. He married Julia Mathilda (Tillie) on November 7, 1912. They had no children.[207]

When Hedman applied for a U.S. passport on November 13, 1922, he stated that his year of immigration was 1903 and that he had lived in Sidney, Montana, Beach, [illegible], North Dakota, as well as in Colton, South Dakota. He had been naturalized as a U.S. citizen July 12, 1911 in Bowman County, North Dakota. His birthplace was first listed as Ragunda, then crossed out and listed as "Hoorn..." (Hörnefors).[208]

In 1923, after a visit to Sweden, he arrived at Ellis Island on August 7 and continued to Colton, South Dakota. In 1953, he and his wife flew to and from Sweden.

In 1930, he lived in Onida, South Dakota (U.S. Census). His and his parents' country of birth were listed as Sweden, and his occupation as "doctor."

He was a member of the local Presbyterian Church and the Masonic Lodge.

Hedman's life was recaptured in periodicals in 1998 and 2007.

In 1998, the *Argus Leader*, Sioux Falls, published a story based on two articles from 1912 and also interviewed Hedman's niece, Delores Cobbett of Murrieta, California, his nephew, retired Dr. Don Anderson of Seattle, and

---

[204] *Nordstjernan*, New York, April 23, 1912, p. 12.
[205] *Hemlandet,* Chicago, May 14, 1912.
[206] www.ancestry.com.
[207] *Ibid.*
[208] *Ibid.* The reference for the next two paragraphs is also from www.ancestry.com.

several Onida residents. Ms. Cobbett said that her uncle never brought up the subject of the *Titanic*.

Anderson commented, "I'm sorry to say he didn't ever say much about it." Anderson was of the opinion that Hedman had received medical training in Sweden and that he also had studied several years at the Palmer School of Chiropractic in Davenport, Iowa, although he never secured his chiropractic license. Anderson guessed that the reason for this was that his English was not good enough to pass the tests.

In Onida, Mr. and Mrs. Hedman were wealthy enough to buy one of the fanciest homes in town, a brick structure that had originally been built for a millionaire from the east coast. "Built in 1910, it had the first electricity in town. Maybe the first of everything. I've got it on the National History Registry," Anderson said.[209]

Two months later, the same reporter interviewed Fred Lehman of Sioux Falls, who owned a book, *Titanic: Triumph and Tragedy.* The book listed the passengers on board the *Titanic*, among them seven from South Dakota. "His interest in the *Titanic* was fanned by stories his Grandma Violet used to tell him, and by a great-great uncle who went door-to-door selling a book called, *Titanic and Other Great Shipwrecks.*[210]

In 2007, a historical journal described Hedman as a settler-recruiter, who was berthed with Malcolm "Sever" Johnson, a [Swedish] concrete worker from Minnesota. The article says the two men went up on deck after the accident and realized the ship would sink. Johnson suggested they should meet their fate together, but Hedman panicked and fled.

When the surviving Hedman arrived at the St. Paul Union Depot he was accompanied by three Swedish immigrants. As they were unable to speak English, Hedman translated for all three. One of the three was six-foot Carl [Olof] Johnson, misidentified as Paul Johnson. Hedman had shared his employer's money with the cash-strapped immigrants.[211]

---

[209]Since Hedman was only 19-years old when he emigrated, it's doubtful that he had any medical experience in Sweden, not even in the military as he was too young to have served. It's not likely he would have been admitted to Palmer College of Chiropractic.

[210] Steve Young, *Argus-Leader*, Sioux Falls, S. D., Tuesday March 10, 1998. Courtesy Ron Johnson, Dalesburg, S.D. Among the seven were the Norwegians Olaus Abelseth and Lena Jacobson Solvang (Mrs. Rasmus Rasmusson, a victim) and the Swedes Johan Ekstrom (victim), Johan Cervin Svensson (survivor), and Johan Svensson (victim).

[211] *Minnesota History.* The Quarterly of the Minnesota Historical Society 60/7 Fall 2007, p. 263. Absent from this group was Karl Johnsson of Killeberg, who may have stepped off the train to go to Camden Station, Minnesota, his destination in the Minneapolis area.

Another tidbit about Hedman was that he served several years as the Surry County coroner and as city councilman. He was described as a colorful little man who spoke broken English with a heavy Swedish brogue. [212]

As recent as 2009, a local newspaper wrote about him:

> A photo in *Minnesota History*, 60/7 Fall 2007, Minnesota Historical Society, with the caption, "Immigrants who survived wreck of Titanic." The immigrants pictured are Oscar Hedman, standing at ease with his hands in the pockets of his black overcoat. He is wearing a light-colored fedora. Anna Sjöblom wears a plain light-colored brimmed hat and a fitted buttoned coat that does not quite cover her long skirt. She carries a purse. Berta Nilsson wears a white hat decorated with large plumes, a short fitted jacket in a light color, and a long flaring dark skirt. Oscar and the girls have narrow faces, while Carl Olof Johnson appears to be broad-faced. Misidentified as Paul Johnson, he wears a gray overcoat and dark fedora. He has his hands in the pockets. Carl Olof is reported to be over 6 feet tall. Oscar appears to be of average height and taller than the women. The photo was from *St. Paul Dispatch* (no longer in business), April 26, 1912. The original photograph is no longer available.

Text below the photo: "Mr. Hedman was bringing over a large party of Swedish immigrants to take farms in the United States. Only ten reached New York. Mr. Hedman brought three of them to St. Paul today, on the way to different points in the Northwest."

In January of 1925, "Dr." and Mrs. Hedman arrived in Onida, South Dakota where he set up a practice as "Swedish Masseur." In the 1920s, Onida still had a Western or cowboy flavor. Dirt roads and one railroad, entering the area in 1910 provided access to the community. Regardless, he seems to have prospered and he lived in the community for the next forty years....

Hedman was well known in the community as a survivor. "Sadly, many of those who made it to safety were not well treated," the article said.[213]

One biographer wrote that Hedman and his wife moved often to avoid getting a citation for practicing without a license. The locals called him "Doc." [214]

Oscar Hedman died July 28, 1961 in Onida, South Dakota from a stroke he suffered while driving his car on Main Street. Witnesses saw how the car

---

[212] Steve Young, Staff Columnist, "Titanic talk refloats tale of Onida's old Doc." *Argus Leader*, Sioux Falls, S. D. Tuesday Jan. 12, 1998 with quotes from two articles, one in *Argus-Leader*, published in 1912, and one in *American News-Dakota News Service* in about 1933. Courtesy of Ron Johnson, Dalesburg, S. D.

[213] *South Dakota Retrospect* "Local heroes and legends," March 1, 2009.

[214] Mr. Oskar Arvid Hedman – Titanic biographies – www.encyclopedia-titanica.org.

slowly turned toward the curb. He was quickly taken to the hospital and died 45 minutes later. The townspeople attended his funeral.[215]

In his last will and testament, Hedman left half of his estate to his wife, Tillie, and the other half to his brother, Robert Hedman, Lidingö, Sweden. As a result, Tillie had to sell her home to pay off her brother-in-law in Sweden. When Tillie died her estate was valued at $88,000. It went to her nieces and nephews.[216]

"We were in the lifeboat for six hours"

Hellström, Hilda Maria

Hilda Hellström

Miss Hellstrom, 22, had planned her emigration for a long time but postponed it when her mother became ill. When her mother died in March 1912, a sister took care of her father, and Hilda left for America. She was initially scheduled to travel on the *Adriatic*, but on account of the coal strike she was transferred to the *Titanic.* (See group photo in the beginning of this section).

She occupied cabin 135 far aft on D-Deck and was rescued in Collapsible C together with Velin Ohman.

Hilda was born December 7, 1889 in Stora Tuna parish, Kopparberg's län, the daughter of August Hellström (born in1857 in Hällefors, Västmanland's län) and Carolina Jansdotter (born in 1860 in Stora Tuna). In 1900 the family lived in No. 32 provided by the Domnarvet Company.[217]

She had two brothers and two sisters. She sailed from Göteborg April 5, 1912 on the *Calypso,* giving her last residence as Stora Tuna, Dalarna. Her destination was her aunt Carolina Johanna Erikson, 1032 Florence Avenue, Evanston, Illinois. The *Carpathia* manifest listed her residence in Sweden as Domnarvet.

The Swedish newspaper *Dalpilen* wrote about her April 23, 1912.

"Among the passengers on the Titanic from Dalarna was Hilda Hellström of Borlänge. She had just celebrated her 23rd birthday and since one year prior she had held a ticket to America with the destination of Evanston, Illinois, where an aunt had promised to care for her…."[218]

---

[215] Part of this information was derived from www.titanicnorden.com

[216] Philip Gowan, "Mr. Oskar Arvid Hedman." Titanic Biography linked to www.encyclopedia-titanica.org.

[217] From the Swedish Church records courtesy Björn-Åke Petersson, Kallinge, Sweden.

[218] From the Royal Library's digitalized newspapers.

The Swedish-American newspaper, *Nordstjernan*, New York, quoted Miss Hellstrom about her experience when interviewed at the Swedish Immigrant Home.

I and my friends were all in bed in our cabin when the collision occurred. We did not hurry when we were told to get dressed. Coming up on deck, we were told that there was no immediate danger, and we Swedes were all calm, but the southerners (meaning southern Europeans) and the Irish made an awful racket. Since we could move around as we wished, I thought it would be a good opportunity to take a look at all the elegance in second class. Therefore, I went on an expedition, which turned out so well that I could see all the luxury in the second class smoking room. Here, they played cards, conversed loudly, and smoked undisturbed. But I thought it was getting cold, so I went back to my cabin to get more outer garments.

This was about ten minutes before the Titanic sank. Up on deck, I managed to get into one of the last lifeboats. In this, there was room for one of my Swedish friends [Velin Öhman].*The boat was otherwise almost completely occupied by Italians. They were half naked in the bone-chilling temperature and the Italian children were almost stiff from the cold. To somewhat protect them, my friend and I took off our coats and wrapped them around the little ones to protect them.*

On the Carpathia the comfort and food varied, but they did what they could for us, and we appreciated everything.

The reporter added:

"She talked calmly and slowly the whole time without any trace of being upset, just like she had related an every-day episode. One could not detect that she had lived through one of the most tragic disasters in modern times. But perhaps it will hit her later."[219]

Later in life, Hilda told her daughter:

I was a 3rd Class passenger aboard the Titanic, and we were cramped for space in the lower berth. I was always curious about just what the rest of the ship was like. I was drawn to the sound of orchestral music, coming from above. I made my way up through the second class level, past men in a room, smoking and playing cards. I found my way up to the main ballroom to

[219] *Nordstjernan*, New York, April 23, 1912.

find my self in the presence of wonderful music playing, and I remained there, unseen by anyone.[220]

When Hilda got into Lifeboat Collapsible C with Velin Öhman, Velin brought out a bottle of brandy and the two women shared it to calm their nerves. She described herself as broke, pale, and skinny.

The paper, Dalpilen, Dalarna, Sweden, published a letter from Hilda on May 7, 1912, addressed to her brother in Stockholm.

A lot has happened since we were together the last time. I never thought that I would live to see the Titanic go under. It was an awful sight, but how I was saved I will never understand. I was so calm the whole time and never thought that it would sink. We were in the lifeboat six hours, so I have not been feeling very well. I expect that I'm thin and pale compared to when I was home. But I never thought I would get to America in such a poor state. But I'm glad that I was saved. We can't leave the home here [the Swedish Immigrant Home in New York] *until we have received clothes and money so that we can manage. I lost everything I owned, so I don't have more than what I'm wearing and it's not that much.*

Yesterday, there were photographers here who took our pictures and today we have seen ourselves in all the papers. And there were people here who talked with us about our voyage, so now it's rather nice. But on board the steamer Carpathia it wasn't that good. The first day they received us kindly, but then they packed us in like hogs.

But one was glad to be there. We have been outside and looked around in the city, and, believe me, they stared at us and everyone feels sorry for us who were on the Titanic. I hardly know what else to write. It's difficult to concentrate enough to write although there is so much to write about.[221]

Hilda reached second class on her own. So did Anna Sjöblom and a Swedish girl as they turned to an emergency ladder meant for the crew. From this viewpoint they could look into the first-class *â la carte* restaurant. Men lodged in the bow climbed another emergency ladder and up the first-class companionway to the boats. Others crashed the barriers. Hundreds milled endlessly around on the forward well deck or the poop deck.[222]

---

[220] Her story told to her daughter, Ellen Larson Centko.
[221] From the Royal Library digitalized collection of newspaper articles. Swedish text, courtesy Margaretha Hedblom, Malung, Sweden. Comment: The *Carpathia* had to make room for 705 unexpected passengers, and it was not a big ship.
[222] Ibid, p, 56.

In New York, Hilda recuperated at the Swedish Immigrant Home. While there, she received $50.00 from the Women's Relief Committee, and a sleeper railroad ticket, plus a small amount of cash from the White Star Line.[223]

Hilda lived with her aunt until she married John Edward Larson on December 7, 1915 in Waukegan, Illinois. Their first address was 1870 Greenbay Road, Highland Park, Chicago. In 1930, the U.S. Census listed the family as living at 1052 Oak Street, Highland Park in Lake County, Illinois. John Larson was 70 and had married Hilda when he was 50. He and his parents were born in Sweden. He had emigrated in 1881 and worked as a caretaker. Hilda was 40, and their daughter, Ellen, born in Illinois, was 8-years old.[224]

Hilda's husband, John Edward Larson, was born in 1860 in Göteborg. [He was 29 years older than Hilda.] Edward died February 24, 1948.

A few weeks before Hilda died March 15, 1962, she moved in with her daughter, Ellen Centco, in Streator, Illinois. She was buried March 18 in Memorial Park, Skokie, Illinois.

"We clung to that door for hours"

Jansson, Carl Olof

Carl Olof Jansson, later Johnson

The 21-year-old immigrant was employed as a carpenter for the Eriksson Brothers in Örebro and was an active member of the socialist labor movement. When he decided to emigrate he did so without permission from the authorities and bought his ticket in Copenhagen, presumably to avoid his military service. He went by train to Esbjerg on Denmark's west coast, where he boarded a ship to England.

Born May 17, 1890 in Korsberga parish, Skaraborg's län, he was the son of Lars Alfred Jansson (born in 1851 in Korsberga) and Charlotta Kristina Svensdotter (born in 1856 in Angeredshestra parish, Jönköping's län).[225]

---

[223] *Nordstjernan*, New York, May 17, 21. 1912.
[224] www.encyclopedia-titanica.org.
[225] From the Swedish Church records courtesy Björn-Åke Petersson, Kallinge, Sweden.

Carl Olof had four living siblings, all born in Korsberga, Erik Valdemar, born in 1884, who emigrated and took the name Manstedt, Alfred Vitalis, born in 1886, Hanna Elisabet, born in 1894, and Sven Ossian, born in 1901.

About his journey, Carl Olof related: "We arrived in Esbjerg at 6 pm., and went through a medical examination before boarding the North Sea vessel. The ones who was [were] ill and did not have the proper papers had to turn back. We had the right papers although they were bought and signed by the Danish director of police.... The North Sea was terrible as always and the boat rocked continuously...." [226]

Carl Olof described his journey on the *Titanic* in a letter to his parents, brothers and sisters, dated *Carpathia,* April, 12, 1912.

The men's cabins for two or four were light, airy, and attractive. He and his friends spent a whole afternoon exploring the ship, and he likened it to a small town.

The ship had a telephone station, wireless station, police station with a cell, infirmary, hospital, three taverns, post office, newspaper office, and toilets in long rows, church, ballroom and swimming-pool. [227]

On Sunday afternoon, Carl-Olof and his friends sat and talked about soon being in New York, but felt that they were so comfortable on board that they were not that eager to arrive at their destination. They only had to open their mouths and "fried sparrows would fly in." Carl Olof compared it to a communistic society like the one they had envisioned as socialists. The hard work in the new country could wait.

In the evening when the bell rang for supper at 8 o'clock, they all went to enjoy the good food, and afterwards they took a stroll on the deck. It was quiet and the ocean was calm and black. Someone said that they were in the graveyard of the Atlantic, the Newfoundland Banks, where a strong current gathered up icebergs. Carl Olof estimated that they were a few hundred miles closer to New York than to England. They were informed that there was no danger for a ship as large as theirs. They all believed it to be true, and having been told that they would arrive early in the morning the next day they all felt safe and went to bed.

But at 11:30 at night they were awakened and ordered to go up on deck. The ship had hit an iceberg, although they were told that there was no danger, he put some clothes on but had no shoes when he ran up on deck to see the icebergs. They could hardly see the water because of the night sky.

They stood on deck for a while until they heard the order for the lifeboats to be lowered. Carl Olof ran back to his cabin to get more clothes, and took time to grab his watch and his waistcoat before the water rushed into his

---

[226] www.titanicnorden.com

[227] The third-class passengers had, of course, no access to the ballroom and the swimming pool.

cabin. Back on deck, he saw his friends standing there with their lifejackets on and "terror etched on their faces." He wondered what would happen to him. He had no lifebelt and couldn't find one. He had no shoes and no cap.

Up on deck, he was met by a revolver and the shout, "Women first." He thought of his mother and her sorrow and was afraid for his sanity. Two Swedish lads stood behind him, "as pale as corpses," because they were doomed to the same fate as he and several hundred more from other nations.

When he jumped, he sank deep down, but came up to the surface again and fought to keep afloat. He then heard a terrible explosion, which he learned was caused by the hot, steam boilers blowing up. "This was what saved us since it tore the boat to pieces and large doors... came off and floated out in the water."

They finally got hold of the raft, wreckage from the ship, which they hung onto, but after awhile there were so many on it that it sank resulting in a wild fight for survival in the water. He says that he was bold enough to push away others to keep above water. "It is terrible but as such a moment it is only a question of your own life."

He remembered the ropes being lowered from the *Carpathia* and tied around his waist. On the rescue ship they were cared for in the best possible way, received medical attention, and after about a day and a half they felt quite well.

They were allowed to go ashore without any fuss or restrictions. They were given food and clothes and a place to stay for four days. On Monday evening, they made their way to their various destinations. They were given tickets and money. He says that they had not been lacking anything since they reached land, but the disaster would long be remembered.[228]

In a letter to his brother on April 25, he wrote, "If all emigrants had to go through what I have gone through, there would not be as many wanting to leave Sweden...." [229]

Minnesota History Quarterly carried an article in 2007 headlined, "Voices Cast Upon the Sea: Minnesota's Titanic Passengers," in which Carl (Olof) Johnson was misidentified as Paul Johnson in an old photo from 1912 together with Oscar Hedman, Anna Sjoblom (Finland Swede), and Berta Nelson. Mr. Hedman was bringing over a large party of Swedish immigrants, but only ten of them reached New York, the article said.

Johnson had just arrived on deck as the *Titanic* began its fatal dive. Sucked under, then thrust upward, he emerged among countless bodies, "so

---

[228] From a letter that Carl-Olof sent to his home in Sweden. Published in *Letters from the Titanic*, Stockholm, Sweden, 2000 by Claes-Göran Wetterholm. According to Lee Merideth, Carl Olof was rescued in Collapsible A.

[229] www.titanicnorden.com

many of them and so close together that they looked like a black floor that one could walk on." He saved himself by swimming to an overturned boat [The overturned boat was Collapsible B] [230]

Nordstjernan also wrote about Karl [Carl Olof] "Jansson" from Örebro [his last address in Sweden]. His worst impression while swimming around in the water was seeing two Swedish girls throw themselves in the water from a lifeboat. The girls had seen two friends on the rapidly sinking steamer and evidently had become so upset about the fate awaiting them (their friends) that they lost their minds.[231]

The paper *Hemlandet*, Chicago, May 21, 1912, described Carl Olof as 6'3" and weighing 205 pounds.

Chicago American wrote on April 25, 1912. "Carl Janson passed through Chicago together with Lundstrom (Thure Edvin), Oscar Hedman, Karin Abelseth [Norwegian], and Anna Sherblom (Sjöblom, Finnish):

Remarkable strength of Carl Janson, another of the surviving passengers of the Titanic, kept him alive in the frigid ocean for six hours, hanging to a door with twenty others after the ship sunk. Janson reached Chicago today, and told the terrifying experiences when the queen of the seas went down.

Janson is twenty-one years old and a robust young man. He was a third-cabin passenger and after the wreck was nearly frozen to death. When he reached New York the White Star Line gave him a cheap suit of clothes, an overcoat and $I0 in money to sign a release of the Line from further damages. Janson lost $50 and all the luggage on the boat.

Janson had seen Chief Officer Murdoch shoot himself just before the last boat was launched," he said. [The chief officer was Henry T. Wilde.] He gave a graphic story of the sinking of the great liner with its human freight." [232]

I had gone to bed," said Janson, "and was asleep when I was awakened by the stewards, who called out that the ship had struck an iceberg, but that there was no great danger. They told us, however, to get up. That was about

---

[230] *Minnesota History,* see previous reference., p. 263.

[231] This incident has not been reported by anyone else and Carl Olof did not mention it again. It may have been incorrectly attributed to Karl Janson of Örebro instead of Karl Janson of Killeberg.

[232] Even if he saw an officer shoot himself, it was unlikely that he would know his identity, but on board the *Carpathia*, he may have heard others describe the man as the chief officer. Lee Merideth writes that contrary to the James Cameron movie, *Titanic*, Murdoch did not commit suicide. Murdoch was engaged to be married after the New York voyage and was last seen in the water by Harold Bride near Collapsible B. He likely died in the water.

11:30 [!], *or more than an hour and five minutes after the Titanic had struck the iceberg.* [The *Titanic* struck the iceberg at about 11.40 p.m., *Titanic* time].

I arose and dressed, even putting on my overcoat before going on deck. There did not appear to be any great excitement in the steerage quarters. I went to the top deck. No one attempted to stop me. [In his letter to his parents he wrote that he wore only his waistcoat.]

Women and children only were allowed to come out of the steerage after that. Shortly before the last boat was launched I glanced toward the bridge and saw the chief officer place a revolver in his mouth and shoot him self. His body toppled overboard. [See footnote.] *I waited for the last boat to leave and then jumped overboard myself. I was swimming not more than twenty feet from the ship when she upended and went down. The Titanic did not break into two, though there were two explosions. I saw her propellers as she went under. The suction was small. A door from the deck was flung near me and I grasped it with more than twenty others. We clung to that door for hours. One by one the others slipped off and sank.*

The water after the sinking of the Titanic was dotted with persons and floating ice. The cries and moans continued for hours. I cannot see why more could not have been rescued. It was 7 in the morning when I was picked up.

Janson left on the Chicago & Northwestern Railway to-day for Swedesburg, Neb., where he has a brother.[233]

Another article, published in Omaha, chronicled the fates of two Nebraska men who were on the *Titanic*, Emil Brandeis, an Omaha business man, and the Swede, Carl [Olof] Johnson.

About Johnson, the paper described him as a penniless immigrant who carried everything he owned in a suitcase. Seeking a new life in America, his destination was Wahoo, Nebraska. The article said Johnson was a 21-year-old carpenter by trade, who had left his native Sweden to escape mandatory induction into the Swedish military. He slipped over to Copenhagen and booked a trip to America. He scheduled his departure on the *Titanic* on the urging of a booking agent who said it was the finest liner ever built.

He caught a cattle boat from Copenhagen to Southampton, England, where he got his first look at the 'queen of the seas.' Johnson had described

---

[233] *Chicago American*, Chicago, article posted on www.encyclopedia-titanica.org in January 2011. Janson was a new immigrant and did not know English, so someone must have interpreted the story for him. Note that the officer who allegedly shot himself is identified as the chief officer. The chief officer was Henry T. Wilde. His wife and two children had died two years earlier, leaving him with four children under ten years of age. Lee W. Merideth writes that Wilde may have been the officer who shot himself. The *Titanic* hit the iceberg at 11.40 p.m. Titanic time, so he could not have been notified at 11.30. Compare with the letter he wrote to his parents related above.

the *Titanic* as "nothing like the cattle boat that we came over on from Copenhagen." Johnson, a third-class passenger, thought he was traveling in luxury. He spent his last evening on the *Titanic* smoking his pipe and talking with his fellow Swedish passengers about Sweden and America. After dinner on roast pork and boiled potatoes, he smoked his last pipe of the day. Johnson said that after the first warning, he could have rolled over and gone back to sleep had not a steward rapped on their door and told them to go atop.

When Johnson felt the cold on deck, he went back to his cabin to get his overcoat but did not make it because he found the deck awash in fast-rising water.

Johnson described the white signal rockets fired into the night sky, the cries and poignant goodbyes as husbands and wives were separated, and the quiet desperation of those remaining on the sinking ship.

The article says all men were equal—all facing almost certain death. The *Titanic* class system had broken down as Johnson climbed to first class. He jumped over the rail into the dark 28-degree water. Not wearing a lifebelt, but a good swimmer, Johnson fought to keep away from the frantic hands trying to pull him under. He said he watched as the ship reared for the last time, the stern pointing straight up in the air, before slipping beneath the waves.

According to the same source, Johnson reached Collapsible B, where more than a dozen men already struggled to climb on top. Johnson was among 28 men able to crawl on to the overturned boat....To confirm that it was Collapsible B, he later named a "ship's steward"Lightover," who also was on the overturned boat. [Second Officer Lightoller]. ...

The survivors from Collapsible B were supposedly the last to be picked up by the rescue ship *Carpathia*. Carl Olof was said to have suffered just a few bruises and scratches from his six-hour ordeal. After a generous swig of whiskey, he could rest at last.

The man who had left Sweden to escape his military service was drafted into the U.S. Army in World War I and transported back to Europe to serve on the front lines in France. Once again, he survived and returned to Wahoo, where he became a contractor known as "Titanic Johnson."[234]

His draft registration, dated June 5, 1917, described him as a single man and self-employed carpenter. Physically, he was tall, of medium build with blue eyes and light hair.[235]

Carl Olof married Edith J. Syverson on May 23, 1938. The couple was childless. He died March 23, 1978 of cerebral hemorrhage in Wahoo, Nebraska. His wife died in December the same year.[236]

---

[234] Henry J. Cordes, World-Herald Writer, *Sunday World-Herald*, Omaha, Neb., Jan. 25, 1998. Article courtesy of Ron Johnson, Dalesburg, S.D. The paper does not refer to its sources.

[235] www.ancestry.com

Was he murdered or not?

Johansson, Oscar Leander

The 26-year-old Oscar's dream of America began with high hopes, but turned tragic in the end. He never married. It was alleged that he was murdered in 1928 by the husband or boyfriend of a woman with whom he had an affair. The *New York Times* reported on April 19, 1925 that Oscar Palmquist, 42, Lenox Avenue had drowned in a pond in Beardsley Park. He had been missing since March 23.

Born June 26, 1885 in Villstad parish, Jönköping's län, he was the son of Knut Johansson (born April 30, 1834 in Villstad) and Johanna Matilda Abrahamsdotter (born July 4, 1845 in Villstad). Oscar emigrated from Qvarnaryd Östra Villstad, March 23, 1912. His brother, Anders Wilhelm Knutsson [later Andrew Palmquist], born November 6, 1881 in Villstad, emigrated earlier and lived in New Haven, Connecticut.[237]

The Swedish newspaper, *Kristianstadbladet,* lists Oscar Johansson as departing from Copenhagen. Lee Merideth lists him as Oscar L. Johansson rescued in Lifeboat No. 15, which allowed men. Oscar said he was in the cold water long enough for one of his knees to be affected. He applied for aid from the Swedish Consulate, but his request was denied because he had already received $200.00 and because he had suffered from a knee injury since he was 13 years old, which probably would have prevented him from entering the United States the usual way. The consulate concurred that even if the *Titanic* had not foundered, he likely would have been unable to work. Oscar lived in Bridgeport, Connecticut, and worked as a toolmaker.[238].

The Swedish-American newspaper, *Hemlandet*, mistakenly wrote that Oscar's name was Axel, but correctly stated that he was the brother of Andrew Palmquist, Poplar Street, New Haven, Connecticut. It also says that Johansson was saved in an unusual manner by grabbing on to a door. He had attached two lifebelts to his body. A girl in a lifeboat threw him a shawl that he held on to until he and others were picked up by the *Carpathia*.[239]

---

[236]Claes-Göran Wetterholm, *Letters from the Titanic*. Postal Museum Publication No. 48, Stockholm, 2000.

[237] Information courtesy of Björn-Åke Petersson, Kallinge, Sweden. Anders changed his name to Andrew Palmquist and Oscar then did the same.

[238] www.encyclopedia-titanica.org.

[239] *Hemlandet*, Chicago, April 30, 1912. Since Oscar is not reported to have recuperated at any of the charity places in New York where the other Swedes stayed, his brother may have picked him up in New York.

On the *Carpathia* passenger manifest, he was listed as Oskar Johannsen, traveling to a "Friend" [actually his brother] Andrew Palmquist, 65 Poplar Street, New Haven, Connecticut. In the records of Bethesda Lutheran Church, New Haven, Connecticut, he is listed as Oscar Leander Johnson "Mr. Titanic," together with his brother Andrew Palmquist. He dropped his membership in the church on February 2, 1914 when he moved to Bridgeport. Having changed his name to Palmquist, Oscar apparently lived in Stamford, Connecticut, for a while. The records state that his brother, Anders William (Andrew) Palmquist, emigrated from Villstad in 1900. Andrew left the congregation in 1917.[240]

When Oscar registered for the WWI draft in Bridgeport, Fairfield County, his middle name was misinterpreted as "Larder." The 33-year-old resided at 18 Montgomery Street in Bridgeport. He had declared his intention to become a citizen. He worked as a toolmaker at Bryant Electric Company in Bridgeport. His nearest relative was his mother in Sweden. Oscar is described as tall and slender with blue eyes and brown hair. He had a stiff knee. The registration was signed September 12, 1918.[241]

Descendants of his brother Amandus and wife Gertrud were interviewed by the *Connecticut Post*, April 14, 1998 after Cameron's movie, *The Titanic*, had been released. They said that they had always known that Oscar was killed by a jealous man and then thrown into the pond.[242]

His death on March 27, 1925, however, was referred to as an accident. Articles in *New York Times* and *Bridgeport Post* reported that he had drowned. *New York Times* wrote on April 19 1925:

"Surviving the Titanic disaster April 14 [15], 1912, by swimming for hours in the icy waters until picked up by a rescue ship, Oscar Palmquist of 42 Lenox Avenue was drowned in six-feet of water in a pond in Beardsley Park onto which he is believed to have wandered. Missing since March 23, Palmquist's body was discovered in the pond today."[243]

Oscar lived near his siblings in Bridgeport. He was buried at Mt. Grove Cemetery, Bridgeport, Connecticut.

---

[240] Swedish-American Church records on microfilm. Bethesda Lutheran Church, New Haven, Conn.

[241] www.ancestry.com

[242] www.titanicnorden.com. *Emigranten Populär* shows that Amandus Knutsson, 19, sailed from Göteborg May 1, 1896. He was from Villstad and went to New Britain, Conn.

[243] www.titanica-encyclopedia.com. After a visit to Sweden, Andrew Palmqvist sailed from Göteborg in 1909. His destination was New Haven, Conn. He is listed as being 28-years old and living in America. Source: *Emigranten Popular.*

Skipper's son was shipwrecked twice

Johansson, Oscar W. Olsson

The 32-year-old married Swedish American had emigrated in 1905 and worked on ships carrying iron ore on the Great Lakes. The skipper was a Norwegian by the name of Petersen.

In 1911, Oscar returned to Sweden and on New Year's Eve of that year, he married Maria Abrahamson. But because earnings were low on Orust, he wrote to his former boss, Captain Petersen, who arranged for him to sail on the *Bulgaria* (from New York) to Detroit, but since Oscar was delayed arriving in New York due to the *Titanic* disaster and also by helping a boy finding his parents, he missed the *Bulgaria* and boarded another ship, which ran aground. Captain Petersen did not know where Oscar was and reported him missing, but Oscar had saved himself wearing only his underwear. He later said the two incidents caused him to develop problems with both his stomach and nerves.[244]

Born September 8, 1879, in Skörbo, Myckleby parish, Orust, Göteborg's & Bohus län, Oscar was the son of Johan Oskar Olsson (born in 1849 in Myckleby) and Britta Maria Emanuelsdotter (born in 1846 in Myckleby). In 1890 and 1900, the family lived in Lunna, Myckleby. Oskar had two brothers, Olof Emanuel, born in 1874 in Myckleby, and John Melin born in 1888 in Myckleby.[245]

As a young man, Oscar had worked as a sailor on the schooner *Edit,* captained by his father out of Uddevalla. Swedish embarkation records include Oskar W. Johansson, 32, residence America, as having sailed on the *Calypso* from Göteborg April 5, 1912 with the destination of Detroit, Michigan.

The *Carpathia* listed him as Oscar Johanson, 22 [32] married, from Stillingsö, Sweden. His destination was a friend, Anthony Peterson, Detroit, Michigan.[246]

Oscar's travel companions on the *Titanic* were Karl Johan Johansson and Samuel Niklasson from Myckleby, both of whom perished. Oscar was rescued by Collapsible A.

Oscar recuperated at the Swedish Immigrant Home in New York and told his story to *Nordstjernan's* reporter:

---

[244] This information may have come from an unidentified newspaper and an article headlined, "Man saved from "Titanic lost between New York and Detroit."

[245] From Swedish Church records courtesy Björn-Åke Petersson, Kallinge, Sweden.

[246] Manitowoc may have been Peterson's residence while Detroit was his business address. He was probably identical with the skipper who was Oscar's employer. On the *Carpathia's* survivor list, Johanson is listed as 22-years old when it should be 32.

I have been a seaman and during my years at sea I have experienced several dangerous episodes and one shipwreck. So I'm used to it. But, horrible scenes like the one that played out on board the doomed Titanic, I have never witnessed before, and I hope I never will… I stood midships when the ship sank, and I knew what was going to happen. Shortly before I went overboard, a few crewmembers and I tried to release one of the collapsible lifeboats…. We got it loose but could not get it to open up. It was flat like a raft. These lifeboats are surrounded by a layer of cork that makes them float easily. A Swedish fru stood beside me—I don't recall her name—with her two children. She asked me to try to save them, and this I promised her. When the waves covered us, I hopped overboard with both children. I could hold on to them for a while, but then I was pulled down from the suction of the ship and hit one of the chimneys and with a sorrow in my heart, I let the children go. Eventually, I was able to crawl up in the flattened boat that floated nearby. Suddenly, it capsized, and we were in the water. When we managed to come back up on it, we were only 12 left. I don't know how many we were from the beginning…. For 4 ½ hours we stood there until all 12 of us were rescued by a lifeboat. About our treatment on the Carpathia I have only good things to say. They did what they could for us.[247]

Svenska Tribunen Nyheter, Chicago, reported the following about him:

… he was awakened in steerage by a scraping and breaking jolt. He ran up on deck… the band played some popular melodies… the officers ensured the passengers that there was no danger. They told me to go back to steerage…. I followed their advice. An hour later, the Titanic sank. I jumped into the ocean, and when I surfaced I was close to a collapsible lifeboat. It was empty and I held fast to it for two and one half hour and was then rescued.[248]

[247] *Nordstjernan*, New York, April 23, 1912, p. 7. There was no Swedish mother with two children who perished, but there were mothers who were lost together with more than two children. Mrs. Pålsson traveled alone with four children. Wennerstrom wrote that he was asked to hold on to two of Mrs. Pålsson's children, but lost them when the water rose. Perhaps she asked Oscar W. Johansson to hold on to the other two and lost them as well?

[248] *Svenska Tribunen Nyheter*, Chicago, Apr. 23, 1912. Lee W. Merideth lists Oscar W. Olsson (Johansson) 28, as being from Chicago and going to Chicago. Rescued in Collapsible A. Recent discussions on www.encyclopedia-Titanica.org suggest that he was rescued by Collapsible B along with his fellow Swede Ernst Persson.

When Oscar reached the *Carpathia*, he went down to the engine room to get warm. As soon as he arrived in New York, he sent a telegram to his wife that said, "Saved, Oscar."

The Woman's Relief Committee in New York gave him $50.00. The Swedish Consulate in Chicago issued a new passport for him May 9, 1912 to replace the one he had lost on the *Titanic*.

Oscar moved back to Sweden for good in 1918 and worked as a rigger for the Allmag Ship Yard. Upon his retirement, he ran a small hotel together with his wife. He died at the Trolltorp Old People's Home on Orust April 5 1967.[249]

He had changed his surname to Johansson, because he didn't think that the Americans pronounced Olsson correctly and also to follow the tradition of patronymic surnames. (His father's first name was Johan.) [250]

Her husband fainted when he heard the good news

Johnson, Elisabeth (Alice)

Mrs. Oscar W. Johnson, 24, nee Backberg, was a Finland Swede, married to a Swede. In the first part of 1911, she received news from Finland that her father was on his death bed and wished to see her and her children. Her father died before she could leave, but she still decided to visit her mother and siblings and also her husband's family in Ramkvilla, Sweden.

Born January 24, 1885 in Helsingfors, Finland, she was the daughter of Stefan and Amanda Backberg. She had five brothers and one sister. Alice is included here because she was married to a Swede and belonged to the Swedish-American community in St. Charles, Illinois.

When Alice was 17 years old, her father arranged for her to marry Karl Victor Nefling. The marriage took place in Finland November 16, 1902, but the union turned out to be an unhappy one. To get away from it, Alice immigrated to Chicago, where she met and fell in love with Oscar Johnson. This prompted her divorce, which was granted May 31, 1907. She then married Oscar, and their first child, Harold, was born January 28, 1908. The second child, Eleanor, was born September 23, 1910, also in St. Charles.

While visiting her husband's relatives In Ramkvilla, Sweden, Alice met Elin Braf and Helmina Nilsson, and accompanied them on her return voyage

---

[249]www.encyclopedia-titanica.org. Oscar may have returned to Sweden shortly before he was required to register for the WWI draft on September 12, 1918. He was not found in the registration records under either the name of Olson or Johanson.

[250] Various sources including www.encyclopedia-titanica.org

to America. They left Sweden via Malmö and sailed to England on a ship belonging to the United Steamship Company.

All five were asleep when the *Titanic* collided with the iceberg. Carrying Eleanor, Alice led them up on deck. Elin and Helmina saw to Harold. A man held Eleanor so that Alice could step into the lifeboat. Helmina followed, but Elin was frozen in place with fear and unable to move. She held on to Harold so tightly that he had to be pried from her. Elin never got into a lifeboat and perished. Alice turned her head away when the *Titanic* sank. [251]

An article in *Chicago Daily Tribune,* April 18, 1912, relates how her husband fainted when he learned the good news:

Merchant faints from happiness… when he learns that his relatives were saved from the shipwreck. Special from Aurora, Illinois. Oscar W. Johnson, 32 years old, a businessman residing in St. Charles, Ill., fell down in a faint that lasted 30 minutes when a telephone call from Aurora let him know that all women on the Titanic had been saved. [Not all women, but more importantly to him, his wife and children].

Johnson's wife and two small children, Harold 4, and Eleanor, 1, and his two sisters were booked as passengers on the giant ship and none of their names have been on the list of the saved. Mrs. Johnson had been away from home for one year. Her little girl was born while she was overseas, and the child's father had not seen her. [This is incorrect as she was born in St. Charles in September of 1910.] *He expected to meet his family in Chicago tomorrow. He had just renovated his home as a surprise for his wife.*[252]

Another source states that Oscar went to New York to meet his family. See next.

In New York, Alice was cared for at St. Luke's Hospital, where Red Cross gave her money and a new trunk. Her husband, Oscar Johnson, had come by train to New York to meet his family. On April 24 they traveled to Chicago and on to St. Charles, where many friends and relatives met up to welcome them home. Baby Eleanor still suffered from exposure to the cold winds in the lifeboat. Four-year-old Harold, who had been left by the rail until someone passed him to his mother in the boat, was the life of the party.[253] [Another child, Herbert, was born in 1913.]

---

[251] www.titanicnorden.com
[252] *Ibid.*
[253] http://genealogytrails.com/ill/

Alice and her children passed through Chicago on April 25 on her way to St. Charles. She later appeared in a play in Elgin at a special *Titanic* presentation.[254]

Oscar Johnson was born in Sweden in about 1882 and had emigrated in 1901, four years before Alice. When the Census was taken in St. Charles in 1910, he was naturalized and listed as a bowling alley manager. He died of consumption October 31, 1917 at the age of 35. Alice then married Hans Amundson, who unfortunately died of phenomena within a year, possibly in December of 1918, leaving two children from a former marriage. The once divorced and twice widowed Alice adopted Amundson's children and married Carl Peterson in 1920. Peterson was a widowed farmer with two children.

According to the 1930 U.S. Census, Carl Peterson, 45, was born in Sweden and had emigrated in 1902. The children listed were: Harold, 22, stepson, Clifford 18, son; Einar, 16, son; Hedvig, 7, daughter; Vernon Amundson, 11 (adopted son), and Irene, 4, daughter. All the children were born in Illinois. Alice was the mother of Hedvig and Irene. Carl Peterson died in 1964 and Alice on December 19, 1968. [255]

His mother screamed, "Save my boy."

Johnson, Harold T.

The 4-year-old Harold was born January 28, 1908, the son of Elisabeth (Alice) and Oscar Johnson.

His mother and sister were already seated in a lifeboat while Harold stood on the ship crying. When Alice screamed, "Save my boy," a man standing nearby grabbed the child by an arm and a leg and dropped him 30 feet into the arms of his mother.[256]

Harold died August 10, 1968 at the age of 60 and is buried in Little Woods Cemetery. St. Charles, Illinois. [May actually have died in April of 1968.][257]

Harold and his sister Eleanor

[254] www.encyclopedia-titanica.org.
[255] www.encyclopedia-titanica.org. and http://genealogytrails.com/ill/.
[256] Cris Kohl, p. 53.
[257] www.ancestry.com

The infant girl had no memory of the Titanic

Johnson, Eleanor Ileen

The 1 ½ year-old Eleanor was born September 23 or 29, 1910 in St. Charles, Illinois, the daughter of Elisabeth (Alice) and Oscar Johnson. She was baptized Elenora Ilene on December 9, 1910 at Bethlehem Lutheran Church, St. Charles, Illinois. Her parents were not members of the congregation. She was rescued in lifeboat 15 together with her mother and brother. Eleanor married Delbert Shuman (1909-1981), and they had one son, Earl. She worked at the Elgin Watch Company and later as a telephone operator until retiring in 1962. She died March 7, 1998 in Elgin, Illinois.[258]

Railroad man repelled on a rope to the water below

Johnsson, Karl

Karl Johnsson after his rescue. His cheeks appear to be swollen. Photo courtesy Robert Bracken.

Karl was the son of John, and therefore a Johnsson. He was 25-years old and single when he arrived in New York on board the *Carpathia* in 1912. Before his emigration, he was a railroad brakeman at the Killeberg railroad station in Skåne. Until recently there has been only vague, conflicting information about when and where this man was born. He has been the most difficult Swedish survivor to trace both in Sweden and in the U.S.

Extensive research shows that Karl was born May 12, 1886 in Karhult, Loshult parish, Kristianstad län, the son of *Banvaktare* (R.R. lineman) John Nilsson (born Dec. 12, 1850 in Stockhult, Loshult) and his wife Ingrid Nilsdotter (born August 3, 1854 in Vitseltofta [also spelled Visseltofta¨parish, Kristianstad län). The family resided at Gnubbarp No. 2 in Loshult. Karl had 12 siblings.[259]

---

258 http://genealogytrails.com/ill/

259 Loshult parish records, Kristianstad län, Sweden, researched by genealogists in Sweden. His siblings listed in the 1882-1995 household records were: Sven, born 1877, Blenda Sofia, born 1878, Emil, born 1880, Ida, born 1881, Otto Viktor, born 1883 or 1885, Oskar Bernhard Nikolaus, born 1887, Blenda Maria, born 1889, Anna Matilda, born 1891, Klara, born 1893, and Axel, born 1894. Two more children were born after 1995, Tage, and Gerhard. In 1915 when the father died, Ida, Otto, Oskar, Blenda, Klara, and the under-aged children, Axel, Tage, and Gerhard were living, as was Karl in America. In 1947 when the mother died, only Ida Ljungberg, Blenda, Nyman, and Klara Andersson, were listed as surviving children. Karl was not listed although he was still living in America. The deceased Otto had six children: Silva

Karl Johnsson moved from his home in Loshult in 1906 to Malmö, and registered in Caroli parish, where he lived in block "Thor IV." In 1907, he moved within the same parish to block "Quiding V," where he lived together with his siblings Oskar Bernhard Nikolaus Johnsson, born November 5, 1887, and Blenda Maria Johnsson, born November 18, 1889. His occupation was listed as brakeman. He moved back to Loshult on February 11, 1910.[260]

Karl left Sweden in 1912 without reporting to the authorities, presumably because he wished to avoid obtaining permission from the military. Many young Swedish men circumvented the law by going to Denmark, where they bought a waistcoat containing the necessary papers to enter the U.S.

It was either in Copenhagen or on the *Carpathia* that Karl's surname was incorrectly spelled Janson. On the *Carpathia* manifest, his father's name was incorrectly listed as G. Nilsson when it should have been J. Nilsson. The *Carpathia* manifest, which is part of the Ellis Island records, lists Karl as being from "Killsberg" (Killeberg). The newspapers *Nordstjernan* and *Hemlandet* confirm that he was from Killeberg, located close to Hallaryd, where his travel companion, Olga Lundin, Karl's third cousin (4-*männing*) began her journey.[261]

An emigration certificate (*utvandringsbetyg)* was issued for Karl Johnsson in Loshult on June 14, 1912 when he was already in the U.S.[262]

Karl had no middle name. He was alive and living in America when his father died February 23, 1915, but was not listed as a survivor when his mother had died June 23, 1947.[263] Contacted by telephone, descendants of his siblings in Sweden confirmed that Karl was on the *Titanic* and that he survived by floating on a door. A son of a nephew said, "Karl remained in America, but we lost contact with him." The relatives had no knowledge of any preserved letters from him.

One contributor to a popular website erroneously identified Karl as a brother of Andrew Palmquist, New Haven, Connecticut. Andrew was the

---

Persson, Alva Jansen, Ruth Ling, Sonja Lind Dahl, Elly Severinsson, and Harry Johnsson. The deceased Axel had one son, Axel Axelsson.

[260] Information courtesy Gert Påhlsson. Sources All 45, p. 102, and All 65, p. 99.

[261] The *Carpathia* Manifest. The initial is probably a misunderstanding of the pronunciation of the letter.

[262] Information courtesy of Torsten and Ingegärd Trulson, Loshult Hembygdsförening, Loshult. Such certificates could be requested after the emigrant had left Sweden.

[263] Copies of *bouppteckningar* (probate records) obtained from *Landsarkivet* in Lund. Father's record dated Mar. 24, 1915 and mother's dated Nov. Nov. 24, 1947. Karl's nephew, Axel Axelsson, was the one who stated that Karl remained in America and that the family lost contact with him.

brother of Oscar Leander Johansson, who later assumed the name of Palmquist.[264]

Another source incorrectly lists Karl as a 32-year-old man living in Huntley, Illinois, and returning to Huntley. Huntley was the destination of another Swede, Karl Carlsson, who perished.[265]

Three men from the Hallaryd area traveled with Karl and Olga, namely, Nils Johansson (Olga's fiancé), Albert Augustsson, and Paul Andreasson. Karl and Olga, who were third cousins, were the only survivors of the group. Nils Johansson was Karl's second cousin.[266]

While Karl's travel companions registered their departure in Malmö, Karl did not do so. Having bought his ticket in Copenhagen, he traveled by train to Esbjerg on Denmark's west coast, where he boarded a ship taking him to Parkeston, England. He went on to Southampton by train via London. This route seems to be the one taken by several young men leaving Sweden without the proper papers. Also leaving from Copenhagen were Gunnar Tenglin, Einar Karlsson, Jan [Thure Edvin] Lundstrom, Carl [Olof] Jansson, and Aurora Adelia Landergren.[267]

When Karl fled the doomed liner, only a small part of the steamer's stern was visible. He repelled down a rope to the water below and managed to keep afloat on wreckage until he reached a lifeboat. While swimming, he exchanged a few words with Gerda Dahlberg who fought unsuccessfully for her life nearby.[268]

Olga Lundin, in a letter to Sweden, wrote about Karl: "Kalle did not get into a lifeboat until later but floated on a board in the water for six hours [?], so he was almost dead when he came on board the ship that we are now on." [See Lundin, Olga].

In New York, Karl recuperated at the Swedish Immigrant Home, but was not interviewed by the paper *Nordstjernan*. According to Pastor Lilja, director of the home, Carl Johnson [Karl] received $50.00 from the Women's Relief Committee while staying at the home. The immigrants also received a rail-road ticket to their destinations from the White Star Line, plus a small amount of cash.[269]

---

[264] The website is www.encyclopedia-titanica.org. Bethesda Lutheran Church, New Haven, Conn., lists the two brothers as members. It was Oscar who gave speeches in New Haven about his rescue and not Karl. Björn-Åke Petersson confirmed that Andrew and Oscar were brothers.
[265] Merideth, *Titanic Names*.
[266] Information courtesy Cecilia Månsson, Sweden.
[267] *Kristianstadbladet* and other sources.
[268] *Hemlandet*, Chicago, May 14, 1912.
[269] *Nordstjernan*, May 17 and May 21,1912. The other Karl Janson (Carl Olof) was staying at the Salvation Army.

In the Ellis Island records of passengers arriving in New York on the rescue ship *Carpathia,* Karl reported his destination as "Employer C. A. Smith's Sawmill at Camden Station, Minnesota.[270]

The owner of the mill was Swedish and probably employed many Swedes. In 1912, the same year that Karl arrived, Smith moved his company to Marshfield, now Coos Bay, Oregon. Charles Axel Smith, a native of Sweden, became one of Minnesota's leading lumbermen in the late 19th century.

In Oregon, he began to purchase stands of virgin forest. His agents filed claims to 160-acre tracts of timber and then transferred them to his company. In 1907, his holdings had reached 300,000 acres. The "The state-of-art "big mill" was the envy of other lumber manufacturers. Minnesotans arrived to set up logging camps and transportation systems to supply the mill with logs. It had miles of railroads, rafting facilities, and waterfront docks for loading timber. The finishing facilities were located at Bay Point, California.[271]

A few years later, Charles Axel Smith had overextended his company and incurred heavy debts on the timber land and the building of logging railroads. When the market became glutted and prices dropped, he sold some of its vast timber holdings. In 1916, a creditors' committee reorganized the properties as Coos Bay Lumber Company. In 1918, the C. A. Smith Big Mill was no longer controlled by Smith.[272]

Karl registered for the World War I draft in St. Helens, Oregon as "Chas Johnson," born May 12, 1886, a resident of Kerry, Columbia County, Oregon, and a subject of Sweden, not naturalized or declared, living in Kerry, Columbia County, where he worked as a logger for the Kerry Timber Company. He listed his closest relative as "T" or "I" Nilsson of Sweden, likely his mother, Ingrid Nilsson. He was tall and of medium build with blue eyes and light hair. He signed his name Charlie Johnson at St. Helens, Oregon on September 12, 1918, shortly before the war ended. [This record does not list his year of immigration, but the fact that his date of birth is correct and that

---

[270] Camden Station by the Mississippi River was located in Camden, now a part of Minneapolis.

[271] C. A. Smith Lumber Company in Oregon Encyclopedia-Oregon History and Culture, written by William G. Robbins. Smith was born December 11, 1852 in Boxholm, Östergötland, and came to the U.S. on *S.S. Paris* on May 22, 1867 with his father and sister. He attended public schools in Minneapolis and the University of Minnesota for one year (Passport application, signed June 7, 1912, www.Ancestry.com) and other Internet sites.)

[272] *Ibid.*

the nearest kin is a Nilsson living in Sweden makes it virtually certain that Charles is identical with the *Titanic* survivor Karl from Killeberg.][273]

The following was found about the Kerry Timber Company:

> *The Columbia & Nehalem River Railroad, most commonly known as the Kerry Line, was one of the most famous early 20th century logging railroads in the Northwest. What distinguishes the Kerry line from most of the hundreds of other logging railroads that operated from the late 1800s through the 1930s in Oregon and the Pacific Northwest was the sheer number of logs that were hauled from the woods between 1915 and 1938.*
>
> *Another thing that distinguishes the Kerry line from most other logging railroads was its 1875 foot long tunnel.... A separate spur left the log dump and connected with the Spokane Portland & Seattle RR that ran by the Kerry log dump.*[274]

In 1918, about 400 feet of the south end of the tunnel collapsed causing the line to shot down for several months. A few years later the tunnel collapsed due to sabotage, but was soon restored.[275]

In 1920, according to the U.S. Census for Oregon, Charles Johnson, 33, born in Sweden, worked in a lime quarry in Douglas County, Green Township, District No.153. The census lists him as "transient" and laborer at a lime quarry, the same as the other workers at the quarry. In the column for the year of immigration, it says "un," (unavailable). The camp cook listed below Charles is Jenny Ingram, 22, the daughter of the head of the household, Randolph S. Ingram.[276]

The census was taken April 7, 1930. A few months later, Charles and Jenny were married.

Charles Johnson, 34, and Jenny Ingram, 22, were married by county judge N. J. Steward on June 5, 1920 in Roseburg, Douglas County. Charles

---

[273] Local Board for County of Columbia, State of Oregon, St. Helens, Ore. Roll No. 1852053. www.ancestry.com. Having compared this record with several other registrations, it is clear that the registrants filled out the forms themselves. Charles wrote his in a flowing hand as he penned Nilsson the Swedish way with one long s and one short. September 12, 1918 was the last registration for WWI service, which was for men 18-21 and 31 to 45 years old. Charlie had narrowly escaped having to register with the first men because of his date of birth.

[274] "The Kerry Timber Co. and the Columbia & Nehalem River Railroad." http://www.brian894.com/Kerry railroadhistory.html

[275] *Ibid.*

[276], Charlie's year of immigration is not listed. Problems with the Kerry tunnel might have made him seek employment in the quarry, located 3-4 miles south of Roseburg on Roberts Creek Road.

listed his residence as Portland, Oregon, and Jenny listed hers as Roseburg, Oregon, where she was born September 13, 1897. Portland and Roseburg are 200 miles apart but connected by the Southern Pacific Railroad. It was the first marriage for both. Their dates of birth were not listed.[277]

The 1930 U.S. Census shows Charlie and Jenny living in Jewell, Clatsop County, Oregon:

Charlie Johnson, 43, born about 1887 in Sweden, head of household. Wife, Jenny Johnson, 32. He had married at age 33 [actually at the age of 34], and was the head brakeman for the logging train. [The immigrant from Killeberg was a brakeman on the railroad in Sweden.] A boy by the name of Chas P. Andregg, 12, lived with them.[278]

Jewell, Oregon, was a logging community located at the junction of 103 & 202 near the Nehalem River in the extreme northwestern part of Oregon. The couple lived in the Upper Tide Water Logging Camp.[279]

Their marriage did not last. Jenny Johnson remarried on June 3, 1938 in Kelso, Cowlitz County, Washington. Both she and her new husband, Franklin Sandy, resided in Washington County, Oregon, just south of Columbia River. The marriage return shows that Jenny had been married before and was divorced.[280]

In the 1940s, Johnson lived in Blachly, Lane County, Oregon, where he was known as "Swede" or "Titanic Swede." He worked as a lumberman (poleman) for Blachly-Lane Cooperative Electric Company, located in the Triangle-Lake area of Oregon. Being a poleman meant that he cut down the trees for utility poles and finished them. His coworker Gordon Smith described him as huge and strong as an ox. "He could pick up a pole on his

---

277 Information from the Genealogical Society of Douglas County, Roseburg. Dr. E.V. Hoover signed the Marriage Oath and Certificate stating that he was the physician on June 4 who had examined Chas Johnson and found the applicant "free from contagious or infectious venereal disease." Dr. Hoover was one of the witnesses to the marriage together S. R. Sykis (possibly a county clerk).

278 The boy was listed as a boarder. He was born in Washington, his mother in Iowa, and his father in Washington. His birth record shows "unnamed birth," Jul. 12, 1917 in Seattle, father Oscar Andregg.

279 www.ancestry.com. Charles would have had a birthday between the date of the census and the date of the marriage. To be a brakeman on a logging train was, and still is, the most dangerous job in America.

280 They could have been divorced any time between 1930 and 1938. Certificate of Marriage signed by Jenny Johnson and Frank W. Sandy and Marriage Return also signed by both. They were married by the Justice of the Peace. Jenny died in mid-July 1973. Her second husband, Franklin R. Sandy, was also a logger (b. 1908, d 1964.) Copies received from the Lower Columbia Genealogical Society, Kelso, Washington. Charles was not found to have registered in the fourth registration for the WWII draft conducted on April 27, 1942, which was for men between 45 and 64 years old, the so-called old-man's registration.

shoulder and carry it for a mile," he said. Johnson worked there when other men went to war and was still there when they came back. Johnson told his coworkers about his ordeals on the *Titanic.* He had left his money in his cabin and went back to get it, but it was too late. The water was coming in. Had he recovered the money, he thought he would have lost it in the water.[281]

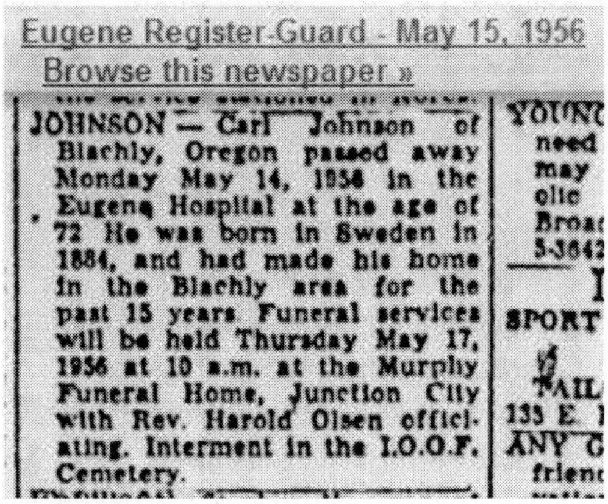
Eugene Register-Guard - May 15, 1956
Browse this newspaper »

JOHNSON — Carl Johnson of Blachly, Oregon passed away Monday May 14, 1956 in the Eugene Hospital at the age of 72. He was born in Sweden in 1884, and had made his home in the Blachly area for the past 15 years. Funeral services will be held Thursday May 17, 1956 at 10 a.m. at the Murphy Funeral Home, Junction City with Rev. Harold Olsen officiating. Interment in the I.O.O.F. Cemetery.

Death notice for Johnson, courtesy Historical Society, Junction City, Ore. His age should be 70.

Johnson shared living quarters, a cabin in the woods, with another coworker, Guy Ramsdale.

A death certificate for Carl [his given name] shows that he was born in Sweden, lived in Blachly, and worked for the power company as a laborer. He died on May 14, 1956 at Sacred Heart Hospital in Eugene, Oregon of broncopnenumonia. He had been ill for two days, but had suffered from carcinoma of the lung for six weeks. Johnson was buried in the Restlawn Cemetery/IOOF, Junction City, Oregon. No head stone found.[282]

"The ship has run aground"

Karlsson, Einar Gervasius

Karlsson, 21, spelled his name Carlson in the U.S. When only half awake, he realized that the engines had stopped. He woke his cabin mate saying, "The ship has run aground." John Asplund, the sailor, answered, "Here in the middle of the Atlantic? Go back to sleep."

He and Asplund hid in the shadows, Einar said, until they got a chance to climb down the ropes into the lowering boat. Afterward, he suffered from rope burns on his hands, arms, and legs. He watched as the ship took its final bow and described it as great flashes of light much like fireworks before deadly silence as the *Titanic* took its final plunge.

---

[281] Information Robert L. Bracken, Titanic International Society.

[282] Research by Barbara Jones, Genealogical Forum of Oregon (Portland). The certificate contains some errors. The informant was Andy Christensen, and he probably did not know Carl's correct age and other details. It was not necessary to be a member of the IOOF to be buried in their cemeteries. There was a Danish Lutheran Church in Junction City, now Faith Lutheran Church.

Born June 19, 1890 at No. 304 in Oskarshamn, Kalmar län, he was the son of factory worker Per Fredrik Karlsson (born October 2, 1859 in Högsby parish, Kalmar län) and Emilia Jonsdotter (born June 18, 1860 in Kråksmåla parish, Kalmar län). Einar was a corporal with the Kalmar Regiment. He emigrated from Oskarshamn, March 27, 1912. There is no notation in the Swedish records about the *Titanic*.[283]

Together with his traveling companion, Johan Asplund, Karlsson bought his ticket in Copenhagen. On his escape from the *Titanic*, he climbed down the ropes to Lifeboat 13. Karlsson's great-granddaughter, Melissa Bendig, said, "He never wanted to talk about the night of the *Titanic*, but what we do know is that he was unable to retrieve his personal belongings and had trouble getting to the lifeboats as he was a third-class passenger."

In New York, Einar recuperated at the Salvation Army Cadet School. While there, he and his friends John Charles Asplund, Gunnar Tenglin, August Wennerstrom, and Carl Olof Jansson, had a group portrait taken.[284]

After the near-death experience, he suffered from nightmares every April. He lived in California, Colorado, New York, and Minnesota, before settling in Nebraska in 1916.

Nordstjernan wrote about Einar:

Einar Karlsson was the one who appeared the calmest and most good-natured. As soon as he had been lucky enough to crawl into a lifeboat, he went to sleep and slept until he was taken aboard the Carpathia.[285]

On June 6, 1917, Einar Carlson registered for the WWI draft in Saunders County, Nebraska. He described himself as alien, single, and a farm laborer working for "Edd" Petersen, Freemont, Nebraska. He had served as corporal in the Swedish Infantry for three years, and was of medium height and build with brown eyes and black hair.[286]

He became an American citizen in 1917, probably prior to his service in the Army. He served in World War I, before returning to Nebraska to farm. Later he worked for the telephone company. Carlson died in 1958 at the age

---

283 Information courtesy Björn-Åke Petersson, Kallinge, Sweden.

284 www.Titanicmannen.se. The Swedish-American newspaper, *Hemlandet*, Chicago, wrote on April 30, 1912, that Karlsson was headed for Brooklyn, New York. See group portrait in *Letters from the Titanic* by Claes-Göran Wetterholm, Stockholm, 2000, p. 20. This portrait shows two Salvation Army officers and four other men, two of them identified as Carl Olof Janson and August Wennerstrom. One of the others is tentatively identified as Einar Karlsson, but it could be Gunnar Tenglin. The smaller man is probably John Asplund.

285 *Nordstjernan,* New York. Apr. 23, 1912.

286 www.ancestry.com.

of 67. His daughter donated his few remaining artifacts to the Titanic Historical Society, including his dining room assignment card.[287]

In 1930, according to the U.S. Census, Carlson lived in Holt County, Ewing Township, District 14, Nebraska. His wife Marjorie, born in Iowa, was 26-years old. Her father was born in France and her mother in Iowa. Their son, Eugene, was 6-years old, and their daughter Margaret M, 5. Both children were born in Nebraska.[288]

"I gave my money and papers to Captain Holm"

Landergren, Aurora Adelia

Adelia gave her money and papers to her traveling companion, Captain John Holm, also from Karlshamn, because she was wearing only a sweater and a vest and had no pockets. Her valuables were lost when Holm went down with the ship. The 22-year-old single woman had bought a ticket to sail on *Fredrik VIII* of the Scandinavia-America Line. On her way to Denmark she met up with John Holm and Mauritz Ådahl and traveled with them. When they arrived at Southampton, they discovered they were re-booked on the *Titanic* because of the coal strike. [See her image in the group photo shown in the beginning of this chapter.]

She was born June 18, 1889 in Karlshamn, Blekinge (parish and county), to Axel Mattsson Landergren (a fisherman born in 1849 in Karlshamn) and Fredrika Karolina Håkansson (born in 1856 in Karlshamn). In 1900, the family lived at No. 382 in the block named "Amerika" in Karlshamn. Adelia had four siblings.[289]

She had been down to her cabin to get her photographs and on the way back she discovered that someone had locked the door leading to the upper decks. Maurtiz Ådahl had waited for her and managed to unlock it so that she could come up again.

In her letter to Sweden, Adelia wrote she had given her money and papers to Captain Holm (John) for safekeeping. Her companions were calm. When they thought it was time for her to get into a lifeboat, they strapped the life vest on her and helped her into Lifeboat 13.[290]

In New York, Adelia recuperated at the Swedish Immigrant Home. While there, she received $50.00 from the Women's Relief Committee. Adelia also received $75.00 from the Red Cross. Her destination was New York.

---

287 www.encyclopedia-titanica.org. Slightly edited).
288 www.ancestry.com.
289 From the Swedish Church records, courtesy Björn-Åke Petersson, Kallinge, Sweden.
290 Claes-Göran Wetterholm, *Letters From Titanic,* p. 14. Only a short excerpt. Captain Holm did not survive.

In 1919, she married Fredrik Johnson at Bodö, Sweden, but they lived in New York. They had no children. Adelia died in New York August 2, 1947 and is buried there.[291]

Count Posse's daughter traveled in first class

Lindström, Sigrid Posse

The 55-year-old countess was a first-class passenger and visitor. She was the niece of the late Swedish Prime Minister Arvid Posse. In 1888, she married Captain Karl Johan Lindström, born in 1849 in Växjö, Kronoberg's län. In 1900, the couple lived in Linköping, Östergötland.[292]

Born December 18, 1856 in Ängelholm Garnisonsförsamling (the Garrison parish) Kristianstad län, she was the daughter of Major Count Knut Lage Posse, born in 1821, and Lovisa Aminoff (1829-1880). Both parents were deceased. Mrs. Lindstrom had three siblings: Countess Ebba Posse married to Captain Sigfrid Freilich, Count Arvid Posse, and Count Christer Posse, who had died in Africa in 1886 while on a Stanley expedition.

In 1912, she lived with her husband in Stockholm, but sailed from Cherbourg, France after a visit to Paris. She was on her way to visit her sister [or daughter] in New York.

While on the continent, Mrs. Lindström had visited with one of her daughters in Berlin, who had recently married a German *skriftställare* (publisher) by the name of Norbert.[293]

On the *Titanic*, she became acquainted with Erik Lind and Håkan Björnstrom-Steffanson, who escorted her to lifeboat 6. She later sued White Star Line for loss of clothing that she valued at 6000 francs. Mrs. Lindstrom, widowed in 1917, died in 1946.[294]

"Oh, how I mourn Nils and the others"

Lundin, Olga Elida

In a letter to Sweden, Olga described how much she had suffered and how she mourned her fiancé, Nils Johansson, and the other men in her group who perished. On the *Titanic*, the 23-year-old woman became seasick and

---

291 www.encyclopedia-titanica.org. Adelia and her husband could not be found in any of the U.S. Censuses for New York.

292 From Swedish Church records courtesy Björn-Åke Petersson, Kallinge, Sweden.

293 *Hemlandet*, May 14, 1912.

294 www.encyclopedia-titanica.org. (In 1920, 6.000 francs would have been worth $375.00, but the value of currencies fluctuated a great deal after WW!).

switched her ticket from third class to second. Her fiancé paid the difference in price. [See her image in the group photo shown in the beginning of this chapter.]

Born January 9, 1889 in Kråkeryd Södergård, Hallaryd, Kronoberg's län, Småland, she was the daughter of Edvard Måhlgren Lundin and his wife, Gustafva Eriksdotter. Her father was a soldier with the Kronoberg Regiment No. 98. He was born in 1865 in Götered, Kronoberg's län. He left Sweden without papers, and in 1907, he was taken off the church books. He had married Olga's mother, Gustava Eriksdotter, in 1888. She was born in 1857 Hallaryd.

Olga had three siblings:[295]

1) Jenny Alfrida, born February 9, 1890. She emigrated in 1911 and lived in Meriden, Connecticut. She returned to Hallaryd in 1918, but emigrated once again in 1920. In 1928, she left for New York from Göteborg on the *Gripsholm*. Having returned to Sweden for good in 1932, Jenny died in Osby, Kristianstad län, September 12, 1968. In 1941, she married Arnold Botvid Jönsson, born in 1900 in Hallaryd. He died in 1975 in Osby, Kristianstad län. Jenny died February 11, 1968 in Osby.
2) Hulda Annette, born in 1892 in Hallaryd. She was married to Olof Persson, and they owned a farm in Hallaryd. He was born in 1885 in Hallaryd and died in 1967. Hulda died in 1987 in Hallaryd. While being cared for at the Ljungby hospital, she recalled that she had a sister, who was on the *Titanic*.
3) Hjalmar Lundin, born in 1900 in Hallaryd, married to Agda Oliva Bengtsson, born in 1900 in Hallaryd. They had one son, Astor.

There is no evidence of Olga having emigrated before 1912, although the Ellis Island records state that her last residence was Meriden, Connecticut. She received her emigration certificate on April 1, 1912, and departed from Malmö on April 5. Her last residence was listed as "Halland," which was supposed to be Hallaryd, Småland. Her destination was her sister, Jenny Lundin, Meriden, Connecticut.[296]

Olga traveled with Paul Andreasson, Albert Augustsson, her fiancé Nils Johansson, and Karl Johnsson. All except Karl were from Hallaryd.

---

[295] Much of the information about Olga's family comes from Cecilia Månsson.

[296] Meriden, Conn. might have been entered in the wrong column. According to Swedish church records, courtesy Björn-Åke Petersson, Olga did not emigrate before 1912. Cecilia Månsson says that it was not unusual that emigrants did not take out their papers the first time they left for America.

Olga and Nils were cousins. His mother, Ingjer (Ingrid Eriksdotter), was the sister of Olga's mother, Gustava Eriksdotter. Ingjer was married to Johannes Karlsson. Their son, Nils, emigrated from Hallaryd in 1903.[297]

Karl was Olga's third cousin (4-*männing*), and not her brother-in-law as stated in other sources. Karl and Nils were second cousins (3-*männingar).*[298]

On the *Titanic*, Olga shared a third-class cabin with Gerda Dahlberg, but because Olga could not stand the sea, her fiancé, Nils Johanson, paid the extra cost to have her moved to second class. After that, Nils and Olga could only see each other from a distance and had to shout to each other. While the ship foundered, Olga and her male travel companions stood near Lifeboat 10 and prayed. Crewmen took her by her hands and legs and threw her into the lifeboat, she said. Karl was the only other survivor of the group.

Olga was taken to the Swedish Immigrant Home in New York, where she received $75.00 from the Women's Relief Committee. She probably also received a railroad ticket from the White Star Line to her destination. [299]

The 1930 U.S. Census lists Olga Lundin, single, as living in Manhattan, working as a servant for the Marzagelli family.[300]

In the 1930s, Olga married Charles Andersson, born in 1891 in Mönsterås, Kalmar län. They had met in Sweden. Due to Charles's deteriorating health, they returned to Sweden in 1963 and settled in Osby, Kristianstad län, probably because Olga's sister, Jenny, and her husband lived there. Charles died February 11, 1964. Olga Lundin Andersson died March 1, 1973 in Osby, Kristianstad län.[301]

Olga wrote a letter to Sweden dated, Atlantic, April 16, 1912:

Dear brother and siblings:

I will now briefly write a few lines to you and let you know that I am alive after great suffering and difficulties. You must have read in the newspaper that the ship we sailed on went under. Oh, Almighty God, how I have suffered on this journey.

Just think, last Sunday night we were awakened by a terrible noise when the ship ran into an iceberg. We all got up, imagine the panic, but still we didn't believe that it would sink.

---

[297] Information, courtesy Cecilia Månsson, Sweden, who says that almost all of the emigrants in this group from Hallaryd came from blacksmiths families. Many immigrants in the Måhlgren family settled in Brainerd, Minnesota.

[298] Information courtesy Cecilia Månsson, Sweden, who had three relatives, perhaps five, on the *Titanic*. One of them was Olga Lundin.

[299] *Nordstjernan*, New York, May 17, and May 21, 1912.

[300] www.ancestry.com.

[301] The information about her marriage was received from Cecilia Månsson, Sweden.

It was the world's largest steamer. I'm so shaken that it's almost impossible to write. I can't collect my thoughts. I'm so nervous and down so I can't do anything. I have the sad message to tell that Nils, Albert, and Paul found their graves in the waves of the Atlantic. Oh, dear Lord, how sad. Imagine it. My pen cannot describe it.

I held Nils with one hand and Kalle [Karl] *with the other. We read and prayed as long as we could and then we decided not to separate but die together. We didn't see another way. Albert and Paul went after* [aft?] *We five were like siblings, and we were to be separated in the waters of the Atlantic. It was 12 o'clock when this happened and within an hour the entire ship had sunk with 3,000* [more like 1,500.]

A bigger disaster at sea has probably never happened. Oh, how I mourn Nils and the others. The last word he said when we had prayed was that he had not only prayed for himself but also for his parents and siblings. There we stood on deck and didn't see anything but death before us.

Then they launched the lifeboats. I was thrown into one. I held Nils by the hand and wanted him to come with me, but they held him back because they were afraid we would be too many. I screamed as loudly as I could and wanted to go back, but then they lowered us.

There I sat in a small fishing boat in the middle of the Atlantic, and I could see only death at any moment. But it was not my time and therefore I am alive. How many were saved I don't know, but no more than 700 out of 3,000. Kalle did not get into a lifeboat until later but floated on a board in the water for six hours, so he was almost dead when he came on board the ship that we are now on. Lord God, we are like pigs. Here are only Japanese ... and it smells ...[302]

The newspaper, *Skandinavia*, wrote on April 24, 1912 about her welcome at her final destination:

Seldom has anyone, whether Swedish or of another nationality, received such a reception as Olga Lundin did last Friday when she arrived in this city [New Haven, Conn.?] *The entire Swedish population here received her with open arms. Reporters from the other newspapers interviewed her and published her picture.*

On April 24, 1912, *the New Haven Evening Register* published a group photo that included Olga Lundin to the left. It did not say that she had arrived in New Haven. The names of the other women were misspelled, but they

302 The letter was published in the paper, *Kalmar,* May 13, 1912, "En smålandsflickas skildring av Titanikolyckan."

were Aurora Landergren, Hilda Hellström, Anna Sjöblom, and Berta Nilsson. The caption read:

"New York, April 22. Among the surviving passengers of the Titanic who were brought here by the Carpathia were five Swedish women who had taken passage in the steerage. They are being cared for at the Swedish Mission pending arrangements for their future movements...." The head of the "Mission" Rev. M. Lilja was included in the picture and identified.[303]

Jennie and Olga Lundin were members of Augustana Lutheran Church in Meriden, Connecticut. Jenny joined June 11, 1911, but removed to Brooklyn, New York. Olga joined the church June 2, 1912, and removed to California March 19, 1913.[304]

Olga might have visited Sweden in 1913. In 1923, she sailed on *M.S. Stockholm* to New York, giving her occupation as baker and her destination as Englewood, New Jersey, which was where her sister Jenny Lundin lived at the time. Olga had a light complexion, dark hair, and blue eyes. She worked as a cook, for, among others, the Norwegian crown prince during his exile during World War II. In 1929, she sailed from Göteborg to New York on *RMS Kungsholm*, arriving November 4.

The 1930 U.S. Census for Manhattan lists Olga Landin, 40, as working for the Frank Marzagelli family.[305]

In the mid-1930s, Olga married Swedish American Charles Andersson, born in 1891 in Mönsterås, Kalmar län. They returned to Sweden to live in Osby, Skåne, where her sister Jenny lived. Charles died February 11, 1964, and Olga died March 1, 1973 in Osby.[306]

According to a newspaper article dated July 10, 1961, she had donated 10,000 Swedish *kronor* to the hospital in Hässleholm in appreciation of good treatment.[307]

"They let me row a while and that was good"

Lundström, Thure Edvin

The 32-year-old Lundstrom told reporters in New York and Chicago about his ordeal. He said that an elderly woman and a young man pulled him from

[303] Copyright 1912 by American Press Association. The pose is the same as in a photo published by *Nordstjernan*. See also photo in the beginning of this section.
[304] Swedish-American church records. Microfilm, SSIRC.
[305] www.ancestry.com
[306] Information Cecilia Månsson.
[307] www.encyclopedia-titanica.org. The exchange rate in 1960 was close to 5 crowns to the dollar. Thus Olga's donation was equal to about $2,000.00.

the water into a lifeboat. He had immigrated to America in 1900, and was a former missionary to China. From 1911 until April 1912, he lived in Gislöf, Östra Nöbbelöf, where he may have worked as a barrel maker.

The paper *Hemlandet,* Chicago, wrote that he had served as a missionary in China for two years. When he became sick with climate fever, he returned to Sweden. He helped his fiancée, Elida Olsson, and several Swedish women to their lifeboats. One of the lifeboats was said to have filled with water causing most of its occupants to drown.[308]

Born March 8, 1880 in Östra Nöbbelöv, Kristianstad län, he was the son of Nils Olsson Lundström (born in 1842 in Järrestad parish, Kristianstad län) and Johanna Österberg (born in 1842 in Gladsax parish, Kristianstad län).[309]

Lundström had five siblings: Mathilda, born in Gladsax 1868, Olof, born in Gladsax 1871, Johan Anton, born in 1876 in Östra Nöbbelöv, and Victor Sigfrid, born in 1882 in Östra Nöbbelöf.

Lundström bought his ticket in Copenhagen. His destination was the residence of his friend, Emil Edward, Fargo Street, Los Angeles. After the Titanic's collision with the iceberg, he helped Mrs. Agnes Sandstrom and her children to a lifeboat and helped other Swedes into another lifeboat, which was said to have filled with water because there were no plugs to seal the holes in the bottom. Having escorted his fiancée. Elida Olsson, to the lifeboat, Lundström believed she was safe.[310]

Lundström is listed as being rescued in Lifeboat 15, but said that he was swimming when taken up by a lifeboat in the water.

He traveled with his fiancée Elida Olsson, two friends, Agnes Sandstrom, Hulda Klasėn, and more than a dozen other people, of which only he and Agnes Sandstrom, and her children, survived. In New York, he was cared for at St. Vincent Hospital.[311]

Lundström's ordeals were described by a *Nordstjernan's* reporter:

---

[308] *Hemlandet*, Chicago, May 14, 1912.

[309] From the Swedish Church records, courtesy Björn-Åke Petersson, Kallinge, Sweden. Östra Nöbbelöv is located on Skåne's east coast in an area called Österlen that was dotted with many little fishing villages.

[310] *Hemlandet*, Chicago, May 14, 1914. All the lifeboats were accounted for later. The paper said that he helped the following people to two different lifeboats. They were Mrs. Agnes Lundström (should be Sandstrom), Klas Klasson, Hilda Klasson, Gertrud Klasson, Elida Olsson, Hulda Verström, and a Norwegian girl, Karen Abelseth. Except for Sandstrom and her children and Karen Abelseth, all of these passengers perished. The paper added that Lundström flung himself into the sea and was eventually taken up by a lifeboat. He was a deeply religious man and it is doubtful that he would lie about how he was saved.

[311] Merideth, "Group Notes," p. 57.

The Swedes kept very calm and collected and never tried to elbow their way forward. Lundstrom had jumped before the steamer sank. He swam around for a long time in the ice-cold water in his lifebelt. Meanwhile he witnessed how three [?] *lifeboats capsized, and said that most Swedes were in those boats.*

When he had been swimming for a long time, a lifeboat came rowing past him, and he tried to hang on to the bow when an elegantly dressed woman brutally hit him in the face with her fist.

He fell back in the water and would surely have perished if it hadn't been for an elderly woman sitting in the stern of the lifeboat, who reached out to him with one hand. She and a young boy pulled him up in the boat.[312]

The following is from *Chicago Daily News*, Chicago, headlined, "Many From Sweden Lost" and attributed to Lundstrom:

After I saw them all safely off, I went back to the third cabin. There were many people from Sweden on board the ship and just a handful of them were saved. I was surrounded by young Swedes, who all seemed willing to die after they had placed their wives and sisters and babies in the boats. I stood there with them a while and then jumped into the sea.

It was frightfully cold, but I was used to it, and I swam for many minutes. Then I was picked up by a lifeboat. There were only 25 people in it. I thought of all those brave young men who were drowned. Then I got extremely cold, but they let me row a while and that was good. At last we were picked up. [313]

Thure Lundstrom, age 38, registered for the WWI draft in Cook County, Illinois, on September 12, 1918 while residing at 4918 Ohio Street in Chicago. He was a Swedish citizen but had declared his intent to become naturalized. He worked as a janitor for the YMCA at 1621 Division Street. His wife's name was Signe. He was of medium height and build with blue eyes and brown hair. He listed one affliction: His legs had been frozen in the *Titanic* disaster.[314]

On September 25, 1919, Thure Edwin Lundstrom petitioned the Chicago court for naturalization while living at 1006 N. Lowler [Lowell?] Avenue. The petition was denied. No reason given. On October 22, 1937 his citizen paper

---

312 *Nordstjernan*, Apr. 23, 1912, p. 7.
313 *Chicago Daily News*, April 24, 1912. Posted on www.encyclopedia-titanica.org by Thomas E. Golembiewsky, January 26, 2011.
314 www.ancestry.com. The fact that his leg had been frozen in the *Titanic* disaster confirms that he had been in the water.

was issued in a Los Angeles court. He resided at 1738 South Berenda Street in Los Angeles.[315]

The 1930 U.S. Census for Los Angeles lists him and his family as follows: Edwin Lundstrom, 50, born in Sweden, alien, carpenter for a construction company. Wife Signe, 41, born in Sweden, alien, daughter Eniz M., 15, born in California, son Louis D, 12, born in Illinois, daughter Helen E., 10, born in Illinois, daughter Ingrid, 2, born in California. Both husband and wife are listed as having arrived in the U.S. in 1912.[316]

Lundstrom worked as parquet floor installer. He died unexpectedly while on a carpentry job in Las Vegas in 1942. His wife Signe Louise Lundstrom died in 1976 at the age of 88.[317] Descendants resided in Grant Pass, Oregon, in 2005.

Engaged woman lost her fiancé

Nilsson, Berta Olivia

Miss Nilsson, 18, was accompanied by her fiancé, Edvard Larson Rondberg. She was rescued in Collapsible D. Her fiancé went down with the ship. [See group photo in the beginning of this chapter.]

Her destination was the home of her sister, Mary Nelson, 55 East Trent Street, Missoula, Montana. After her rescue, she went to Montana by train together with Oscar Hedman, Carl Olof Johnson, and Anna Sjöblom. They were photographed at St. Paul Union Depot.

Born February 22, 1894 in Åsegård, Lysvik parish, Värmland (province and county), she was the daughter of Nils Nilsson (born 1866 in Lysvik) and Ingeborg Johannesdotter (also born in1866 in Lysvik). The church book notes that Berta was rescued from the *Titanic.*[318]

Berta departed from Göteborg on April 5, 1912 on board the *Calypso.*[319] In New York, she recuperated at the Swedish Immigrant Home, where she received $50.00 from the Women's Relief Committee and a railroad ticket from the White Star Line to her destination, Missoula, Montana, and a small amount of cash.[320]

She married William Christensen, a police officer, and they lived in Chicago. Being afraid of the sea, she never visited Sweden. She died December 27, 1976.

---

[315] *Ibid.*
[316] www.ancestry.com. The image is difficult to read.
[317] www.encyclopedia-titanica.org.
[318] From the Swedish Church records, courtesy Björn-Åke Petersson, Kallinge, Sweden.

[320] *Nordstjernan*, New York, May 17 and May 21, 1912.

The obituary in the *Chicago Tribune* stated that the services for Mrs. Bertha Christensen, 88, of 4205 Fullerton Avenue would be in the chapel at 4338 W. Fullerton Avenue. She had died in Northwest Hospital.

The obituary said the deceased was one of the last living survivors of the *Titanic* in 1912. A cousin, who died in the sinking, had put her in a lifeboat before the ship went down. She was survived by two sons, Arthur and Leonard, three daughters, Mrs. Marion McCrum, Mrs. Ruth Gabriel, and Mrs. Dorothy Cherry, nine grandchildren; and ten great-grandchildren. She was buried at Mount Olive Cemetery [Same as the Norwegian survivor Karl Midsjo]. [321]

Third-class dining room where most of the Swedes had their meals.

[321] *Chicago Tribune*, Chicago, Dec. 29, 1976.

Joliet-bound woman saw two lifeboats capsize

Nilsson, Helmina Josefina

Helmina Nilsson

Miss Nilsson, 26, came from a large family and was the last of the siblings to emigrate. She had four younger brothers, Albin, Emil, Frans, and Edvin, as well as a younger sister, Ida, and two older sisters, Alfrida and Hanna. Of these, Albin, Emil, and Edvin had emigrated earlier and changed their names to Lander. They lived and worked in Joliet, Illinois, which was Helmina's destination. Her sister Ida and brother Frans stayed in Sweden.

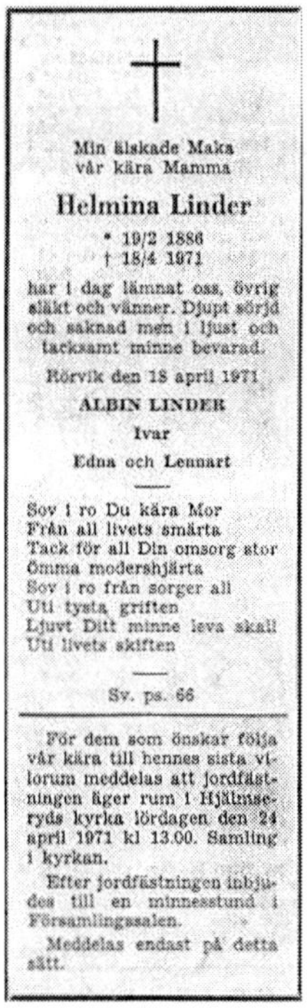

†

Min älskade Maka
vår kära Mamma

Helmina Linder

* 19/2 1886
† 18/4 1971

har i dag lämnat oss, övrig släkt och vänner. Djupt sörjd och saknad men i ljust och tacksamt minne bevarad.

Rörvik den 18 april 1971

ALBIN LINDER

Ivar

Edna och Lennart

Sov i ro Du kära Mor
Från all livets smärta
Tack för all Din omsorg stor
Ömma modershjärta
Sov i ro från sorger all
Uti tysta griften
Ljuvt Ditt minne leva skall
Uti livets skiften

Sv. ps. 66

För dem som önskar följa vår kära till hennes sista vilorum meddelas att jordfästningen äger rum i Hjälmseryds kyrka lördagen den 24 april 1971 kl 13.00. Samling i kyrkan.

Efter jordfästningen inbjudes till en minnesstund i Församlingssalen.

Meddelas endast på detta sätt.

Announcement of death for Helmina Linder. The funeral was held in Hjelmseryd Church April 24, 1971.

Helmina and her sister Alfrida

Born February 19, 1886 in Dragsnäs, Ramkvilla parish, Jönköping's län, Helmina was the daughter of farmers Johan Peter Nilsson (born March 9, 1845 in Ramkvilla) and Anna Kristina Magnidotter (born November 2, 1847 also in Ramkvilla). In 1900, the family moved to the small tenant farm, Åkerslund, belonging to Skärbäck's Bolsgård. Helmina's emigration certificate was dated March 30, 1912.[322]

Helmina and her traveling companion, Elin Braf, left Sweden via Malmö April 5, 1912. On the *Titanic*, Helmina met up with Ernst Aronsson and Gustaf Edvardsson and was pleased that they, too, were headed for Joliet.

Helmina's cabin mates, Elin Braf and Alice Johnson, had fallen asleep when the ship hit the iceberg, but woke with a start. Helmina was still awake. Alice, who knew English, inquired and determined that they needed to leave quickly. Elin, who had crossed the ocean twice, took her time and was left behind. Helmina tossed a shawl around her shoulders and headed for boat deck.

---

[322] Information courtesy Björn-Åke Petersson, Kallinge, Sweden.

Seated in Lifeboat 13, she cringed when she heard the screams of all those doomed as the ship went down. She said she saw two lifeboats capsize near the one she was in. In New York, Helmina, Alice, and her two children recuperated at St. Luke's Hospital. [323]

Helmina Nilsson Linder

In 1917, Helmina married Albin Linder and they had two sons, Ernst and Ivar. In 1920, the U.S. Census showed them living in Joliet, Illinois, District 155. Albin Linder was 31. They returned to Sweden in 1922, where a daughter was born.

Living on farms they had purchased at Brohult and Linnevik, they remained in the area until 1954 when they moved to Rörvik. Helmina died at the hospital in Värnamo April 17, 1971 at the age of 85. She was survived by her husband, Albin, son Ivar, and a married daughter, Edna Lager. [324]

"Not my time to die"

Nysten, Anna

Miss Nysten, 22, had planned to leave Sweden in the summer of 1912, but she had friends leaving in the spring, and they talked her into going with them. Their friends in the Mission Church gave a farewell party for them.

The large Andersson family from Kisa and the Danbom family of three became her travel companions. Anna was the only one of the party who survived. She was one of the few Swedish *Titanic* survivors who married and had children, and was not reluctant to talk about her *Titanic* experience.

---

[323] Cris Kohl, 34, 74, 123.
[324] www.encyclopedia-titanica.org. Also www.titanicnorden.com

Anna Nysten

Born January 22, 1890 in Östra Eneby, Östergötland, she was the daughter of Samuel August Nysten, who owned a farm and a saw mill (born 1848 in Tjärstad, Östergötland) and Maria Sofia Nilsdotter (1863 also in Tjärstad). In 1900, the family lived in Hökhult, Kisa, but moved to Farsbo in the same parish in 1908. Anna had eight brothers and sisters, the five eldest from her father's first marriage, among them Klara, who had emigrated earlier. Three siblings were younger than Anna. She received her emigration certificate on March 29, 1912 and left the farm and family.

Her destination was her sister, Klara Tornquist of Passaic, New Jersey. Anna was employed as a domestic in Hackensack, New Jersey. The next sister, Elsa Maria, born in 1891, moved to New York on September 27, 1912.[325]

All the members of the Anderson and Danbom families perished. Mr. Ernst G. Danbom's body was found and interred in Stanton, Iowa. The Danboms had visited Sweden, and intended to settle in Canada.

A telegram was sent to Anna's father, *herr* S. A. Nysten, Nydala, Kisa, dated Göteborg, April 19, 1912, stamped *Whita Stjärnlinien*, Göteborg. It said that Anna Nysten had arrived in New York aboard the steamer *Carpathia* (signed Carl Eriksson).

Anna left Göteborg on the *Calypso* on April 5, 1912, listing her destination as Passaic, New Jersey. The *Carpathia* listed her destination as employer Mrs. Nielson, Hackensack, New Jersey. Anna was rescued in Lifeboat 13.

Anna Nysten's letter to her parents:

I am now with my sister Klara [Tornquist], *who is married. They have it so nice and good. Their son, who is married, lives in a big house nearby. He met us at the train and drove us up here. They are so kind to me, so you must not think that I suffer although I happened to have a difficult voyage.*

I can hardly describe how it happened. There was terrible screaming and groaning, but you and I ought to thank God that I am alive. I managed to get into a lifeboat because I don't think it was my time to die. I'm supposed to experience more of the world.

---

[325] Information courtesy Björn-Åke Petersson, Kallinge, Sweden.

You have probably read in the newspapers about what happened, but I can tell you a little. The boat hit an iceberg at about 12 o'clock between Sunday and Monday. I can hardly describe how it happened. There was terrible screaming and groaning, but you and I ought to thank God that I am alive. I managed to get into a lifeboat.

There was a terrible jolt, so we nearly fell out of bed. But then they said that it was not serious, so the passengers calmed down until the ship began to sink, and the deck was full of people. You can imagine how it looked. I can hardly describe it. Oh, how terrible it was when everything went dark. When the ship went down we were not far away and we were almost sucked under.

We heard awful rumbling and noise when the boat sank. We sat in the lifeboat from 1:30 until 6:30 in the morning, but fortunately the sea was calm. You can imagine how happy we were to see the steamer Carpathia close in on us and we could come aboard. They were so good to us. We received blankets and coffee and brandy as much as we wanted. But there was still much groaning and crying because most of us had lost a dear relative. It was hardest for those who had lost family members. Many became hysterical.

Now, however, I am at my destination and feel quite well. I hope that you have not worried too much about me because I'm all right. All who were with me after the disaster received everything they needed. I received a nice coat and under garments. I had my money on me, and just think how amazing, I had my food basket with me. No one except me had anything with them. [In the original translation *matkorg* (food basket) was translated as purse.] [326]

In New York, Anna was taken to the Swedish Immigrant Home, where she received $25.00 from the Women's Relief Committee.[327]

Summaries from clippings about Anna published in unidentified newspapers:

Twenty-five years later, Anna related her story to a newspaper reporter. In the resulting article, she said that someone had taken her lifebelt. She stood crying on deck when a sailor gave her his lifejacket. In 1937, she no longer dreamt about the disaster as she used to do. Anna was the only survivor of a party of eleven. (The party listed above.) "I was pushed and pushed," she said. Anna continued. "A sailor threw me into the last lifeboat that was launched. The boat could have held 63 people. We were only about 40." [She was rescued in Lifeboat 13, which was not the last one.]

In an article published in Sweden, it said:

---

[326] Copies of the letter and clippings received from Anna's granddaughter, Marianne Lorenz, Iowa.
[327] *Nordstjernan*, New York, May 21, 1912.

Ernst Danbom had assumed the responsibility of being the "tour conductor" during the journey back for that small group of eleven persons. In this group was also Sofia Nysten (Anna) from Kisa, in the church records known as the only surviving from this group from Östergötland. Sofia Nysten was restless, her friends told her to remain onboard so they could go down with the ship together. "We will go together," they cried and stood close to each other.

But Sofia couldn't be persuaded; she went to and fro on the deck. Suddenly strong arms threw her into the last one of the lifeboats. She cried, "I am freezing so much," and Danbom threw a fur coat over her.

An awful horror came over all in the lifeboat. Should they escape to be drawn down when the ship sank? Unforgettable memories which Sofia always had within her. With broken dreams of success, shipwrecked, alone, abandoned but saved—she was to land in the new country.[328]

Anna says she spent three years in New York with friends. She then came to Boone, Iowa, and a few months later to Des Moines, where she was married. The article, which was published in 1932, also says that for the first three or four years after the disaster, she could not talk about her *Titanic* experience.

In 1953 [1958?], Anna cried quietly as she saw the movie, *Titanic.* To her, it was part of her life. She said that she was impressed by the accuracy of the film and the likeness of Captain Smith and the actor portraying him, Richard Basehart. [Brian Aherne may have portrayed Captain Smith, and Richard Basehart played another part.] Anna thought that the picture was wonderfully done. At one of her trips to Sweden, her ship stopped outside Newfoundland, where Anna says she cried uncontrollably.

The food basket she had brought with her was stolen from her, perhaps for a souvenir. At one time, she says that she was offered $100.00 for it. In New York, a Swedish minister took the Swedes to his home [The Immigrant Home] and also sent a cable to her parents. [Through the White Star Line. See above].

In 1972, Anna Gustafson still spoke of all the excitement aboard the ship as it went down. She saw a man in woman's clothing in the bottom of one lifeboat. She had intended to return to Sweden, but when the *Lusitania* was torpedoed in 1915, she changed her mind and came to Iowa in May of that year. She said she had never flown in an airplane and was too scared to fly. She visited Sweden twice, the last time in about 1952.

---

[328] Olle Friberg, Trollhättan, "Fem små bondebarn följde Titanic i djupet" in *Land*,. Translator unknown. This article suggests that the rest of the party had decided to remain on board and die together.

In an undated letter to a radio reporter, Anna wrote: "For three hours we tossed about on the ocean. Few words were spoken. Everyone was waiting for death. Suddenly someone saw a dim light in the distance. Some thought it was a star. As we came closer, we saw it was a ship. Everyone became delirious with happiness." Four men rowed the lifeboat she occupied.

Anna and her family belonged to First Lutheran Church in Des Moines. According to the church records, her husband, Arvid Gustafson, was born August 11 1889 in Hanglösa parish, Skaraborg's län and had emigrated in 1900. He was received as a member May 29, 1901. Anna had arrived in 1916 from Boone, Iowa. They were married October 20, 1917.

Their children were: Linnea Arvida Sophia, born September 23, 1919 in Des Moines

Arvid Harry, born November 10, 1920, died July 29, 1924

Edgar William, born September 15, 1925

Arthur Sigvard, born August 9, 1929 in Des Moines.[329]

In 1972, Anna's son, William Gustafson lived in Des Moines, Iowa, her son, Arthur Gustafson, in Tulsa, Oklahoma, and her daughter, Linnea, (Mrs. Jack McDermott) in Des Moines, Iowa. 1972). Anna had six grandchildren.

In 1975, there was a short article in the *Des Moines Tribune* and a photo of Anna.

Her husband, Arvid, died in about 1967. Anna passed away March 28, 1977 and is buried in Resthaven Cemetery, West Des Moines. She was survived by two sons, one daughter, six grandchildren, and three siblings, Elise in America, and Agda and Gunnar in Sweden. [330]

Chicago-bound woman looked at the bright stars

Öhman, Velin

Velin, 22, said she was traveling to the home of her uncle, Henry Forsander in Chicago, but he was the man whom she would later marry.

Born March 14, 1890 in Ek parish, Skaraborg's län, she was the daughter of Johanna Sofia Öhman (born in 1862 in Mariestad, Skaraborg's län). In 1900, the family lived in Rudet, Ek parish.[331]

She sailed on the *Calypso* from Göteborg April 5, 1912 as Velin Öhman, from Ek, Skaraborg's län, with Chicago as her destination.

---

[329] Swedish-American Church records. Anna and her husband lived at 836 Boyd Avenue in Des Moines in 1932.

[330] Information courtesy Marianne Lorenz, Iowa.

[331] From the Swedish Church records, courtesy Björn-Åke Petersson, Kallinge, Sweden.

On the *Carpathia* manifest, her closest relatives were listed as her foster parents, Per and Matilda Johnson. She was rescued in Lifeboat C. Her travel companion, Hilda Hellstrom, recalled that Velin brought a bottle of brandy and shared it with her in the lifeboat. As Velin bobbed in Collapsible C, she looked at the bright stars in the sky and wondered if she would ever reach America.[332]

Velin changed her name to Vivian and lived out her life in Chicago. She married Henry Forsander and they had one daughter, Elsie or Elise.[333]

In 1920, the family lived on Lincoln Avenue. The daughter, named Elise, was three years old. In 1930, they lived at a different address in Cook County, District. 2806. Henry was listed as pattern finisher, born in Sweden, and as having emigrated in 1910. Elise was 13 years old. No other children listed. Henry, born in 1883, died July 24, 1963, and Vivian on November 19, 1966.[334]

According to Mrs. Carson, her mother watched the movie "Titanic" on television the Sunday before she died. "She cried when those left on board sang *Nearer my God to Thee,* and went to bed before the movie ended." Mrs. Carson also said her mother dreamt about the sinking ship the night before it actually happened. [335]

The *Chicago Tribune* printed the death notice and announced the service for Mrs. Vivian Forsander, 74, a survivor of the *Titanic,* to be held the following day, November 22, 1966 at the Fern Chapel on 10001 Western Avenue. Mrs. Forsander lived with her only relative her daughter Mrs. Elsie Carson, 2525 West 99th Street. Her husband, Henry, had died four years earlier.

---

[332] Cris Kohl, p. 79.
[333] Posted by Phillip Gowan, Nov. 21, 2001.
[334] www.ancestry.com
[335] Obituary in *Chicago Tribune*, November 21, 1966 linked to www.encyclopedia-titanica.org.

Married man fought for his life and survived

Persson, Ernst Ulrik

Persson, 25, was a married man and father, who had worked as janitor and chauffeur in Stockholm, Sweden. His wife, Anna, and their sons, Ernst Folke and Ernst Tage, arrived in America in October of 1912. Two younger children were born in America. Persson's ordeals are well documented.

Ernst Persson, his wife, and two eldest children. Photo courtesy Mike Pearson

His last address in Sweden was Holländargatan 4 in Stockholm. From Göteborg he sailed on the *Calypso on* April 5, 1912. He listed his occupation as chauffeur, his residence as Södermanland, and his final destination as Chicago.

He accompanied his sister, Elna Persson Ström, and her daughter, Telma Matilda Ström, all headed for Indiana Harbor, Indiana, where Elna Ström had lived for some time. Elna and Telma did not survive. Persson says he was rescued by a boat floating upside down [B] and nearly one meter under water.[336]

Born July 29, 1886, in Wäsby *rote* (ward), Julita parish, Södermanland's län, Ernst was the son of Per Ulrik Persson (born in 1854 in Julita) and Matilda Larsdotter (born in 1859, also in Julita). No record of emigration was found for Persson.[337]

---

[336] www.encyclopedia-titanica.org.

[337] From Swedish Church records courtesy Björn-Åke Peterson, Kallinge, Sweden. His sister had emigrated earlier. See Ström. *Hemlandet*, Chicago, May 14, 1912, wrote that Persson was a gate keeper at the house on Holländargatan. He had acquired tickets to America for his wife and children, but left his family at home.

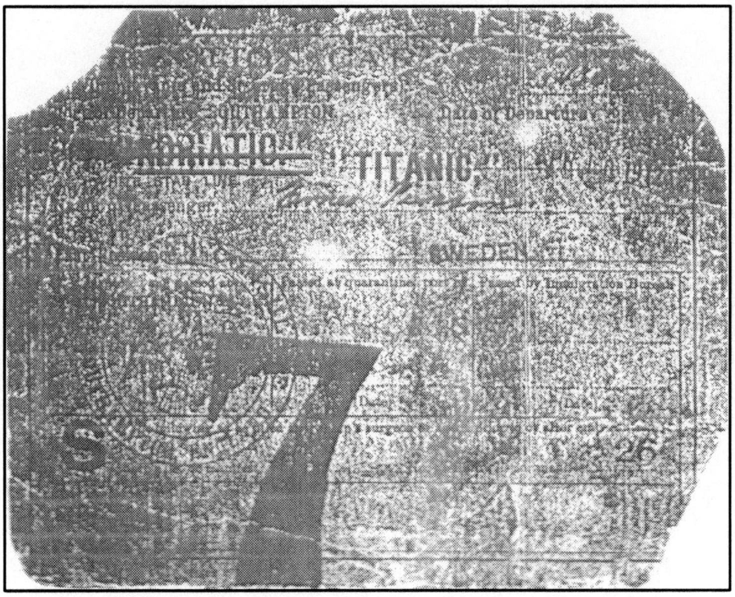

Persson's Titanic ticket showing
Adriatic crossed out and Titanic added.
Courtesy of Mike Pearson.

EMIL KJELLBERG
Konsulterande Ingeniör
Skeppsbron 10, Stockholm 2
Telefoner: Riks 38 67. Allm. 143 03

Kompetensbevis för automobilförare.

Herr Ernst Ulrik Persson

har för mig undergått pröfning of sin kännedom om automobilers konstruktion, skötsel och manövrering och får jag på grund däraf förklara honom beträffande dylika fordons skötsel och manövrering kompetent.

Stockholm den 9 Juni 1911.

Emil S. Kjellberg

Af Öfverståthållareämbetet förordnad besiktningsman för automobiler

Persson's Swedish driver's license,
courtesy Mike Pearson

Ernst Persson's hobby was fishing. Photo courtesy Mike Pearson.

Ernst's great-grandson, Mike Pearson, says that Ernst, his sister Elna, and niece, occupied cabins on G deck.

The paper *Nordstjernan* wrote about Persson:

Our talk with Ernst Person enforces our belief that they (the survivors) have not yet realized what happened to them; that the colossal, horrible scope of the disaster has not yet become clear to them. For instance, when he talked about his sister and his parting with her, he did so quietly, listlessly, and absentmindedly, as in a trance, or under the influence of painkillers. It was the same with the others. But when they awaken, they will have to face the dreadful reality. At the Immigrant Home, they have from the moment they arrived received the very best care, and everything has been done for them in all respects to make it [their stay] as pleasant as possible.[338]

After the tragic event, Ernst wrote a letter to his family in Sweden:

[338] *Nordstjernan*, New York, April 23, 1912, p. 7.

Beloved Parents, Wife, and Children:

You, my beloved, have no doubt heard of the terrible disaster that has occurred. Oh, what a night I have experienced since I last wrote to you. You have probably received the letter I wrote to you from England and the telegram I sent at my arrival. We departed Southampton on the 10th and everybody was happy and content, for food and everything was the best we could wish for.

Then came the terrible night. They woke us up at 12 midnight, and told us to enter the aft deck because we had struck an iceberg. Nobody believed there was any danger because the ship was declared unsinkable. We did not worry until they began to lower the lifeboats. Then there was a panic, and everybody who tried to jump into the lifeboats without permission was shot [His perception]. *Women and children first; the men had to save themselves the best they could.*

When Elna and I came up on deck, all the lifeboats were filled, so there was no chance of rescue. We stood together the whole time, and agreed to accompany each other into the depths. But as the boat [ship] *sank, and the water started to pour over deck, there was a terrible sight and scuffle, and we became separated.*

Then I heard Elna say, "Tell Wilhelm and my parents and brothers and sisters if you get rescued." I didn't see her again because we were all washed overboard. When I entered the water, I sank several meters below the surface. Floating up again, I had a roof of wreckage over my head and clung on for a good while. But then the ship began to sink, so I had to leave the wreckage and try to swim away. Otherwise, I would have been dragged into the depths once again.

As I floated and swam around, I saw how [other] *people in the water tried to save themselves in an overloaded boat. But when they hung on to the sides, the boat overturned with the keel upward, and all drowned. I saw how some people climbed up on it, so I swam to it, and was taken up. Only Italians* [his perception] *were on this boat, and it was so crowded that it floated nearly one meter below the water. There I had to lie for six hours with the water up to my shoulders.*

Then we were taken up in a lifeboat that rowed us to the big boat that had come to rescue us. You cannot imagine how it was as thousands of people lay in the water crying for help and no help was available. But don't grieve too deeply my beloved. We can thank God that any of us got rescued among so many thousands of people who lost their lives. Tears are shed all over the world over this disaster.

But surely it is awful to think that Elna and little Telma no longer exist. I don't know how it will be to come to Wilhelm because I don't believe that she got rescued. There are so many in the hospitals, but I have not seen her name in the newspaper although all rescued are registered. Some of us Swedes are staying at this hotel [Swedish Lutheran Immigrant Home]. *As you can see, we were photographed by all newspapers, movie theaters and all book shops.*

We were well received when we arrived. Three of us had no caps or overcoats, and we were let in first and got dressed from top to toe and received 15 dollars, because I had not a single penny when I disembarked. Now we can stay at this hotel where we get good food and nice rooms, free of charge. All societies and theaters collect money for us, so we probably get more money after a while. So don't worry about me. I feel well though I feared that I would not be able to withstand the [cold] *'bath'. My whole body was stiff when I came up.*

On the boat that rescued us, we were bedded down and could rest two days. Then we had to get up and try to dry our clothes because nobody cared to help us with that. We didn't arrive in New York until Thursday night [April 18], and the disaster occurred on Sunday night. So you can imagine how far we were from land. The boat rescuing us was a real .... It was a boat traveling on Italy with only swarthy passengers. So then you can understand how it was. But we were satisfied to be out of the water. I have posted a card to Aunt Anna. I got her address from Elna by chance. Otherwise, I would not have known where to go because I had no other.

Well, now my beloved, I have given you a brief report about what had happened. You will get more information later on because it is impossible to put any more of these sheets in the envelope, and I don't have any other paper. I hope you are all healthy and don't grieve too much so that you become ill from it. I will find work and save money because I will probably come home again. I will not expose my beloved wife and children to the same voyage that I went on. So farewell for a while. I shall write as soon as I arrive in Chicago. You will then get my address, so I can hear from you. My warm greetings and solace to you my beloved in Sweden from your castaway son, husband, and father of our small boys.

(signed) *Ernst*

Postscripts penned on the edges of the last three sheets:

I cannot describe in words how awful everything was. You have to try to imagine it—the last moment I saw my dear sister stand there with little Thelma tightly in her arms.

I wish I could send you a paper with our photographs, but all are sold out, and we cannot take the ones they have here. I am pictured almost full size in one paper—the best photograph I've seen of myself.

You, my dear wife, got to be with me in the water. Yours was the only photograph I had, and it stayed fast in my pocket. The first I did when I was on a dry surface, I took it out and looked at it. I began to cry, but then I thought that you smiled at me, and I became calm."[339]

Ernst Persson's struggles have been well documented. On one website I found the following:

... Persson held his sister's [hand], and in the other he held the little girl's. The liner sank slowly, inch by inch, foot by foot. All of a sudden a wave came and flushed them overboard. The suction of the sinking ship sucked them into the deep. As long as possible, Persson held fast to his sister's hand, but finally he had to let go. At once, he began to float upwards.

He says that he had been under water at least two minutes and was very weak. He had no hope of seeing daylight. Suddenly, his head hit something hard, and the jolt gave him renewed strength. He understood that he had reached the surface and that debris stopped him from emerging. By using his last strength, he managed to free himself from the obstacle, and breathed once again. He had a lifebelt around him, which held him up. He found a floating plank and rested on it for a while. In the distance he could see a fully loaded lifeboat and began to swim toward it.

When he came closer, the boat capsized abruptly because so many desperate people looking for rescue clung to one side and tried to get up. Together with several others, he hung fast to the capsized lifeboat. At least 50 people tried to crawl on to the boat, but were pushed aside without mercy. Here one had to try to save ones own life without mercy to others who were pushed away.

---

[339] Ernst Persson's letter written in New York April 20, 1912 to his family in Sweden. Older English translation edited by the author of this book, March 2008 with addition of postscripts, not previously translated. Letter courtesy, Mike Pearson. In this letter, it appears that Persson climbed up on Collapsible B. Some sources say that 30 people were taken off the upturned boat.

Person's most gruesome memory was that wherever he swam, with every stroke his hands pushed against corpses with distorted faces, and they were so close that they almost made him lose his mind. When he finally was taken up by the Carpathia he had been in the ice cold water about six hours.[340]

In New York, Ernst recuperated at the Swedish Immigrant Home, where

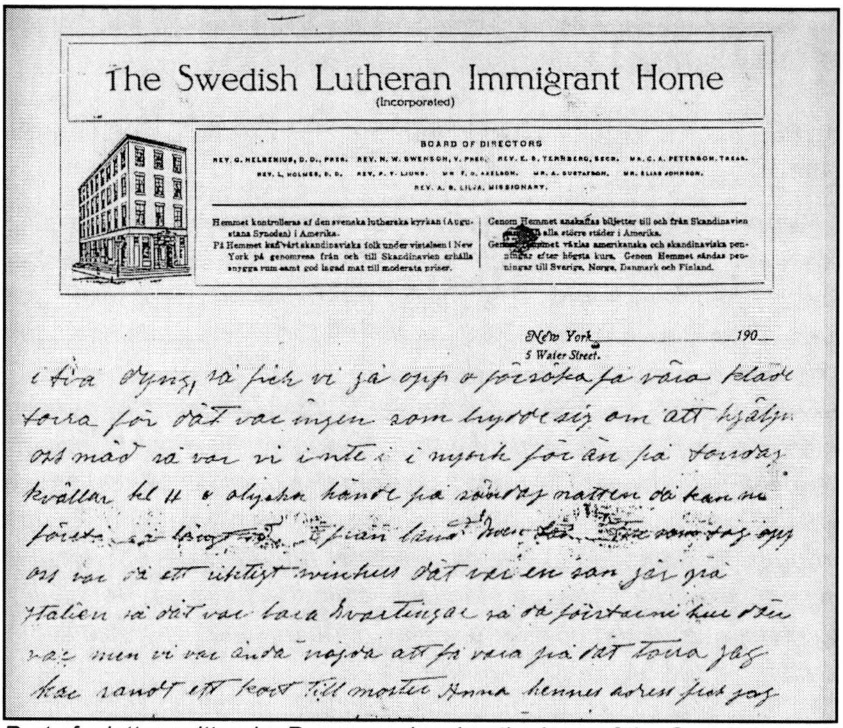
The Swedish Lutheran Immigrant Home
(Incorporated)

BOARD OF DIRECTORS

REV. G. NELSENIUS, D.D., PRES. REV. N. W. SWENSON, V. PRES. REV. K. B. TENNBERG, SECR. MR. C. A. PETERSON, TREAS. REV. L. HOLMES, D.D. REV. P. T. LJUNG. MR. F. O. AXELSON. MR. A. GUSTAFSON. MR. ELIAS JOHNSON. REV. A. B. LILJA, MISSIONARY.

Hemmet kontrolleras af den svenska lutherska kyrkan (Augustana Synoden) i Amerika.
På Hemmet kan vårt skandinaviska folk under vistelsen i New York på genomresa från och till Skandinavien erhålla snygga rum samt god lagad mat till moderata priser.

Genom Hemmet anskaffas biljetter till och från Skandinavien ... alla större städer i Amerika.
Genom Hemmet växlas amerikanska och skandinaviska penningar efter högsta kurs. Genom Hemmet sändas penningar till Sverige, Norge, Danmark och Finland.

New York ______ 190__
5 Water Street.

Part of a letter written by Persson, showing the logo of the Swedish Lutheran Immigrant Home. Courtesy Mike Pearson.

he received $75.00 from the Women's Relief Committee. From the White Star Line, he received a railroad ticket to his destination and a small amount of cash.[341]

The reports vary somewhat, but the questions might have been different, and Persson may have added something that he had forgotten in previous interviews.

A report in *Chicago Daily News* told how he was saved after floating around in the ocean hanging on to a thick plank for over an hour after the Titanic sank. [The story] was told to-day by Ernest Persson, 26 years old, a Swede, who arrived in Indiana Harbor from New York … to his brother-in-law

[340]http:// www.titanicacentury.com/interviews.
[341] *Nordstjernan*, New York, May 17 and May 21, 1912. He could not have survived if immerged in water for six hours.

William Strom, whose wife and daughter, Thelma, 3 years old, went down with the ship. Strom went to New York in an effort to find his child among the unidentified little ones who were rescued.

"My sister and Thelma arrived on deck just after the last boat had left the vessel," began Persson. "In a short time the water was knee deep.Suddenly, the boat gave a lurch and we were thrown into the sea. I went under, it seems about ten times and each time was brought up by the suction of the sinking of the ship. I grasped a plank and looked around for my sister and niece, but they had disappeared."

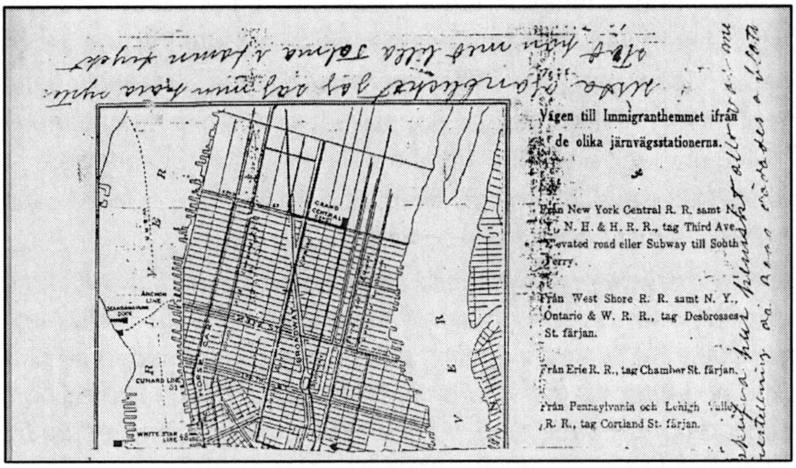

A postscript written by Persson on a map showing the location of the Immigrant Home where he was staying. On the bottom of the sheet there was a warning for "runners," who tried to swindle newcomers.

In about an hour I saw an overturned lifeboat, which was filled with men. I begged them to take me on, but they refused, saying that if they did, they would all be hurled off into the water. Finally, we all saw another lifeboat with women and children in it. It wasn't full, however. We called to them and begged them to take us in. The seamen in charge refused, saying that the work of pulling them over the side of the boat would upset it.

A woman stood up and pleaded with the seamen. I afterward learned that this woman was Mrs. John Jacob Astor. After a time the sailors consented, but the men on the overturned boat were first taken off. Then I climbed on the deserted craft and was later taken into the safer one."

We had one man with jet black hair with us. He lost his wife and five children. After we were taken on board the Carpathia I saw that his hair had turned snow while. A short time later he died from exposure."[342]

---

[342] *Chicago Daily News*, n.d. Republished on the website Nordikfolk.com with no date for the newspaper article. Mrs. Astor was in Lifeboat 4. Mike Pearson said some of

Ernst Persson, a survivor of the Titanic wreck is in Indiana Harbor having arrived yesterday in company with William Strom of 3905 Grapevine Street, an employee of the Standard Forging Company. Mr. Strom had been to New York to search for his little daughter Thelma, age 3, who in company with Mrs. Strom and the latter's brother, Mr. Persson, had taken passage on the ill-fated steamship. Mr. Strom knew that his wife had perished, but he had hoped that he might find the girl among the unidentified children rescued. His search for the little one proved fruitless and [he] *has now given up all hope of ever seeing her again.*

Lake County Times also carried an article about Pearson:

Persson was one of a number of men saved through the intercession of Mrs. John Jacob Astor, who pleaded that they be taken into the lifeboat on which she was a passenger. [Mrs. Astor was in Lifeboat 4.] Probably none of the survivors of the awful disaster had a more harrowing experience than Persson. Arriving on deck after the last of the lifeboats had been lowered away he saw his sister and little niece swept to their doom by a swell caused by the sinking ship, which carried him down with it.

He never saw the women or the child again, although he himself came up to the surface after what seemed to him to have been a plunge of 10 feet down into the water. He seized a floating plank which happened to be near him and looked about for his sister and the baby, but although scores of men, women and children were struggling in the water about him, buoyed up by life preservers, he failed to distinguish the ones he sought.

He had not been in this position long when he noticed an overturned lifeboat nearby, with a number of men clinging to it. He made for it as best he could and managed to get a hold on it. Others to whom the disabled craft represented a possible means of escape also made for the boat, but with less success. A score of more who grabbed for the boat were beaten back by those already in possession who feared for their own safety if they permitted any more to weigh it (down).[343]

---

the Swedes had celebrated the night before and it might have helped them survive in the cold water. See account for Agnes Sandstrom, which says that she left her cabin together with Elna Strom and her daughter.

343 www.nordikfolk.com. The date of the paper is not listed, but since Persson had just arrived in Indiana it was probably dated about a week or two after the sinking. Colonel Gracie wrote that he was transferred to Lifeboat 12, which then took them to the *Carpathia*. The occupants of the lifeboats are not always correctly reported as the list was compiled at a later time.

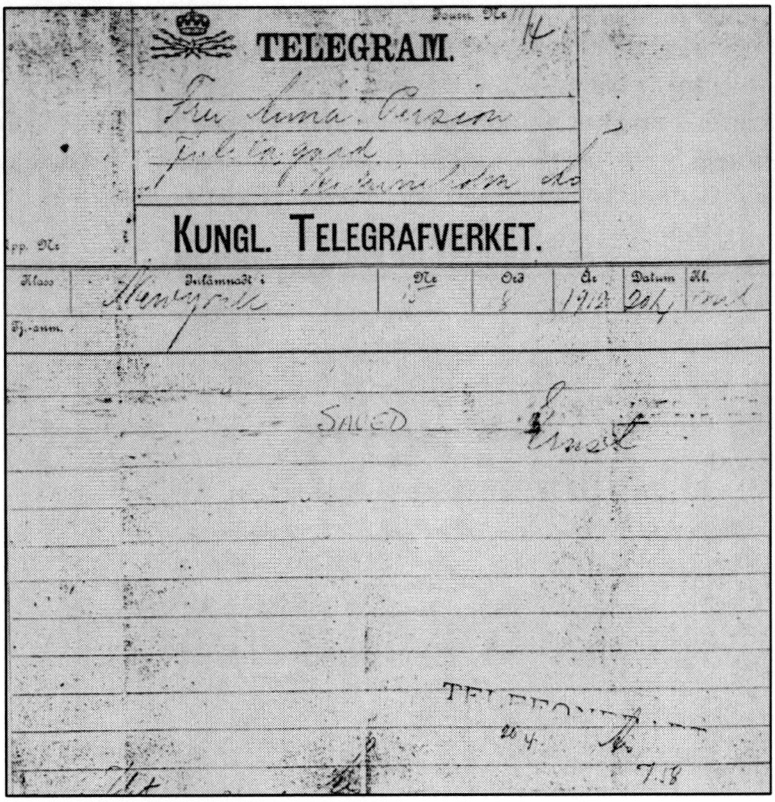

TELEGRAM.

KUNGL. TELEGRAFVERKET.

SAVED — Ernst

The telegram Ernst sent to his wife saying he was safe.
Courtesy Mike Pearson

In 1914, Ernst spelled his name Ernest Pearson and lived with his family at 3725 A Carey Street, Indiana Harbor, Indiana. He worked as a bricklayer at the Standard Forgings Company, where William Ström also worked. The family later settled in Hammond, Indiana.

Ernst Ulrik Persson, 29, registered for the WWI draft in Lake County, Indiana, on June 5 (probably in 1918) while residing at 3719 Michigan Avenue, East Chicago, and working as a furnace heater at Standard Steel Forging Co. Listing a wife and three children, he was described as being of medium height, slender, with blue eyes and brown hair. It was noted that his left hand had been deadened by a piece of steel.

In 1930, the U.S. Census for Hammond, Lake County, North Township, lists Ernest Pearson as being 40 years of age, a renter, and bricklayer for the Forging Plant. His wife, Anna, 45, was listed as being born in Germany (probably incorrect) and her parents as being born in Sweden. The children listed were Ernest F, 22, pipefitter at the Gas plant, Ernest T., 20, bricklayer at Oil Refinery, Berthel, 14, and Edith 10. The two eldest were born in Sweden.

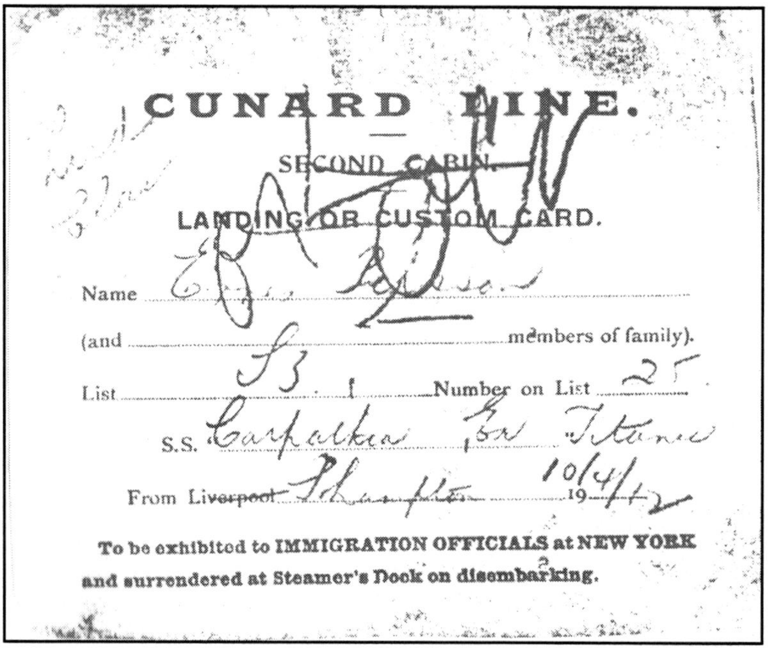
CUNARD LINE.

SECOND CABIN.

LANDING OR CUSTOM CARD.

Name

(and .... members of family).

List 53 Number on List 25

S.S. Carpathia for Titanic

From Liverpool 19

To be exhibited to IMMIGRATION OFFICIALS at NEW YORK and surrendered at Steamer's Dock on disembarking.

Persson's landing card shows that he was on board the Carpathia of the Cunard Line out of Liverpool. "Second cabin" was crossed out. Liverpool was also crossed out and replaced with S. Hampton. Titanic and the sailing date of April 10 was added. Document courtesy of Mike Pearson.

Persson also registered for the WWII draft, at the age of 55, while residing at 4929 Hickory Avenue, Hammond, Indiana. His employer at the time was Universal Cement, East Chicago. His contact person was Ernest Pearson, Jr., 668 Spruce Street, Hammond.[344]

Ernst died of heart failure, October 17, 1951, at the age of 65, and is buried in Elmwood Cemetery in Hammond.[345]

---

[344] www.ancestry.com. During WWII men were required to register up to the age of 64.

[345] See also www.nordikfolk.com

"Everything was magnificent on board"

Sandstrom, Agnes Charlotta

Agnes Sandström

Agnes's maiden name was Bengtsson. She was a 24-year-old Swedish-American, who had immigrated from Forserum, Jonköping's län, May 1, 1905 and had lived with her husband in San Francisco since 1908. After the *Titanic* tragedy, the family returned to Sweden for good.

Born November 8, 1887 in Lerbäck parish, Örebro län, she was the daughter of Bengt Bengtsson (born June 15, 1849 in Pjätteryd, Kronoberg's län) and Mathilda Lovisa Eriksson Öman (born August 25, 1857 in Lerbäck). On April 5, 1912, Agnes sailed on the *Calypso* from Göteborg with her two young daughters, listing their residence as America and destination as New York.

Other sources listed her final destination as San Francisco. She was married to Hjalmar Sandstrom, who had emigrated in 1907 at the age of 24 from Ås, Jönköping's län with New York as his destination. They had two daughters, Marguerite and Beatrice (See entries below).

Agnes and her daughters had been visiting relatives in Hultsjö and were on their way to San Francisco. On the *Titanic,* she shared cabin G 6 with Elna and Thelma Strom. (See story of Ernst Persson).

After the collision, Agnes guided Elna and her daughter up on deck, but in the confusion they lost sight of each other. Agnes entered Lifeboat 13 with her children, while Elna Ström and her daughter perished. In New York, Agnes and her children recuperated at St. Vincent Hospital and continued their journey to California about one week later, passing through Chicago on April 20.

In an interview recorded in Sweden, Agnes recalled how magnificent everything was on board, how good the food was and how beautifully it was served. She said that she and her travel companions were like one big family and were having a good time. There was music and dancing although she did not participate because she had two small children. She enjoyed watching the activity. One woman was busy knitting a sweater for her husband in America and wanted to finish it before she came home, but she did not survive.

Agnes had gone to bed when she felt a jolt. She thought they had collided with another ship because of blinding fog. A steward knocked on their door telling them that they had hit an iceberg, but that the damage had been repaired so they should not worry. A little later the steward came back and said that they should put their life vests on. She wondered how she could do that when she had to carry a little one. She hung it over one arm and never put it on.[346]

Agnes died December 1, 1985 in Bruneby parish, Östergötland, Sweden at the age of 98. Her husband, Hjalmar Sandström died in Sweden on October 9, 1927.[347]

Four-year-old girl grew up in Sweden

Sandstrom, Marguerite Rut

The 4-year-old girl was born March 23, 1908 in San Francisco, the daughter of Agnes and Hjalmar Sandstrom. She was rescued in Lifeboat 13 with her mother and sister.

The family returned to Sweden in the fall of 1912. Marguerite later married Otto Pettersson and lived in Bankeryd, Småland. She died August 15, 1963.[348]

Infant girl had no memory of the Titanic

Sandstrom, Beatrice Iren

The infant daughter of Agnes and Hjalmar Sandstrom was born August 9, 1910 in San Francisco. She was rescued in Lifeboat 13 with her mother and sister. The family moved back to Sweden in the fall of 1912. Beatrice lived in Motala, Östergötland, Sweden.[349]

After her mother's death in December 1985, Beatrice took on the role of telling her mother's story. She said it was not until 1962 that the local media became interested in interviewing the family. Before that the topic was not discussed. Beatrice accompanied Claes-Göran Wetterholm to some of his lectures and also to Boston in 1988 for a meeting. She received much

---

346 www.titanicnorden.com
347 Information courtesy Björn-Åke Petersson, Kallinge, Sweden.
348 www.encyclopedia-titanica.org.
349 www.encyclopedia-Titanic.org.

attention even though she spoke only Swedish. She was the last Swedish *Titanic* survivor to pass away on September 4, 1995.[350]

Boy turned away from lifeboats twice

Svensson, Johan Cervin

The 14-year-old boy traveled alone to join his father and sister in Alcester, South Dakota, where he changed his name to John C. Johnson.

He was born March 5, 1898 in Knäred parish, Halland (parish and county), the son of Sven Peter Johansson (born I 1868 in Knäred) and Elisabeth Jönsdotter (born in 1864 also in Knäred). In 1900, they lived in Lagerud, Knäred.[351]

Johan Svensson, later John C. Johnson. See also image in the group photo shown in the beginning of this chapter.

Johan Cervin had six siblings, Anna, Jenny, Rudolf, Leonard, Reinhold, and Gösta. His father and sister, Jenny, had settled in Alcester, South Dakota in 1911, and the rest of the family intended to follow. Johan sailed on the *Calypso* from Göteborg, April 5, 1912 as Cervin Svensson from Knäred, destination Alcester, South Dakota.

When Johan was ready to leave, his mother sewed 15 *kronor* (About $4.00) into his jacket lining as spare cash. He later recalled that when the *Titanic* began to sink he found his way to the first-class boat deck. After being refused twice, he finally got into lifeboat 13, the third boat he had tried to enter.

The *Red Wing Daily Republican* wrote that the young man was an orphan. The caption read, "Two French babies and a Swedish boy were left orphans by the Titanic Catastrophe." The boy's photo was inserted in a photo of the two French infants that were cared for by Miss Margaret Hays. The paper incorrectly named the 14-year-old boy Sven Svenson. It said that his father was lost on the *Titanic* and that his mother had died a year ago, but both his parents were alive, his father in South Dakota and his mother in Sweden.[352]

---

[350] Claes-Göran Wetterholm, "Titanic International mourns Beatrice Sandström: Swedish *Titanic* survivor passes away at age 85" Voyage, No. 21, Summer/Autumn, 1995, Freehold, NJ, p. 45.

[351] From the Swedish Church records, courtesy Björn-Åke Petersson, Kallinge, Sweden.

[352] Microfilm issue of the paper dated April 29, 1912, p. 3. The two French infants, Edmond R. Navratil, 2, and Michel M. Navratil, 3, had been placed in a lifeboat by their father, who had kidnapped them from the mother. Once the mother found out

On board the *Carpathia* he was at first treated as a first-class passenger, but his clothes betrayed him and he was sent down to steerage. His uncle, Isak Johnson, met him in New York. His photograph appeared in the paper *Nordstjernan*.

In New York, young Cervin recuperated at the Swedish Immigrant Home, where he received $35.00 from the Women's Relief Committee. From the White Star Line he received a railroad ticket to his destination, plus a small amount of cash.[353]

People in the Dalesburg area in South Dakota called him "Titanic Johnson." Shortly after he had arrived in the Beresford-Wakonda area and found a job as a farmhand, he walked into the Dalesburg Lutheran Church southwest of Beresford and presented his emigration certificate from the Lutheran Church in Sweden. The church kept the document and discovered it in 1998 after the movie *Titanic* by James Cameron had reignited the interest in the ship, according to Ron Johnson, who is not related to "Titanic Johnson."[354]

A newspaper in Vermillion, South Dakota, wrote about him shortly after his arrival in the area:

....

Young Johnson is now making his home with Victor Swensson on the latter's farm out in Prairie Center, and his father is working for Charles Swenson also of Prairie Center. The boy's father came to this country a few years ago, and had but recently sent for his son to join him in America....

... when the subject of this story had an opportunity to jump into one of the lifeboats he was without cap, shoes, or overcoat.... Young Johnson succeeded in getting word to his father that he was safe, and it was a joyful meeting between the two when the lad arrived here a week ago last Saturday....

He is well educated in his native tongue, talks readily of his experiences on the trip both before and after the accident, and has written a long account of the happenings of the journey to his mother who is still in Sweden. Despite

---

where they were she came to New York to claim them. The father, who perished, had traveled under the false name of Hoffman, which made the children more difficult to identify.

[353] *Nordstjernan*, New York, May 17 and May 21, 1912.

[354] The emigration certificate is issued for Johan Cervin Svensson, son of homestead owner Sven Peter Johansson and his wife Elisabet Jönsdotter, Lagered 3. It said that he was born March 5, 1898 in Knäred, Halland County and that he was moving to North America from Knäred. It was signed by *kyrkoherde* (head pastor) Hellden and dated March 29, 1912. Copy courtesy Ron Johnson, Dalesburg, S.D. It was stamped by *Poliskammaren* in Göteborg Apr. 4, 1912, a day before Cervin left Sweden Representatives of the Police Department in Göteborg and Malmö checked so that the people leaving Sweden had the appropriate papers, which was the main reason why the men of military age avoided this step and went to Copenhagen instead.

the harrowing experiences he underwent, and the exposure he endured after seeking refuge in the lifeboat, he is now in good physical condition He is a lad of promise, and will in time make a good American citizen....[355]

The article in a Sioux Falls newspaper went on to state that the young man was aboard the ship because his father, Sven Petter Johanson, worked on a farm north of Vermillion and had sent for his 14-year-old son to join him. According to the article, John Johnson had a daughter, Joy Johnson. She lived in Long Beach, California.[356]

Johan Cervin Svensson's journey

I was a boy of fourteen when I left some of my family in Sweden. I was traveling alone to join a sister and my father in the United States. I left Knäred, Sweden by train for Gothenburg. Then I took a small combination freight and passenger boat to Hull, England. From there I went on the Southampton by way of London. I will always remember the beauty of the English countryside. There were acres of glass hothouses. The roads were made of white limestone. Hedgerows lined the fields and pastures. We arrived in London aboard an elevated railway. From it I could look down and plainly see Buckingham Palace and Big Ben. I will always remember those landmarks.

When I reached Southampton, I settled down in a second rate hotel. I would wait four days for the TITANIC to sail. Finally, the day arrived. I believe it was a Sunday. The ship was really big. Her four smoke stacks were so large a double track railway could run through them.

All the passengers, baggage and freight were loaded. Lines were cast off and the gangplank was raised. We headed out across the Irish Sea to Queenstown, Ireland. We picked up some passengers from a small boat so we wouldn't have to tie up there. Now we were ready to start for the open Atlantic. There was not much to see. Two days out we met the Lusitania, another ship that was doomed.

About three days out I noticed the sailors acting strangely. At the time I didn't pay much attention, but I heard later that the sea gulls had deserted our ship. When they do that it means a ship is doomed according to an old sailor legend. The air was getting cooler because we were heading for the ice fields on the afternoon and evening of April 14, 1912. At about eight o'clock, a

---

[355] "Saved from the Titanic Vermillion Visited by One of the Survivors of That Awful Marine Catastrophe," *The Dakota Republican*, Vermillion, S.D., Thursday May 9, 1912.

[356] Steve Young, Staff Columnist, "S.D. man survived Titanic's plunge," *Argus Leader*, Sioux City, South Dakota, Sunday March 22, 1998.

group of us got together for a little visit. Among this group was a rancher from South Dakota. He was about forty-eight years old.

He had been back to Sweden to bring his father to live in America. I think the older man was about seventy-two years of age. The conversation turned to the TITANIC. The younger man pulled a souvenir picture of the ship out of his pocket. He looked at the picture for a moment and said it had been predicted that the biggest ship afloat was going to sink on her maiden voyage. He said, "I hope it isn't this one." They were both lost).[357]

About 9:00 p.m., I went to my cabin to retire. About 11:25 p.m. I was awakened by someone knocking at the door of the cabin. Since I was unable to understand English I didn't know what it was all about. (The ship had struck an iceberg at 11:10.)

In the meantime some of the men in my cabin had gone out to find out what was wrong. They came back to get their life belts. It didn't take me long to get on the ball and get my lifebelt and scramble up on deck. I walked through a corridor when I noticed some wet tracks. Some of the crew must have been down below to check the damage. This didn't stop the sailors that were standing in the alley way from laughing at us for taking our life belts along. I got up on main deck. The third class people were milling around.

As we looked out over the water on port side we could see some lights from SS California at about 18 kilometers away. We kind of figured we would get some help. Later I found out that the captain on the CALIFORNIA had warned Captain Smith, on the TITANIC, that they were laying still during the night on account of ice. He had suggested that Smith do the same. From what we heard Smith told him to get to and stay put. So we didn't get any help.

About that time they sent up some rockets, three or four. We didn't seem to sink so fast at first. The rear deck was really lifting up out of the water when the stern went down. Most of the folks didn't seem to think that TITANIC would go down.

It was about midnight when they started to set out lifeboats. They lowered the first boat. Lord Ismay got in and gave the order, "Women and children first!" People were very reluctant to get in because there was such a strong belief that TITANIC was unsinkable. [Ismay got in one of the last boats, Collapsible C.]

One lady with three children was standing near me. I told her she better get in a boat. She told me that she wouldn't get in the boat until she found out

---

[357] The two men were John Ekstrom and his father Johan Svensson. See "The Swedish Victims."

what they were going to do with her trunk. They all lost their lives. I met the woman's husband in New York.[358]

In 1967, when Johnson came to Vermillion to attend his brother's funeral, there was another article about him. His brother, Rudolph, had died at the age of 67. John C. Johnson was 69 and a retired construction welder still living in Long Beach, California. The article said that John and Sven [John's father was Sven Johansson] changed their surname to Johnson in 1915 when they began to farm at Dalesburg. Sven died in 1937. [The interview in 1912 refers to John C. as Johnson or John.]

Recalling the night of the sinking of the *Titanic*, John said he saw inexperienced crew members fail in the operation of lowering a lifeboat. It resulted in a boatload of would-be-survivors scattered in the icy ocean. [Unconfirmed although there is a story about a lifeboat that was thought to have filled with water because the hole in the bottom had not been plugged. See the Lundstrom story.]

According to the article, the mother arrived from Sweden in 1914, but this is incorrect. The emigration certificate issued in Knäred July 31, 1914, was for the father, Sven Peter Johansson, Lagered 3 [John C's father], born February 10, 1868 in Knäred and four of his children. Although the father had emigrated earlier, he must have gone back to Sweden due to his wife's illness because she died on May 13, 1914 and never made it to America. He then took his remaining children with him and returned to South Dakota.

Another episode told by Johnson involved a woman who got into a lifeboat while a man held her two small children. The boat began to swing out on its davits and as the man attempted to board the boat with the children, one of them fell from his grasp. He got safely aboard with the other child. [This story seems to be a variation of a similar episode in which the dropped child was saved.]

When there was room for one more in a lifeboat, Johnson jumped about 10 feet to get into the boat that had a 50-person capacity.

He said he could see from the lifeboat how water began to flow into the smoke stacks. He heard explosions. He could also see the ship's three screws and rudders as the stern struggled briefly before sinking under the water.

The younger siblings were added later on the back of the certificate. They were John Rudolf, born September 9, 1900, Leonard, born September 17,

---

[358] "The Words of Dalesburg's 'Titanic Johnson' a.k.a Johan Cervin Svensson." Typed document, courtesy of Ron Johnson, Dalesburg, S.D.

1902, Reinhold William born April 3, 1905, Gösta Hilding, born January 23, 1908. All were born and baptized in Knäred. Later, someone had added the names of the older children, who had emigrated earlier, Anna Emelia, born February 21, 1894, and Jennie Linnea, born December 31, 1895.

According to this young survivor, it was 10 a.m. before the *Carpathia* reached them. It was his opinion that the *California* was only about 18 kilometers (11 miles) away and appeared to be motionless and that the ship failed to understand the coded wireless pleas for help or the firing of flairs by the *Titanic.*[359]

In South Dakota, Johan changed his name to John C. Johnson and worked as a farmhand. Having traveled to Michigan and Kentucky, he settled down in Long Beach, California, where he worked in a ship yard. He was not found in the draft registrations for either WWI or WWII. He visited Sweden in 1961 and died July 4¸1981 in Long Beach.[360]

---

[359] *Vermillion Plain Talk*, Dec. 11, 1967. Article courtesy of Ron Johnson, Dalesburg, S.D. The *Carpathia* arrived on the scene at about 8.30 a.m. One kilometer equals 0.62 miles.

[360] www.encyclopedia-titanica.org. Svensson left Göteborg Apr. 5, 1912. *Emigranten Populär* 2006.

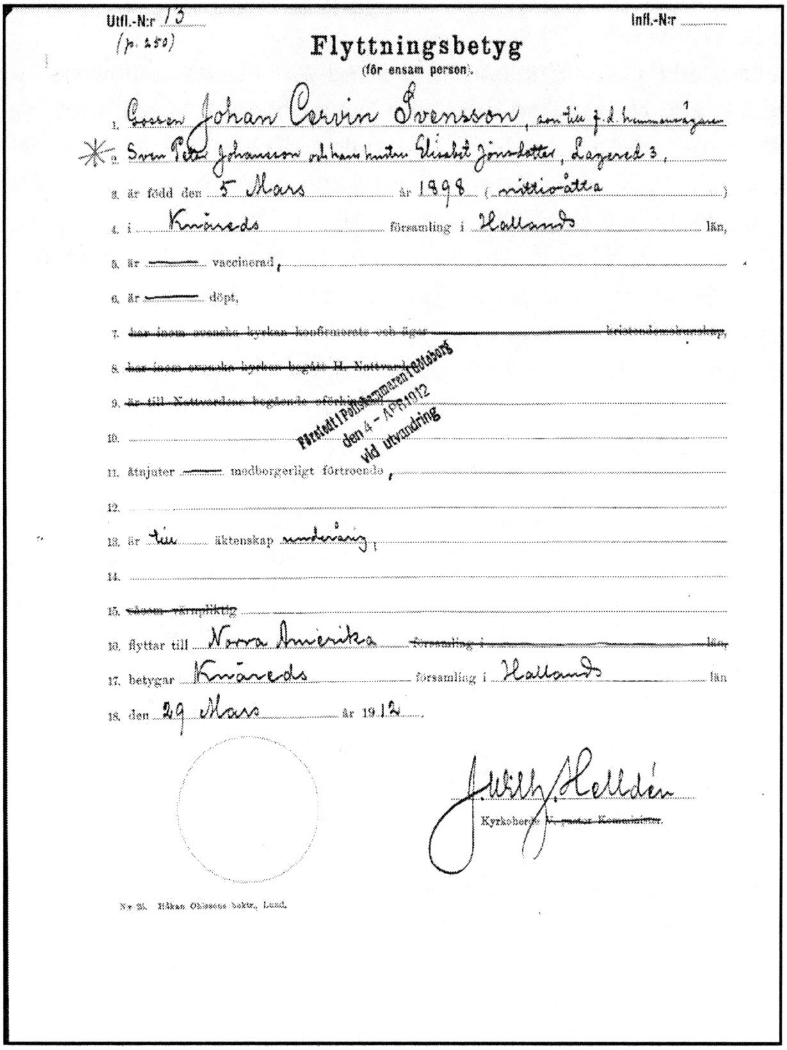
Utfl.-N:r 13
(p. 250)
Infl.-N:r

Flyttningsbetyg
(för ensam person).

1. Gossen Johan Cervin Svensson, son till f.d.
2. Sven Peter Johansson och hans hustru Elisabet Jönsdotter, Lagered 3,
3. är född den 5 Mars år 1898 (nittioåtta)
4. i Knäreds församling i Hallands län,
5. är — vaccinerad,
6. är — döpt,
7. ~~har inom svenska kyrkan konfirmerats och äger kristendomskunskap,~~
8. ~~har inom svenska kyrkan begått H. Nattvarden~~
9. ~~är till Nattvardens begående förhindrad~~
10.
11. åtnjuter — medborgerligt förtroende,
12.
13. är till äktenskap underårig,
14.
15. ~~värnpliktig~~
16. flyttar till Norra Amerika ~~församling i län,~~
17. betygar Knäreds församling i Hallands län
18. den 29 Mars år 1912.

J. Willy Helldén
Kyrkoherde ~~V. pastor Komminister.~~

N:r 25. Håkan Ohlssons boktr., Lund.

Johan Cervin Svensson's emigration certificate issued March 29, 1912.

“The lifeboats were all gone”

Tenglin, Gunnar Isidor

The 29-year-old married man had lived in Iowa previously, but had returned to Sweden to marry and start a family. Buying his ticket in Copenhagen, his destination was Burlington, Iowa, where he had settled when he first arrived in America at the age of 16. He later said the area where he lived in southeastern Iowa was inhabited by three thousand Swedes and that there were four Swedish churches in Burlington, five including West Burlington. His wife and son arrived in 1913.

Until he could speak English, he worked with crews cutting ice on the Mississippi River. He learned English while working at the Horace Patterson farm. Having promised his mother he would be back in five years, he returned to Stockholm in 1908, where he married Anna Amelia Andersson. Their son, Gunnar, was born in Stockholm January 16, 1911. A year later he made plans to return to Burlington. He purchased his ticket in Copenhagen and travelled via Esbjerg, Denmark to Southampton in the company of August Wennerström and other Swedes.

Born March 2, 1887 in Johannes parish, Stockholm, he was the son of Gustav Valfrid Tenglin (born in 1860 in Nysätra parish, Uppsala län) and Hilda Carolina Blom (born in 1860 in Södermanland län). The family lived in the block Geten, House No. 11.[361]

Tenglin said he considered third class on the *Titanic* equal to first class on most other steamers. He shared a cabin with August Wennerström, who also survived.

They had just come back from a party, and he had taken off his shoes to go to bed when they both felt a thud. He put his jacket on, but left his shoes in his bunk and his lifejacket under his pillow. He never returned for them.[362]

In 1912, the *Burlington Daily Gazette* wrote about Tenglin's rescue and quoted him as having said the following about the situation when he came up on deck:

The lifeboats were all gone; it looked to us as if we were doomed to perish with the ship when a collapsible lifeboat was discovered. This boat would hold about fifty people and we had considerable trouble getting it loose from its fastenings. The boat was on the second deck and the ship settled the question of its launching as the water suddenly came up over the deck and the boat floated.

There must have been fully 150 people swimming around or clinging to the boat and we feared it would capsize or sink. We had no oars or anything else to handle the boat with and were at the mercy of the waves, but the sea was calm. There was no way to sit down and we stood up in knee-deep ice-cold water, while those on the edges pushed the frantic people in the water back to their fates, it being feared they would doom us all.

The vivid story was told in several paragraphs. One statement of special interest for this publication read: "A big Swede named Johnson was kept

---

[361] From Swedish Church records courtesy Björn-Åke Petersson, Kallinge, Sweden.
[362] *Ibid.*

busy throwing the corpses overboard as we desired to make the boat as light as possible to increase its buoyancy."[363]

On January 1, 1998, *Burlington Hawk Eye* published a story about Tenglin while the fictional movie *Titanic* played in the Westland Mall: The story was based on an interview with Mrs. Mildred Tenglin and her son, named Gunnar after his father, and an older article published in 1962 in *Keokuk Daily Gate City* on the 50th Anniversary of the sinking.

The 1998 article said an officer on deck engaged Tenglin as an interpreter because he knew English. Tenglin thought that it saved him because he was still on deck translating the officer's commands to other Swedes. Otherwise, he said, he may have been below when the ship went down.

Tuxedoed men jumped over the side into lifeboats, the article said. This was confirmed by Second Officer Lightoller. (See also the profile of Björn-ström Steffanson.)

The article said, "At one point, Tenglin had a seat in a lifeboat, but left it for a woman and two children to take his place. He helped set up four coll-apsible life rafts, stepping into the last one as the deck of the great ship reached the ocean surface."

When the *Carpathia* arrived in New York, the American Red Cross and the Swedish-American Society took pictures of the immigrants and turned them into postcards. Tenglin sent one of those picture postcards to his mother in Sweden, mailing it from Burlington April 29, 1912. The card had been returned to the Tenglins, and Gunnar's wife, Mildred, had kept it although she had never had it translated. Meanwhile, Tenglin's daughter-in-law, who lived in Detroit, Michigan, mused about how the *Titanic* had changed their family's history.[364]

Tenglin was rescued by Collapsible A as stated in the above articles and also by Merideth in his *Titanic: A Complete List of the Passengers and Crew.*

An unidentified newspaper wrote that Tenglin was pulled from the water by the occupants of Collapsible A. His relatives believed he had perished until they received a telegram from him. In New York, he was taken in by the Salvation Army's Cadet School and given $25.00.

He arrived in Burlington, Iowa, on April 24 and stayed at first with J. E. Moberg on South Marshall Street. His wife and son arrived in New York on March 6, 1913 on *Hellig Olav* from Copenhagen. Mrs. Anna Tenglin was 30, and the son, Gunnar Jr., was 2-years old. Their last address in Sweden was Västmannagatan 85, Stockholm.

---

[363] There were many big Swedes on board. It could have been Oscar W. Johansson, who was on Collapsible A.
[364] *Ibid.*

The 1915 Iowa State Census shows Gunnar Tenglin living in Des Moines, Iowa. His World War I draft registration in Des Moines June 5, 1917, shows Gunnar Isidor Tenglin as being 30-years old and born in Stockholm. He was a molder's helper at Murray Iron Works in West Burlington. Although he had a wife and a child, he did not claim an exemption. He listed no previous military experience. He was tall and of medium build with light blue eyes and brown hair.[365]

Gunnar Tenglin held various jobs. He was a plant engineer at the old Showers Bros. Plant. He was a gas worker in the utilities plant that supplied Burlington with gas, and he also worked at the Burlington Railroad shops. In 1937, when J. I. Case came to Burlington, Tenglin was the first man to be hired. He became a millwright and stayed on until 1959 when he retired. Tenglin resided with his wife at 1321 Burlington Street. Mrs. Tenglin died March 11, 1968.

In 1930, the U.S. Census shows him residing with his family in Burlington, Iowa. He was 42 at the time, owned his home, had his first citizen papers, and worked as a fireman at Wholesale Furniture. His wife Anna E. was 40. Their son Gunnar D. Jr., 19, was a woodworker at Wholesale Furniture.

In 1972, Gunnar's brother, Einar, 79, and great nephew, Rune, 32, came from Sweden to visit Gunnar. Sixty years had passed since the two brothers had seen each other, and Gunnar found it so difficult to speak Swedish that Rune had to act as interpreter.

Gunnar Tenglin passed away February 6, 1974 at the age of 86 in Burlington Memorial Hospital. Following a protestant service at Prugh's Chapel conducted by Rev. Donald Turkleson, he was buried in Aspen Grove Cemetery on February 9. He was survived by his son Gunnar S. Tenglin, three grandchildren, and four great-grandchildren.[366] The son, Gunnar S., lived on Iowa Street in Burlington with his wife.

---

[365] www.ancestry.com

[366] www.encyclopedia-titanica.org. Ref. *The Burlington Daily Gazette*, Iowa, 25 April 1912. *The Burlington Hawkeye*, 5 June 1972, 7 Feb. 1974, and 2 Jan. 1998, and Wetterholm. Slightly edited. Tenglin had emigrated from Stockholm län in 1903 at the age of 16. His destination was Burlington, Iowa. *Emigranten Populär.*

Seaman advanced to captain in WW II

Tornquist, William Henry

Tornquist, 25, a naturalized Swedish American living in Boston, Massachusetts, emigrated in 1902 at the age of 16. He sailed from Göteborg October 17, as Joh. W. Björklund, listing his last residence as Örebro and his destination as Boston, Massachusetts. Having arrived in Boston, he reported his destination address as that of his sister, Jenny Tornquist, Boston. She was his half sister and born Maximiliana Jenny Katarina Törnqvist on November 7, 1875 in Örebro before her mother's marriage to Björklund. She emigrated in 1892 and worked as a maid in Boston. William also had a half brother, Carl Alfred Björklund (born in 1863 in Örebro in his father's first marriage), and a brother, Einar Julius Björklund, born 1880 in Örebro.[367]

Tornquist was born March 25, 1886 as Johan Vilhelm Henry Björklund in Hedvig Elenora parish, City of Stockholm, the son of Carl Johan Björklund (born May 18, 1829 in Annelund, Solna parish) and Vilhelmina Larsson (born 1844 in Viby, Örebro län).

His parents were married in Nikolai parish, Örebro, Örebro län in 1878 and lived there before moving to Bromma, Stockholm. From Bromma, they moved to Hedvig Elenora parish, Stockholm, Uppsala län. Johan Vilhelm Henry emigrated October 2, 1902 from Södermalm, Örebro, Örebro län. In the U.S., he dropped his first name, Johan, and used William as his first name. He also assumed his sister's surname of Tornquist. He joined the Navy and after that went to sea on American Merchant Marine ships.[368]

On May 28, 1905, William arrived in New Orleans, Louisiana on *S.S. Homer* from Santos and Rio de Janeiro, Brazil, as a seaman. [369]

On June 28, 1909, William officially changed his surname to Tornquist in the US District of Massachusetts. He was single and resided at 46 Howard Street. E. Braintree. His sister, Jenny, was found both in the 1900 and 1910

---

[367] From the Swedish Church records, courtesy Bo Björklund, Stockholm, Sweden (no relation) and *Emigranten Populär* (Swedish passenger records).

[368] From Swedish Church records courtesy Bo Björklund, Kista, Sweden. No relation and information courtesy of his son William Harvey Turnquist, Walnut Creek, California.

[369] www.ancestry.com. He and another Swede were listed as deserting seamen. In other words, they jumped ship, which was not uncommon among seamen. Compare note 365.

U.S. Censuses. She died in Bridgeport, Connecticut on November 23, 1954.[370]

In 1911, William and his sister, Jenny, sailed together from Göteborg September 8 on the *Calypso* to Hull, England. From Liverpool, they sailed on the *Zeeland*, arriving in Boston September 21. The *Zeeland* belonged to the Red Star Shipping Line, which employed William. He was listed as a sailor with "papers."

In 1912, Tornquist was one of six employees of the American Line who traveled on a free ticket, "deadheading" back to New York because their assigned ship was docked due to the coal strike. Of the six, only Tornquist survived.[371]

According to a family member, the ship Tornquist sailed on to England had been sold to English shipping interests. When he and four other American seamen delivered the ship in Southampton, the American Steamship Company purchased tickets for them on the *Titanic* for their return trip to New York. Tornquist was a non-commissioned officer.[372]

Tornquist said he was rescued in Collapsible A. Merideth lists him as being in Lifeboat 15 or in A.

The Ellis Island records incorrectly list his ethnicity as Belgian-German. The Boston District Court replaced his American citizenship papers, lost on the *Titanic*. No registration for the WWI draft was found in an online search.

In 1923, William "Thurquist "(spelling varies), born in Sweden, U.S. citizen, arrived in New York on the *Kroonland* of the Red Star Shipping Line as Jr. 3rd officer, and on November 28, he arrived in San Francisco as 3rd officer. He was identified as having brown hair and blue eyes. On December 31, 1924, he arrived in New York from Havana and Panama Canal and reported his destination as his home on 181 Street, New York City.

On May 18, 1925, he arrived in New York on the *Manchuria* as first officer going home to his wife, Lottie A, 187 Pine Hurst Avenue, New York. On August 28, 1925, he arrived in San Francisco from Havana and Panama Canal on the Manchuria as 1st officer.[373]

---

[370] In the 1900 Census for Cambridge, Mass, Ward 5, Middlesex County, Jenny was found as a servant for the Mandell family on Auburn Street. In the 1910 U.S. Census, she was found in Brookline, Norfolk, Mass, as Jennie K. Turnquist, 34, working as a parlor maid for the Dane family that had eleven servants. In 1909, she was found as having arrived in Boston from Southampton, September 18, on *St. Louis*. She listed her nearest relative as Nils Fredriksson, Bondegatan 23, Stockholm. Her destination was Brooklyn, New York.

[371] Merideth, "Group Notes," p. 57. Merideth did not name the stranded ship.

[372] E-mail to the author from William Harvey Turnquist, Walnut Creet, California, March 7, 2011.

[373] www.ancestry.com.

When William Henry died September 13, 1946 in Long Beach, Los Angeles, California, his surname was spelled Turnquist. He had one son, William Harvey Turnquist.[374]

Name: William Henry Turnquist
Service Info: CAPT US NAVY WORLD WAR II
Birth Date: 25 Mar 1886
Death Date: 13 Sep 1946
Cemetery: Golden Gate National Cemetery
Cemetery Address: 1300 Sneath Lane, San Bruno, CA 94066
Buried At: Section G Site 2211-A[375]

His wife's name was Novelle (Lottie A.) Turnquist. Her last residence was 98112 Seattle, King County, Washington. She was born March 9, 1892 and died February 10, 1988.[376]

Controversial editor wrote about the disaster

Wennerström, August Edvard

August Wennerström, photo courtesy Gerald Wennerstrom

The 27-year-old Wennerstrom's surname in Sweden was Andersson. He had worked for several newspapers in various towns in Sweden, expressing his socialist views. When he decided to emigrate, he skipped Sweden by buying his ticket in Copenhagen and changing his name to Wennerstrom.

Born April 24, 1884 in St. Maria parish, Ystad, Malmöhus län, Skåne, he was the son of laborer Knut Andersson (born in 1858 in Ingelstorp, Kristianstad län) and Elna Månsdotter (born in 1842 in St. Olof parish, Kristianstad län)[377]

He was employed by his hometown paper, *Ystad Allehanda.* In 1902, he was associated with *Ung-socialisterna* (Young socialists). In October 1904, he moved to Karlskrona, Blekinge, to work for the paper, *Blekinge Folkblad.* He told the chief editor

---

374 www.encyclopedia-titanica.org. This source also says that Tornquist had been a master builder in Örebro before his emigration, but it should be noted that he was only 16 at the time. It also said that he earned a degree in navigation.
375 U.S. Veterans Gravesites, ca. 1775-2006, www.ancestry.com
376 www.ancestry.com.
377 From the Swedish Church records courtesy Björn-Åke Petersson, Kallinge, Sweden.

that he had received an order for printing a pamphlet, but did not describe the contents. When a board member saw how inflammatory the text was, he tried to stop the printing, but the printing continued at night. The pamphlet, "*Gula Faran*" (The Yellow Threat) was published in December 1905 and was confiscated the same day.

Even the socialist paper *Arbetet* declared its opposition to the contents. One month later, *Blekinge Folkblad* was accused of *majestätsbrott (*approx. unlawful slender of the king.) The leading article called King Oscar II, "the king of robbers." Three other well-known men were given similar 'titles.' But perhaps worst of all, the well-loved hymn, *Närmare Gud till Dig* (*Nearer my God to Thee)*, was called a travesty while the the Christian Holy Communion was ridiculed. When August Andersson was summoned to the trial in January 1906, he had left Karlskrona, and the man who took his place assumed full responsibility for the contents of the pamphlet.

August moved to Karlstad, where he became a controversial man in the social democratic press. Officially, he was hired as the manager of the printing shop at *Värmlands Folkblad,* but he also filled in as editor when needed. He suggested the paper hire Ivar T. Vennerstrom as its chief editor, and while the new boss was in America for three month, August filled in for him as chief editor. Ivar Vennerstrom later became the Minister of Defense (1932-36) and served as governor of Värmland (1936-45).

During their time in Karlstad, August and Ivar became close friends and shared everything, including collars, shirts, and underwear. August was criticized by his colleagues for his work methods, but it did not prevent them from praising him when he suddenly left the paper in January 1909, just before the General Strike that led to the paper's demise.

August next went to Malmö, where he became the boss for a printing shop for which he issued stocks. Having begged for and borrowed money, he still ran out of funds. On March 17, 1912, he was back in his hometown, Ystad, likely working as a typesetter at *Ystad Allehanda*. Although he did not have the money for the ticket to America, he decided to emigrate and set the date of departure as April 2. Somehow, he managed to raise the funds.

He avoided going to the pastor of the parish to ask for an emigration certificate by buying his America ticket in Copenhagen. At the same time, he assumed the surname of his friend and boss, but spelled it Wennerström. He traveled the same route as Tenglin, Lundstrom, Asplund, Karl Johnson, and many other Swedish men of military age.[378]

---

[378] Excerpted and translated from Lars Engwall, "Arbetarhistoria."

August Wennerström with his wife, Naomi. Photo courtesy Gerald Wennerstrom, who owns the copyright.

Ivar Vennerstrom later described his former colleague as an adventurer with an unstoppable optimism bordering on irresponsibility. When Ivar learned of the *Titanic* disaster and browsed the list of survivors, he was surprised to see his own surname, but soon realized it was August who had assumed it, only spelling it differently.[379]

Wennerstrom was rescued in Lifeboat A. At Ellis Island, he is listed as having arrived from Ystad, Skåne.

The paper *Nordstjernan* introduced Wennerstrom before it published his article in his own words:

"The Swedish newspaperman, Mr. Aug. E. Wennerstrom was on board Titanic when the steamer sank, and he has for *Nordstjernan* written the description below of this horrifying disaster."

August Wennerstrom's own story:

At noon on the 10th of April, the Titanic—the world's largest steamer—weighing 45,000 ton, left the port of Southampton admired by thousands of people. It headed first to the French war port of Cherbourg, where hundreds

[379] *Ibid.*

of postal sacks and a large contingent of Italians were transferred from a smaller steamer.

We then headed for Queenstown on the Irish coast and took on mail and passengers. We finally entered the Atlantic with 4,000 postal sacks, 1,320 passengers and a crew of 890. Now we had the opportunity to explore the giant Titanic that had cost ten million to build, and we were amazed. Only praise and no criticism. Large, airy salons, elegant cabins, splendid dining rooms, with lots of tasty food at the right time, as the skånings [people living in Skåne] *say.*

Passengers, who had traveled many times on ships owned by various companies, expressed their delight about all the comfort, the good order and cleanliness, yes about everything.

But then we lived the life in what could be likened to a small genial city, dancing, playing, singing, and awakening early in the morning to the crowing of the rooster, because we did have such farm animals on board. In addition, we had various country and city accommodations like a jail, an infirmary, midwives, nurses, doctors, ministers, a bakery, a hospital, post offices, etc.

As mentioned, we had everything on board except stores. One could almost imagine being in a comfortable communistic place, where one only needed to open ones mouth, and cooked sparrows would fly in.

To swim in the Atlantic is probably something that most people fear, but a warm bath on the Atlantic in third class of the Titanic was truly a wonderful and absolutely first-class experience and as comfortable as at Sveabadet [a bathhouse] *in Stockholm. We Scandinavians really enjoyed the bath tubs.*

Everything, like cabins, dining rooms, parlors, and decks, were inspected twice daily, morning and evening, by the ship's doctors who were accompanied by high ranking officers. And one could tell by the looks of the anxious crew that these inspections were thorough.

On Friday the church bells peeled for the Catholics and on Sunday a worship service was held.

Yes, everything was well arranged and the only discomfort came from the people referred to by the Scandinavians as the swarthy (expletive), namely the Italians and the Polish when they were allowed in the parlors and other public places. Yes, about them we should talk quietly. [Remarks omitted]. *These people ought to have access only to the promenade deck in third class, while the Scandinavians, Germans, English, French, Japanese and other cultivated people should be able to move around freely among themselves.*

On Sunday evening, we went to bed, happy and satisfied for a pleasant day. We heard that we could expect to arrive in New York on Tuesday, but it was of little interest to us then because we were in paradise and why should we hurry when we had it so good and had everything we needed.

Sunday evening 11:15 p.m.

Hello! Are you awake! Go up on deck! The ship has hit an iceberg was the call that went out through all doors and in the corridors.

We got up and dressed as if it were morning and took the matter calmly. Walked up on the stern deck, where we managed a little dancing when the crew ensured us that there was no danger. We made fun of the Italians who came up in their night shirts dragging large trunks and lifebelts. Others withdrew to the saloons, lit their pipes, knocked at the bar and wanted a drink feeling morning fresh. An English missus sat down by the piano with her little girl beside her. The spirit was as high as the evening before.

The calm was strengthened when crewmen went around and said that the lifebelts were no longer needed. However, my friend, Tendin [Tenglin] *and I got the idea of going back to our cabin. Oh my! What did we see? The whole crew standing in the corridor with lifebelts on. The stokers came up and the steam engines no longer worked. Everything stood still. The steward ordered us to turn around and leave. When asked if it was the matter of life or death, they laughed and referred to the watertight compartments, which certainly would stop the ship's demise even if the whole bottom went out.*

Still, the lifeboats were lowered and filled with women, children, and crew. Men could not enter them, at least not officially.

Some lifeboats took 80 people while others only a small number. One of them had only 15 or 16 people. Titanic was no longer under command, the pumps stood still, and the ship never did have a search light. The first officer yelled to the helmsman, "Save yourselves if you can because the disaster is unavoidable." In the same moment he put the pistol in his mouth and lay dead on his post.

[The First Officer was William Murdoch] Although there were rumors that he committed suicide, this was never confirmed as his body was not found. Wireless operator Harold Bride said he saw Murdoch alive in the water.]

The boats were still being lowered and disappeared in the night. The Irish were down on their knees praying. The Swedes went from boat to boat and tried to board or looked for lifebelts, quiet and calm, knowing that rescue was possible. [Other passengers] *had become totally crazy, hollered and screamed, not knowing what to do. Everything was chaos.*

Here and there a Swede called out, "Goodbye, friends, it's no use to fight it. I die willingly." I remember especially my friend, Lundahl from Småland, an elderly man, who had lived 25 years in America. He said goodbye and went away to lie down patiently waiting for death to free him.

The English lady mentioned earlier calmly remained by the piano with her child and died there.

The Titanic sank deeper and finally, at the height of the noise, prayers, crying, and calls for help, another lifeboat was discovered, a collapsible up on the bridge. [Wennerstrom was saved in Collapsible A]. *Crewmen pulled it down on the first class deck, but in the same moment, the water came rushing into the first class rooms, and within the minute a large wave covered the top deck of the Titanic. About 1,600 people were washed overboard followed by everything that was loose on deck.*

I and a few friends were thrown up on the just lowered lifeboat, which was cast loose in the bow by the water, and soon thereafter the stern was also free and the next wave carried us away from the ship's four funnels. We encountered and picked up at least 150 people [?].

The Titanic continued to sink and the funnels filled with water, the steam engines exploded and the force threw us out in the open sea and we drifted about around the ship. Not comprehending the situation, we saw the Titanic rise straight up with the bow deep in the water and the stern and its 5-ton propellers up in the air. In the blink of an eye, the Titanic, the world's largest steamer, is no more. It sinks thousands of feet into the deep, and its electric lights cast a last sheen.

But now we can see the disastrous consequence, or rather the spectacle in its full light. Thousands of people fight convulsively on the surface, reaching for anything that can save them. Prayers, calls for help, and insanity.

The scene cannot be described in writing and surely it cannot be imagined. The lifeboats were gone and we drifted in our water-filled and damaged, so-called lifeboat among the still living and striving, the dead bodies, and the wreckage until about half past two o'clock when our boat capsized and all of us, about one hundred, were thrown into the Atlantic, fighting the same fight as thousands of our comrades. After about half an hour, about fifty of us managed to get up in the boat, which was still filled with water. It had been so since one o'clock when the fight for our lives began.

The screams around us slowly subsided, and the dead bodies floated so closely that one could imagine walking on them, and in our wondrous craft one after the other fell down and died. Three had already become insane and had to be held. A man from Helsingborg—who died on the Carpathia—became totally gray-haired in less than 30 minutes. His wife had held on to the gunwale with one hand and me with the other, but after half an hour she gave up her breath and the Atlantic became her last resting place. This occurred before the eyes of her husband, but he had lost his senses and could not do anything. He stared ahead and didn't change his expression. [Gerda and Edvard Lindell. Edvard may have died in the lifeboat.].

We, the survivors of those who had been swept away, continued to drift among dead bodies and wreckage, and intermittingly our own boat lightened as we could heave those who had died overboard.

Our infernal screams then brought a sailboat from Carpathia [Officer Lowe from the Titanic, who had rigged a sail on his lifeboat.] *to us at half past six, and we were rescued from our wet element. By then we had stood in water up to our middle for six or seven hours and also been in the cold sea for half an hour. Only twelve of us were left of the 150 who had clung fast in the beginning. We left our dear water-filled and damaged craft with three dead bodies that we had not thrown overboard.*

As we arrived on the Carpathia we were glad to find a few Swedes who had managed to swim all night and were safely aboard the Carpathia. [They may have floated on wreckage, but they could not have been in the water all night.]

On the Carpathia we were fed and cared for as well as possible. The crew as well as the first and second class passengers did their utmost to make it comfortable and pleasant for us. These passengers made clothes of blankets for the naked children, treated them to sweets, and did all they could.

On the other hand, we suffered immensely from the awful squalor of the [One nationality named]. *And then the food! The ship's provisions were … not for civilized people. The steward and the officers regretted it and did what they could.*

When we had safely arrived in New York on the 18th at nine o'clock in the evening, we had reason to proclaim, Oh, freedom, the wonderful proud word, the most beautiful word of all, etc.

New York, April 19, 1912.

Aug. E. Wennerstrom.[380]

More by Wennerstrom from a lecture quoted in literature. Here he is called Andersson:

The second explosion threw us across the ship and miraculously landed us next to a collapsible boat, which had heretofore been overlooked. We did not have to push it off deck because by that time the Titanic was under water and we floated on top of her. The Titanic bow turned downward and its stern rose higher and higher. A third explosion damaged the bottom of our canvas boat that still floated due to its railing of cork while the Titanic sank bit by bit. More and more people came to the boat that Andersson was in and because

---

[380] *Nordstjernan*, New York, Apr. 23, 1912, p. 16. The woman who let go of the gunwale reportedly was Gerda Lindell. Wennerstrom and other Swedes criticized the manners and appearance of people of certain nationalities. The www.encyclopedia-Titanica.org site writes that Wennerstrom tried to save Alma Pålsson and her children and also Gerda Lindell, whose hand he grabbed. But she was too weakened by the cold and he was unable to hold on to her any longer.

it was so heavily loaded, the boat turned all the way around. After a while he managed to get back to his floating device, which soon filled with people. The boat was overloaded and we had only a couple of oars. We were forced to either stand or sit still. The only motion we experienced was when those who had died were thrown overboard to give the living more room and lighten the load.[381]

Wennerstrom also sent a letter to *Kristianstadbladet*, published in his home province of Skåne, on April 20, 1912, from which I have translated one paragraph:

"A Swede by the name of August Wennerstrom, who is among the saved, has related the following:"

Just as the ship was about to sink, I got hold of a collapsible lifeboat, which was stored behind a funnel. Together with three other men, I got it released and all four of us hopped overboard with the boat. It capsized four times, but each time we managed to get it on the right keel again. While we drifted about I saw at least 200 people floating in the water. All of them drowned. At last, my comrades and I were taken up by the Carpathia."[382]

According to one website, Wennerstrom met Alma Pålsson and her children, also from Skåne, as the *Titanic* began to sink. He tried to hold on to two of the children, but lost them when they came into the water.[383]

The former socialist, journalist, and typographer settled in Culver, Indiana. He married Naomi Johnson, whom he had met at the Salvation Army in Chicago. In the 1920 U.S. Census the family is listed as living in Union Township at which time August was the foreman at a military school. His wife, Naomi, was born in Illinois, but her parents were born in Sweden. In 1930 the couple had six children: Leo E, 14, Clarence W. 12, August E. 10, Knight L. 8, Billy R. 7, and one daughter E.A. Leonora, 7. (The girl named Ann married a Mr. Gibbons. Another child was born later.) By then, the father was listed as supervisor at a school. He was 46 and his wife 36.

One of the many grandchildren is screen-writer Gerald Wennerstrom, Kent, England. He is the son of August Jr., who was born in about 1920. August Sr. also had a son in Sweden, Knut Haglund, who in turn has many descendants. Wennerstrom is unique among the Swedish immigrants on the *Titanic* in that he fathered many children.

---

[381] From writings in Swedish by Lars Engwall.
[382] The letter might have been longer.
[383] www.encyclopedia-titanica.org.

August Wennerstrom registered for the WWI draft on September 1, 1918 in Marshall County, Indiana. A citizen of Sweden, he was described as tall and slender with blue eyes and brown hair. He also registered for the WWII draft at which time he was 58-years old and living in Culver, Marshall County, Indiana.[384]

Wennerstrom died in Fort Wayne, Indiana, November 22, 1950 of a cerebral hemorrhage while at work at the State School. His grandson, Gerald, related how August happened to get that job. The Culver Military Academy was waiting for another man at the train station, but when he didn't show up, August was hired instead. When asked if August abandoned his socialist views, the grandson said, "Yes and no."

Even though he wrote about King Oscar of Sweden in a negative way, he had his picture hanging in his home and spoke respectfully of him. Gerald Wennerstrom says his grandfather was the superintendent of buildings and grounds at the Culver Military Academy for nearly 30 years and later started a seed and landscaping store. He worked as superintendent of the grounds for the State School in Fort Wayne when he died. [385]

---

[384] www.ancestry.com. The last registration during WWII was for men up to the age of 64.

[385] Courtesy Gerald Wennerstrom. Also historical records on www.ancestry.com.

The Swedish victims

The Mansion House Fund mentioned at the end of each victim's profile was started by the Lord Mayor of London, April 17, 1912. The British King and Queen contributed to the fund and so did many other prominent men and women. The fund received $26,500 in donations on the first day and then continued to grow from contributions, large and small. It became the surest and fasted source of compensation for those who had lost a breadwinner. Family members of almost all the Swedish victims received an average of about 875 Swedish crowns (£48.00 or about $230.00) from the Mansion House Fund. The families could also apply for damage claims from the White Star Line, but those funds were not paid until 1914. The information about the amounts received by relatives in Sweden in Swedish crowns is from the website www.encyclopedia-titanica.org. The conversion to American dollars is by the author at a conversion rate of 3.75.

The fact that the third-class-single men were lodged in the bow and single women in the stern made it difficult for relatives and friends to reach one another at the time of the disaster.[386]

When the call came for everyone to go to the boat deck, mothers struggled to dress their sleepy children. The entire Anders Andersson family with five children perished. An emigrant recruiter, Mr. Danbom, related to them by marriage, had enticed them to emigrate although they were well situated in Sweden. As the only American in the group, Mr. Danbom became the natural leader. He warned the others of the expected surge that would pull the lifeboats down with the ship. The adults decided they would all meet death together. The children had no say.

Three of the five Asplund children did not get in the lifeboat with their mother. Selma Asplund said she wished they had all died together as planned. Three of their boys, aged 5-14, perished along with their father.

Mrs. Pålsson, whose husband lived in Chicago, traveled alone with four children and asked a Swedish man to hold on to two of her children. He did so, but lost them when the deck flooded with water.

---

[386] The *Titanic* had forty open berths (men's dormitory) in third class; the rest had cabins, usually with four berths in each. Families could stay together in small cabins with a washstand between the beds.

The entire Skoog family of six was lost. They were on their way home to Iron Mountain, Michigan, after an extended stay in Sweden.

The names of the passengers sailing on the Wilson Line steamer *Calypso* from Göteborg to England were found on the ship's manifest as referenced in the Preface.

Carl Asplund's water-damaged wallet recovered from his body. Photo courtesy Andrew Aldridge, Henry Aldridge & Sons.

The oldest Swedish victim was a 74-year old man, and the youngest a 4-month-old baby boy. The 74-year-old Johan Svensson cried when his son came from South Dakota to take him along on the return trip. The father had no close relatives left in Sweden. The 4-month-old baby, Gilbert Danbom, was born in Sweden, while his parents were staying with relatives. The baby perished along with his parents. The Andersson children are probably in the front row of the photo to the left.

According to survivors, the two families had decided to die together.

Farewell party in Kisa before the emigrants left. Photo courtesy of Günter Bäbler, Switzerland.

The carpenter's watch had stopped at 2:34 a.m.

Ådahl, Mauritz

Mauritz Ådahl and his wife Emelia (Emely), wedding photo, courtesy Swedish Emigrant Institute, Växjö, Sweden

The 30-year-old married Swedish-American had met his future wife, Emely, in Västerbotten while on a job assignment. They had planned to emigrate together, but the idea did not sit well with Emely's parents. Mauritz returned to Asarum and emigrated from there in 1903. Emely worked at the hospital in Umeå until 1906 when she emigrated to join Mauritz. They were married September 14, 1907 and two daughters were born to them in New York.

Born June 15, 1881 in Asarum parish, Blekinge (province and county), Mauritz was the son of the carpenter Ola Månsson Ådahl (born in 1840 in Åryd parish Blekinge) and Elsa Persdotter (born in 1840 in Asarum).[387]

The 1910 U.S. Census for Brooklyn, Ward 27, Kings County, New York, includes Mauritz Odahl, 28, housepainter, his wife, Emely, 29, daughter Vera, 1 ½ years old, and baby daughter, Georgia, two months old. Emely would rather live in Sweden, so later that year, she and the children lived with Mauritz' parents in Asarum. When his father had died in May of 1911, Mauritz also made the move. Working as a carpenter, he bought a piece of land in Asarum and planned to build a house. Short of funds, he decided to return to America to earn more money for the construction.

Mauritz and his traveling companion, John Holm, met up with Adelia Landergren in Denmark. She was also from Karlshamn. Due to a coal strike in England, the three were transferred from another ship to the *Titanic.*

Before his departure, Mauritz wrote to his wife about the change of ship: "Well, my little darling. I am still in Southampton." He explained the delay and why they had been transferred to the White Star Line's largest ship, the *Titanic,* scheduled to depart the next day at noon on its maiden voyage. He

[387] From the Swedish Church records, courtesy Björn-Åke Petersson, Kallinge, Sweden.

ended his letter, "Hope that all goes well and that I soon can be home again with my darlings, my all in this world."[388]

After the collision, Mauritz escorted Adelia Landergren up to boat deck, helped her into Lifeboat 13, and stepped back. Mauritz Ådahl's body was later recovered by the MacKay Bennett (#72). His watch had stopped at 2:34 a. m., 14 minutes after the *Titanic* sank. He was buried at sea April 24, 1912. Described as having fair hair and a light moustache, he wore a dark suit, brown socks, and a striped shirt. Among his belongings were a silver watch and chain, a pipe, a book, comb, knife, key chain, cuff links, a ring marked M. A. and 100 *kronor* in cash. The valuables were sent to his wife in Sweden. In 1995, his grandchildren decided to donate the items to Sweden's only *Titanic* museum located at the Emigrant Institute in Växjö, Småland.

The Mansion House Fund paid 1,784 crowns (about $475.00) to his wife and children in January of 1913 and 509 crowns to his mother (about $135.00). In October 1914, his wife, children, and mother received 6,006 crowns (about $1,601.00) in damages. All damage claims were paid by the White Star Line. The widow supported the family by sewing flags. She died in 1947.

When the Ådahl grandchildren found out that their grandfather had been buried at sea rather than in Halifax, they honored him by laying a wreath at sea from a vessel named "*Nadir*." [389]

Married woman on her way home to Minnesota

Ahlin, Johanna Persdotter

Mrs. Johanna Ahlin, 40, was a Swedish-American married woman, who had immigrated in 1905. In 1912, she had visited her parents and was on her way home to her husband and two sons in Akeley, Minnesota. Her brother, Johan Pettersson, a new immigrant, also perished.

Born June 21, 1871 in Västermo parish, Södermanland (province and county), she was the daughter of Per Larsson (born in 1839 in Västermo) and Anna Stina Larsdotter (born in 1842 in Arboga, Västmanland's län).[390]

In the 1910 U.S. Census, the Ahlin family was found to be living in Chicago, Cook County Ward 26. John Ahlin, 39, had emigrated in 1903. He worked as a stock keeper at a dairy. Johanna, also 39, was listed as having

[388] From www.titanic-norden.com.
[389] www.encyclopedia-titanica.org.
[390] Swedish Church records, courtesy Björn-Åke Petersson, Kallinge, Sweden.

immigrated in 1905. They had two sons born in Sweden, Gunnar, 10, and David, 8.[391]

On March 17, 1905, the family sailed from Göteborg with their residence listed as America and their destination as Chicago.[392]

In 1912, Mrs. Ahlin sailed with her brother on the *Calypso* from Göteborg April 5, 1912, with her residence listed as America and her destination as Chicago. Their bodies were never found.

For health reasons, Johanna had been on an extended visit to Sweden since May of 1911. Her husband, John Ahlin, was from Bärsta in Öja parish, Södermanland.[393]

The Mansion House Fund paid 875 crowns to her husband and sons, and on June 4, 1914, her husband received 455 crowns in damages, for a total compensation of about $355.00. When the consulate in New York tried to contact Mr. Ahlin, March 10, 1919, the letter was returned with the comment, 'Moved, new address unknown.[394]

They decided to die together

Andersson, Anders Johan

The Andersson family. Photo courtesy Günter Bäbler, Switzerland

[391] www.ancestry.com. Lee Merideth lists her destination as Akely, Minnesota.
[392] *Emigranten Popular.*
[393] *Hemlandet*, Chicago, May 14, 1912.
[394] Claes-Göran Wetterholm, *Titanic*. Prisma, Stockholm.

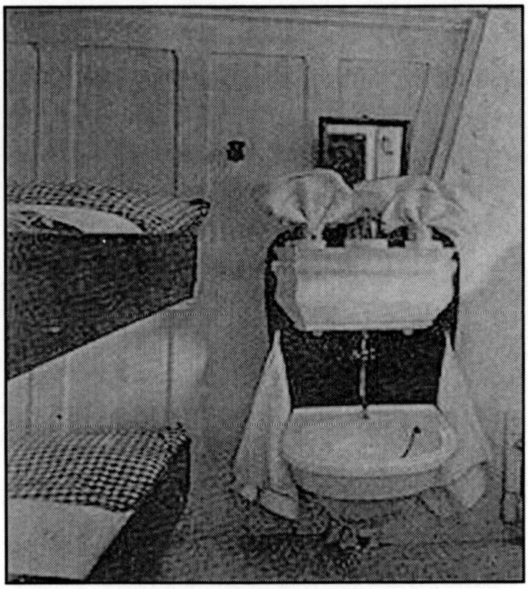
Third-class cabin like the one the Andersson family occupied. There were two more bunks on the right side.

The 39-year-old Andersson was the head of a large family. Although he was a well-to-do farmer in Kisa, he and his wife had been enticed to emigrate by Mr. and Mrs. Danbom. Mrs. Danbom and Mrs. Andersson were sisters. Another sister lived in Winnipeg. The Anderssons intended to settle in Canada.

Born January 21, 1873 in Åtrasmåla, Horn parish, Östergötland (province and county), Anders Johan was the son of Carl Johan Andersson (born in 1839 in Tjärstad parish, same county) and Kristina Lovisa Andersdotter (born in 1850 in Västra Eneby parish, same county).[395]

Anders Johan Andersson and Alfrida Brogren were married June 25, 1898. They had five children: Sigrid, Ingeborg, Ebba, Sigvard, and Ellis. The Anderssons owned a farm in Kättestorp, Horn, Kisa, but sold it before emigrating. Alfrida's brother gave a farewell party for them at which members of the Bränntorp Mission Church were present.

The Andersson family was accompanied by Mr. and Mrs. Danbom, and Miss Anna Nysten, another Kisa resident, who had decided to travel with the two families. Anna was the only survivor of the group. The Anderssons were headed for Sturgeon Creek, St. James, Canada.

Fifty years later, Titanic survivor Anna Sjöblom recalled that while she was still on board the *Titanic*, she had seen a Swedish couple and their five children kiss each other goodbye and jump overboard.[396]

---

395 From Swedish Church records courtesy Björn-Åke Petersson, Kallinge, Sweden.
396 Nick Barratt, *Lost Voices from The Titanic.* Palgrave MacMillan, 2010, p. 145. Quoted from a letter that Anna wrote to Walter Lord on July 18, 1955, for his book, *A Night to Remember.*

Anders Johan's mother and siblings sent a touching letter to the Swedish Foreign Office, dated September 21, 1912. They expressed the thought that no one could possibly imagine what the doomed people had gone through. Neither could anyone express the pain of the relatives who had lost loved ones that way. Their only consolation and hope was that they would meet again at the end of times.

The letter ended with this plea, "We are humbly asking for compensation for what our beloved brought with them in goods and travel money totaling 5,000 *kronor*".[397]

The Mansion House Fund paid 875 crowns to Mr. Andersson's mother, and 912 crowns to his seven siblings. In 1914, his mother received 456 crowns in damage claims. The total compensation amounted to $598.00.

Farm wife dreamed of Canada

Andersson, Alfrida Konstantia

Mrs. Alfrida Andersson, nee Brogren, 39, was the wife of Anders Johan Andersson. She and her husband had sold their farm in Kisa and planned to settle in Canada. They were headed for the home of her sister, Mrs. Zachrisson, St. James, Manitoba, when the entire family perished.

Alfrida was born December 25, 1872 in Åtrasmåla, Horn parish, Östergötland, the daughter of Magnus Peter Constantin Brogren (born 1831 in Horn) and Anna Lena Johansdotter (born 1845 in Kisa parish, Östergötland).[398]

They sailed on the *Calypso* from Göteborg on April 5, 1912, with their residence listed as Kisa and their destination as Winnipeg, Manitoba.

Alfrida perished along with her husband and five children. Her sister, Anna Danbom, and her husband and small child also perished. Anna Nysten was the only survivor of the party from Kisa.

An article in the *Manitoba Morning Free Press* on Saturday, April, 20, 1912, said that two Winnipeg families were believed to have been passengers on the Titanic, Mr. A. G. [J.] Anderson, his wife, and five children, and Ernest Danbom, his wife, and small child. Mrs. Anderson and Mrs. Danbom were sisters of Mrs. Zachrisson of Harcourt Street, St. James.

Mrs. Anderson had written a letter shortly before leaving expressing concerns about sailing on a new ship that had never crossed the ocean, but it

---

[397] www.titanicnorden.com.

[398] From Swedish Church records courtesy Björn-Åke Petersson, Kallinge, Sweden.

was not likely that her premonitions had prevented them from sailing with the new liner. But Mrs. Zachrisson said she hoped something unexpected might have happened to prevent them from leaving.

Mr. and Mrs. Anderson were on their way to Winnipeg with their children and Mr. and Mrs. Danbom and their baby were headed for California, but later intended to return to their home in Stanton, Iowa, the article said.[399]

Alfrida's mother received 462 crowns in damage claims and an additional 185 crowns in claims for a total compensation of $173.00.

Eleven-year-old girl lost to the sea

Andersson, Sigrid Elisabeth

The 11-year-old girl was the eldest child of Anders and Alfrida Andersson of Kisa. She was born April 16, 1900 in Kettestorp, Kisa parish, Östergötland.

Nine-year-old girl lost at sea

Andersson, Ingeborg Constantia

The 9-year-old girl was the daughter of Anders and Alfrida Andersson of Kisa. She was born April 16, 1902 in Kisa parish, Östergötland.

Six-year-old girl lost to the sea

Andersson, Ebba Iris Alfrida

The six-year-old girl was the daughter of Anders and Alfrida Andersson of Kisa, born November 14, 1905 in Kisa parish, Östergötland.

Four-year-old boy lost to the sea

Andersson, Sigvard Harald Elias

The 4-year-old boy was the son of Anders and Afrida Andersson of Kisa. He was born July 21, 1907 in Kisa parish, Östergötland.

---

[399]*Manitoba Morning Free Press*, Winnipeg, Canada, Apr. 20, 1912.

Two-year old girl lost to the sea

9. Andersson, Ellis Anna Maria

The 2-year-old girl was the daughter of Anders and Alfrida Andersson of Kisa. She was born January 19, 1910 in Kisa.

Two men waited for her in Michigan

Andersson, Ida Augusta M.

Miss Andersson, 38, was headed for Manistee, Michigan, where two widowers were interested in marrying her, and where she was expected to care for ten motherless children. Ida was single and worked as housekeeper at the Lagmansbro farm, Vadsbro, Södermanland.

Born November 24, 1873 in Svenstorp parish, Skaraborg's län, Ida was the daughter of Johan Anders Carlsson.[400]

Ida Andersson Photo Axel Janson, Ray, Mengot, N.D.

Ida had three sisters, Elizabeth, Hilda, and Hilma Susanna. The sister Hilda was married to Axel Johnson Sr. of Michigan, but died in childbirth on March 7, 1909.

While raising her own seven children, Hilma in Michigan also took care of her brother-in-law's three children. Her husband's brother's name was Andrew. Ida's destination was given as that of her sister Hilma S. Peterson, at 408 Sibben St., Manistee, Michigan. Ida was expected to help with the care of the motherless children.[401]

Ida sailed on the *Calypso* from Göteborg on April 5, 1912, with her residence listed as Vadsbro, Södermanland, and destination as Manistee, Michigan.

---

[400] Swedish Church records, courtesy Björn-Åke Petersson, Kallinge, Sweden.
[401] www.titanicnorden.com

The Mansion House Fund paid 874 crowns to Greta Olsson, a sister-in-law in Ingelstorp, Sweden. Ida's father, Johan Carlsson, received 924 crowns in damage claims, for a total compensation of $480.00.

Hartford Swede was on his way home

Andersson, Johan Samuel

The 26-year-old-Swedish American had visited his parents and was on his way home to Hartford, Connecticut. His specific destination was c/o Alex Anderson, 1415 Broad St., Hartford.

Born December, 11, 1885 in Stommen, Härja parish, Skaraborg's län, he was the son of Anders Gustaf Andersson (born 1839 in Härja) and Anna-Sofia Lundström (born in 1857 in Vättak parish, Skaraborg's län). In 1900, Samuel lived at Stommen, Härja, but moved to Linköping, Östergötland's län, on March 23, 1907. The church book noted that he had died in the *Titanic* disaster.[402]

Samuel sailed on the *Calypso* from Göteborg on April 5, 1912, with his residence listed as America and his destination as New York.

The Mansion House Fund paid 874 crowns to his father. The White Star Line paid 1,822 crowns in damage claims to his parents, for a total compensation of $719.00.

Blacksmith and his friends were like siblings

Andreasson, Paul Edvin,

The 20-year-old emigrant was a blacksmith. He was on his way to his brother Ernst Nelson, 8109 Sherman Avenue, Chicago. Departing from Malmö April 5, he reported his last residence in Sweden as Hallaryd.[403]

His travel companions on the *Titanic* were Olga Lundin, Nils Johansson, Albert Augustsson, and Karl Janson/Johnsson of Killeberg. According to the surviving Olga, the five were as close as siblings.

Born March 29, 1892 in Kalvshult, Hallaryd parish, Kronoberg's län, Paul was the son of Andreas Nilsson (born in 1856 in Hallaryd) and Emma Pålsdotter (born in 1864 in Göteryd parish, Kronoberg's län). There were three other children in the family. Paul received his emigration certificate on March 15, 1912.[404]

---

402 Swedish Church records, courtesy Björn-Åke Petersson, Kallinge, Sweden.
403 *Emigranten Populär.*
404 From the Swedish Church records, courtesy Björn-Åke Petersson, Kallinge, Sweden.

In a letter to Sweden's Foreign Office, Paul's father wrote that his son had carried travel funds of between 500 and 600 crowns and asked to be reimbursed. Their small farm barely supported the family, and his wife was grief stricken and ill. Paul had left for America hoping to be able to support his parents in their old age.[405]

The Mansion House Fund paid 872 crowns to his parents. In October 1914, they received 924 crowns in damages, for a total compensation of $479.00.

Relative in Joliet awaited the young man

Aronsson, Ernst Axel A

The 24-year-old single emigrant traveled with Gustaf Edvardsson. Both were of military age and probably bought their tickets in Copenhagen. Aronsson's destination was the home of his uncle, Claes Bengtson, 200 Ridgewood Avenue, Joliet, Illinois.[406]

Born June 21, 1887 in Tannåker parish, Jönköping's län, Gustaf was the son of Aron Bengtsson (born 1865 in Tannåker) and Ida Charlotta Nilsdotter (born 1864 in Jälluntofta parish, Jönköping's län). Ernst Axel Algot emigrated March 29, 1912 from Hörset, Berga parish. Earlier in 1912, he lived with his parents, who had six younger children. The church book noted that he perished in the sinking of the *Titanic*.[407]

His parents were poor. His father wrote to the ministry of foreign affairs April 30, 1912, pleading his case. The Mansion House Fund paid 875 crowns to his parents. They also received 2,217 crowns in damage claims, for a total compensation of $825.00.

---

405 www.titanicnorden.com with reference to Cecilia's Place and www.encyclopedia-titanica.org. Most immigrants brought only $25.00 in cash, which they were required to show at Ellis Island.

406 *Hemlandet*, May 14, 1912, Chicago, wrote that Claes Bengtson was his brother.

407 From the Swedish Church records courtesy Björn-Åke Petersson, Kallinge, Sweden.

Body of husband and father found

Asplund, Carl Oscar

The 40-year-old Carl Asplund, a married farmer and family man, had lived for several years in America. He perished along with three sons while his wife, one daughter, and one son were saved. He had paid £31 7s, 9 d for a cabin for his family.

Carl Oscar Asplund was born May, 7 1871 in Alseda, Jönköping's län, the son of Gustaf Samuelsson (born 1842 in Alseda) and Kristina Adelina Jonsdotter (born 1844 in Skede parish, Jönköping's län).[408]

He married Selma May 9, 1896 at Gethsemane Lutheran Church in Worcester, and the four eldest children were born in that city. Asplund and his sons, Carl Edgar, 5, Clarence Gustaf Hugo, 9, and Filip Oscar, 13, perished, while his wife and two children survived. The youngest son, Edvin Roy Felix, was born in 1909 when the family lived in Alseda (See photo of Carl and Selma, and Lillian and Felix in "The Swedish Survivors.").

The family wished to return to Worcester, especially the eldest son, Filip Oscar. If the rest of the family stayed in Sweden, he would return alone when he was old enough, he said. The parents then decided to sell the farm to get money for the journey and return together. Carl's relatives in Worcester assured him that he could get his old job back at Spencer Wire Works.[409]

The emigration contract, Asplund signed with Carl Eriksson, certified emigration agent, listed the emigrants as follows: Charles Asplund, 40, Selma Asplund, 37, Oscar, 11, Gustaf, 7, Carl, 5, Lillian, 5, and Felix 3, all with their last residence noted as America. The White Star Line agreed to undertake to forward them from Göteborg to Worcester, Massachusetts for the sum of 795 *kronor* (about 212 USD. They would get 10 cubic feet of storage space on the steamer and 150 lbs weight by railway. More guarantees followed in case the emigrants would be denied entrance to America. Carl Eriksson's name stamp was dated 5 April, 1912, and so was the name stamp of the representative for the police in Göteborg, who checked the emigrants' papers. Charles Asplund accepted the contract and signed it in his own handwriting April 5, 1912.[410]

Asplund also needed an "Emigrant Inland Forwarding Order," for the journey from New York to Worcester. It was found on his body along with

[408] From the Swedish Church records courtesy Björn-Åke Petersson, Kallinge, Sweden.
[409] www.titanicnorden.com. Carl had a sister in Worcester and Selma had three sisters living there with their families.
[410] The contract was found in a shoebox after Lillian's death. Source: Voyage No. 64.

other items. The White Star Line paid the railroad tickets for the surviving Selma, Lillian and Felix.

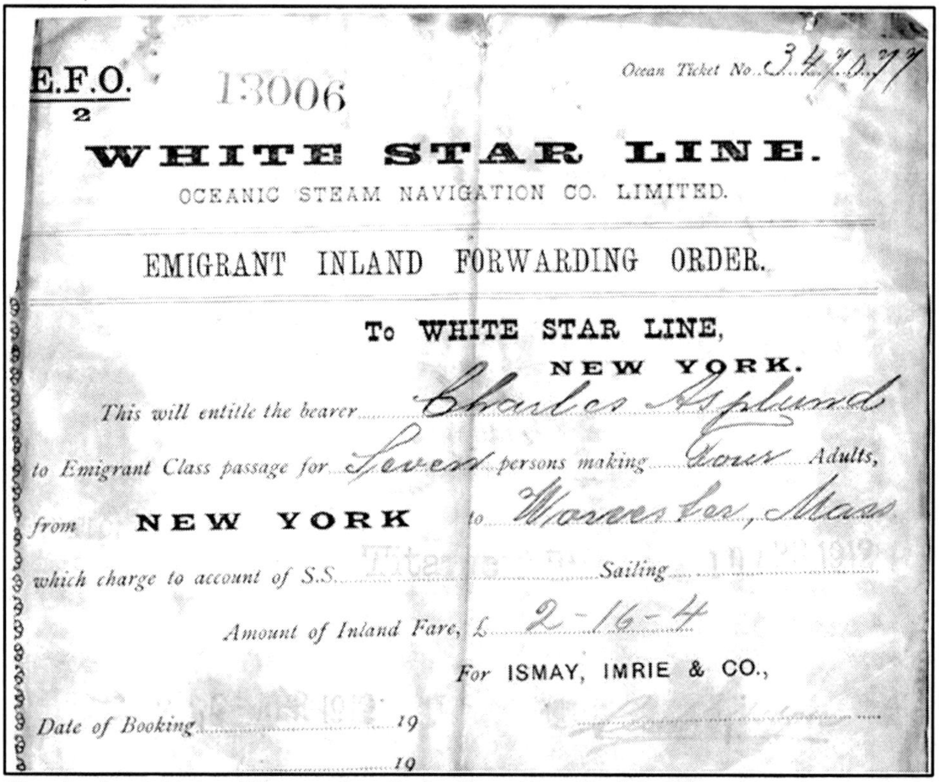

E.F.O. 2 13006

Ocean Ticket No. 347077

WHITE STAR LINE.

OCEANIC STEAM NAVIGATION CO. LIMITED.

EMIGRANT INLAND FORWARDING ORDER.

To WHITE STAR LINE,
NEW YORK.

This will entitle the bearer Charles Asplund

to Emigrant Class passage for Seven *persons making* Four *Adults,*

from NEW YORK *to* Worcester, Mass

which charge to account of S.S. Titanic *Sailing* 10 APR 1912

Amount of Inland Fare, £ 2-16-4

For ISMAY, IMRIE & CO.,

Date of Booking 19

The Asplunds' Inland Forwarding Order from New York to Worcester. Image courtesy Andrew Aldridge, Henry Aldridge & Sons.

The family sailed on the *Calypso* from Göteborg April 5, 1912, all listed as American residents and their destination as Worcester, Massachusetts.[411]

The family boarded the *Titanic* and crowded into a cabin with four bunk beds and a washstand in the narrow space between the bunks. Their final address in Worcester was 151 Vernon Street, Worcester. Life aboard irritated Carl, who remarked that the passengers did nothing but drink, dance and play cards. "If we make it ashore, it should be the last time we sail the Atlantic," he said.

On the night of the collision, the vibration woke Selma, and she roused her husband. Carl dressed to find out what was going on. He decided to wake the children and dress them. In a cabin for four, there were four life vests and they needed seven. Selma later said that they borrowed one from a crewmember and thus had five, one each for her and her husband and the older children.

---

[411] The youngest child, 3-year old Felix, was born in Sweden.

Up on deck, the two youngest children were torn from her and placed alone in a lifeboat crying, she said. Someone yelled, "Bring the children's mother down." Before, she knew it, she was in the boat, looking back and seeing her husband leading their three remaining children in search of another lifeboat, or so she thought.

Keys recovered from Asplund's body. Courtesy Andrew Aldridge, Henry Aldridge & Sons

Carl's body was recovered (#142) dressed in a brown coat and vest, striped trousers, and black boots. The effects recovered were a gold watch, two note books, a gold chain and locket, a brooch marked" F of A.", keys, a knife, and a plain gold ring. There were no marks on his body or clothing, and no money or papers of value were found on the body. He was buried in the Old Swedish Cemetery in Worcester.

Carl carried all of the family's important papers, Selma said, as well as the profit from the sale of their farm. She thought it was strange that he had all seven tickets, but no cash. They also lost their luggage that included three large trunks filled with belongings and table silver from home. Neither the widow nor Carl's mother appear to have claimed compensation, but on March 8, the Mansion House Fund paid 2,699 crowns to Selma and 875 crowns to Carl's mother for a total compensation of $953.00. (See Selma, Lillian, and Felix Asplund in "The Swedish Survivors"). [412]

[412] www.encyclopedia-titanica.org. The Swedish-American newspaper, *Hemlandet*, Chicago, reported that Asplund's mother in Alseda was a widow.

Thirteen-year-old boy lost to the sea

Asplund, Filip Oscar

The 13-year-old Filip was the eldest son of Carl and Selma Asplund. He was born December 12, 1898 in Worcester, Massachusetts. His wish was to return to America when he was old enough. This prompted the entire family to leave. His mother and two sisters were rescued while he, his father, and two brothers perished. His body was not found.

Nine-year-old boy lost to the sea

Asplund, Clarence Gustaf Hugo

The 9-year-old boy was the son of Carl and Selma Asplund, born September 17, 1902 in Worcester, Massachusetts. His body was not found.

Five-year-old boy lost to the sea

Asplund, Carl Edgar

The 5-year-old boy, born Oct. 21, 1906 in Worcester, Massachusetts, was the son of Carl and Selma Asplund. His body was not found. While his twin, Lillian, was saved, his father kept him and his two older sons with him on the deck, telling his wife that they would come in a later lifeboat.

The friends stood together and prayed

Augustsson, Albert

The 23-year-old single new emigrant had worked as a blacksmith assistant for three years in his home community before emigrating. He came from a family of blacksmiths. Augustsson bought his ticket in Malmö, stating his destination as Bloomington, Illinois. His travel companions were Paul Andreasson, Nils Johansson, Karl Johnsson (of Killeberg), and Olga Lundin.

Albert Augustsson. Photo courtesy Günter Bäbler. Switzerland

Born October 10, 1889 in Kråkeryd, Hallaryd, Kronoberg's län, he was the son of August Petersson (born 1865 in Hallaryd) and Johanna Andersdotter (born 1857 in Visseltofta, Kristianstad län). Albert lived with his parents and four siblings on a small rented farm (croft) in Kråkeryd and emigrated from Kråkeryd Södergård, March 30, 1912.[413]

His body, if recovered, was never identified. The Mansion House Fund paid 875 crowns to the parents. In 1914, his parents also received 1,908 crowns in damage claims for a total compensation of $742.00.[414]

Sawmill worker wished to settle in Moline, Illinois

Bengtsson, Jon Viktor

Jon Bengtsson. Photo courtesy of Günter Bäbler, Switzerland

The 26-year-old emigrant had worked on the railroad in Denmark from 1909 to1910, and later worked at a saw mill near his home.

Born July 7 1885 in Knäred parish, Halland (province and county), he was the son of Bengt Karl Kaspersson (born in 1848 in Fagered parish, Halland) and Anna Katarina Bengtsdotter (born in 1839 also in Fagered). In 1900, the family lived in Lagered, Knäred.[415]

He had four brothers. One of his brothers, Emil, lived at 607 5th Avenue, Moline, Illinois, which would have been Jon's final destination.

---

[413] From the Swedish Church records, courtesy Björn-Åke Petersson, Kallinge, Sweden.

[414] *Emigranten Populär* lists him as emigrating from Hallaryd, Kronobergs län. *Hemlandet*, Chicago, wrote on May 14 that Augustsson was on his way to his uncle, Swan Peterson, 1006 W. Taylor Street, Bloomington, Ill. He was said to have carried 500 crowns in cash. If true, it was highly unusual for a new emigrant to bring that much money.

[415] From the Swedish Church records, courtesy Björn-Åke Petersson, Kallinge, Sweden.

Jon Bengtsson sailed on the *Calypso* from Göteborg on April 5, 1912. He was listed as Jon Bengtsson from Fagered, Halland, and his destination as Moline, Illinois.

Emil's son, John Benson, formerly of East Moline, died August 11, 2004 in DePere, Wisconsin. The funeral service was at First Lutheran Church in Moline, where he had been an active member. Benson's obituary said that he was named after an uncle, who had perished on the *Titanic*. John Benson was the treasurer of the Order of Vikings and was known for his beautiful tenor voice. Benson's survivors included his wife, Hazel, daughters Dena Elek of San Francisco, Lynda Cameron of Green Bay, Wisconsin, and grandchildren.[416]

The Mansion Fund paid 875 crowns to Bengtsson's parents. They also received 1,366 crowns in damages, for a total compensation of $598.00.[417]

Man from Stockholm was promised work in New York

Björklund, Ernst Herbert

The names of the relatives in New York who had promised work for this 18-year-old emigrant from Stockholm are unknown.

Born March 1, 1894 in Skeppsholmen parish, Stockholm, he was the son of flag officer Carl Johan Björklund (born in 1846 in Karlskrona *Admiralitet* parish, Blekinge) and Erika Kristina Johansdotter (born in 1850 in Långemåla parish, Kalmar län). Ernst Herbert had five older siblings: John Emil Helge, born 1877 in Catharina parish, Stockholm, Carl Eugene, born in 1881, Jarl Harald, born 1883, Elsa Victoria, born 1885, in Skeppsholmen, and Gurli Carolina, born in 1887, all in Skeppsholmen parish.[418]

The family lived at Grefgatan 62, Stockholm. Björklund sailed on the *Calypso* from Göteborg April 5, 1912, with his residence given as Stockholm and his destination as New York.

The Mansion House Fund paid 875 crowns to his parents, who also received 911 crowns in damage claims, for a total compensation of $476.00.[419]

---

[416] Quad City Times, Aug. 15, 2004.
[417] www.encyclopedia-titanica.org.
[418] From the Stockholm Church records, courtesy Bo Björklund, Stockholm, Sweden.
[419] www.encyclopedia-titanica.org.

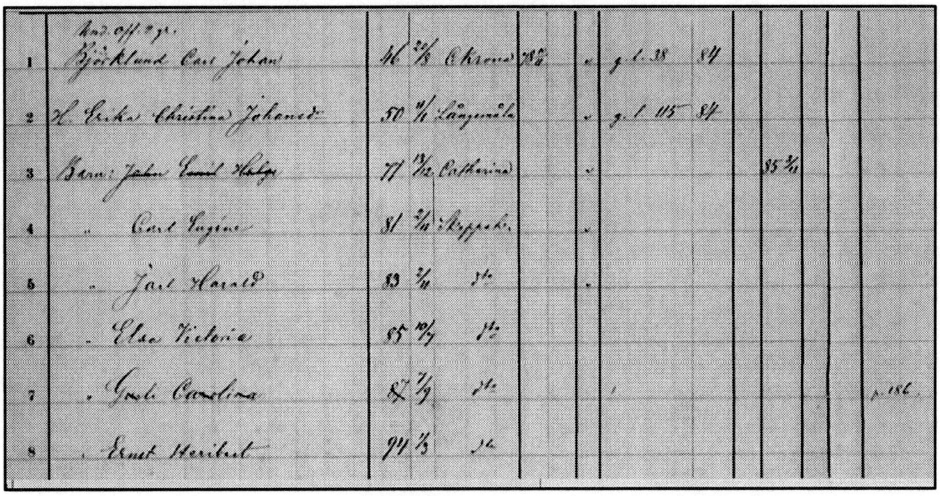

	[illegible]					
1	Björklund Carl Johan	46 20/8	[illegible]	g. l. 38	84	
2	H. Erika Christina Johansdr	50 4/11	[illegible]	g. l. 115	84	
3	Barn: John Emil Helge	77 13/12	Catharina		85 3/11	
4	" Carl Eugène	81 3/4	Skeppsh.			
5	" Karl Harald	83 3/4	d:o			
6	" Elsa Victoria	85 10/7	d:o			
7	" Greta Carolina	87 7/9	d:o			p. 186
8	" Ernst Heribert	94 1/3	d:o			

Photo copy of the Björklund family record in Skeppsholmen parish, 1885-1896, p. 130, courtesy Bo Björklund, Sweden.

The young miss froze with fear on the boat deck

Braf, Elin Ester Maria

Miss Braf, 20, traveled with Helmina Josefina Nilsson from Ramkvilla, who survived.

According to Helmina, Elin, who had been in the U.S. one year earlier, was bringing a doll to give to her niece. When facing a shipwreck, she froze with fear on the boat deck and refused to get into a lifeboat. Her sister, Annie Hammer, living at 1006 Rosco Street, Chicago, waited in vain for her.

Elin Braf. Photo courtesy Gunter Bäbler, Switzerland

Born October, 16 1891, in Spinkabo, Ramkvilla parish, Jönköping's län, Elin was the daughter of Johan Magnus Braf (farmer and solider born April 4, 1850 in Bäckaby) and Mathilda Lovisa Persdotter (born September 9, 1853 in Ramkvilla). On December 7, 1910, Elin moved to Hultsvik in Korsberga parish, Jönköping's län, and emigrated from there. No notation was made about her death on the *Titanic* in the Swedish church records.[420]

Elin sailed from Malmö April 5, 1912 with her residence listed as Korsberga and her destination as Chicago. [421]

The Mansion House Fund paid 875 crowns to her parents. They also received 911 crowns in damage claims, for a total compensation of $476.00.[422]

Butler going back to Worcester

Brobeck, Karl Rudolf

Brobeck, 22, had lived in the U.S. previously. He is not listed as departing from Sweden, and probably bought his ticket in Copenhagen. His destination was Axel Sandqvist, 3 Whipple St. Worcester, Massachusetts. When he last lived in Worcester, he worked as a butler in hotels. Having returned to Sweden, he worked as a painter and janitor in Stockholm and Norrköping.[423]

Born January 2, 1890 in Norrköping, Östergötland's län, he was the son of police officer Karl Edvard Brobeck (born in 1864 in Seglora parish, Älvsborg's län) and Anna Sofia Blomkvist (born in 1866 in Hjorted, Kalmar län). Rudolf had seven siblings, all living in Sweden. On March 12, 1912, he received a moving certificate to Adolf Fredrik parish in Stockholm, but changed his mind and returned the certificate. He lived with his parents and siblings and emigrated from either Matteus or Norra parish in Norrköping.[424]

On April 9, Karl sent a card from Southampton to a person in Worcester, named Sandquist, saying that he would sail soon. He did not mention the

[420]From Swedish Church records, courtesy Björn-Åke Petersson, Kallinge, Sweden. No earlier records have been found of Elin Braf embarking from Sweden or arriving at Ellis Island.
[421] *Emigranten Populär.*
[422] *Ibid.*
[423]There is no record of him having sailed from Sweden, but he might have sailed from Denmark both times.
[424] From Swedish Church records, courtesy Björn-Åke Petersson, Kallinge, Sweden.

name of the ship, and therefore his friend did not know that he had sailed on the *Titanic.*

His parents received 875 crowns from the Mansion House Fund. Later, they received 911 crowns in damage claims, for a total compensation of $476.00.[425]

Tourist might have stayed in the U.S.

Bryhl, Kurt Arnold Gottfrid Lustig

Kurt Bryhl's surname in Sweden was Lustig, but both he and his sister, Dagmar, traveled in second class under their grandmother's surname Bryhl. The 25-year old was described as an adventurous young man, who had seen the world as a seaman. The paper *Hemlandet*, Chicago, wrote on May 14, 1912, that Karl Gustaf (Kurt) accompanied his sister and her fiancé to serve as their translator.

Born March 2, 1887 in Ulricehamn, Älvsborg's län, he was the son of public prosecutor Edvard Gottfrid Lustig (born in 1857 in Grönahög parish, Älvsborg's län) and Ida Jenny Gustafsson (born in 1859 in Höreda parish, Jönköping's län).[426]

Kurt is listed as having departed from Göteborg, April 5 on the *Calypso* together with his sister, Dagmar Bryhl, both from Skara, with the destination given as Rockford, Illinois.

One Rockford newspaper reported that he had qualified to enter Uppsala University, but then heard the call of the sea and for several years worked as a seaman, and also lived in Paris. He was described as "a care-free young man who had seen much and who was preparing to settle down and put his wide experience to use in the calmer affairs of life."[427]

Kurt, Dagmar, and her fiancé, Ingvar Enander, had intended to visit America, but Kurt might have changed his mind and stayed.[428]

There is no record of compensation to the family.

The siblings' destination was their uncle, Oskar Lustig in Rockford, Illinois. Dagmar, who was saved, said that Kurt had been wearing a gray suit on the night of the sinking. His body was not found. Dagmar mourned him deeply, but said that the heaviest burden fell on their father.[429]

---

[425] www.encyclopedia-titanica.org.
[426] From the Swedish Church records courtesy Björn-Åke Petersson, Kallinge, Sweden.
[427] From the *Rockford Republic* as quoted on http://genealogytrails.com/ill.
[428] *Rockford Republic*, April 25, 1912.
[429] *Chicago Daily Tribune* (Illinois), 17 April 1912.

Married man left his family in Sweden

Carlsson, August Sigfrid

The 28-year-old Carlsson was a married man. After he had left Sweden, his first-born son died, and shortly thereafter another son was born. The paper *Hemlandet* reported that Carlsson rented a farm in Östred, where his wife continued to live after his departure. Before that, they had owned a farm in Hunestad. His parents lived in Klef, Dagsås. Two sisters lived and worked as domestics in Varberg. Carlsson was on his way to his brother in Minnesota, presumably to earn money that he could share with his wife at home.[430]

Born February 12, 1884 in Dagsås parish, Halland (province and county), he was the son of Karl Magnus Johansson (born in 1844 in Älvsered parish, Halland) and Johanna Beata Andreasdotter (born in 1839 in Fagered, Halland). On December 27, 1907, August Sigfrid married Julia Bernhardina Stenström. Julia was born in 1839 in Fagered, Halland. Their first child, a son, died September 6, 1912, five months after his father had perished on the *Titanic.* Another son, Karl August Julius, was born 13 days later on September 19, 1912 in Öströd, Dagås.[431]

Having left his home on April 1, Carlsson departed April 6 from Copenhagen by train to Esbjerg, and sailed from to England. He was officially declared dead on March 8, 1920.

The Mansion House Fund paid 2,699 crowns to his widow and 875 crowns to his parents. His family and parents also received 5,466 crowns in damage claims, for a total compensation of $2,411.00.[432]

---

[430] *Hemlandet*, Chicago, May 21, 1912. It was not uncommon that heads of Swedish families emigrated to work in the U.S. to supplement their family's income.

[431] From the Swedish Church records, courtesy Björn-Åke Petersson, Kallinge, Sweden.

[432] www.encyclopedia-titanica.org.

Coachman bought a Danish waistcoat

Carlsson, Carl Robert

In 1908, Carlsson worked as a coachman for hire in Falkenberg. Having finished his initial military training, the 24-year-old was registered with the military authorities and needed permission to leave. Rather than doing so the legal way, he left Sweden without papers and bought what was known as a "Danish waistcoat," that included the necessary papers. He and his travel companion, Nils Hilding Jönsson, then sailed to England from Esbjerg on Denmark's west coast.

Born January 19, 1888 in Vessige parish, Halland (län and province), Carl Robert was the son of Emanuel Carlsson (born in 1854 in Vessige) and Anna Beata Bengtsdotter (born in 1857 also in Vessige). The family farmed at Lassagården, Sörby, Vessingebo, Halland.[433]

While waiting for the *Titanic* to sail, he sent a post card from Southampton to his home with a picture of the *Titanic* with a message saying, "...if I had known that it would go so smoothly, Anna could have come with me..." Anna was his sister, the youngest of his four siblings.

He was headed for the home of relatives in Huntley, Illinois. Although the Carlson family had declared that they were not in need of money, the Mansion House Fund paid them 875 crowns. The parents also received 1,366 crowns in damages, for a total compensation of $598.00.[434]

Sea Captain traveled in first class

Carlsson, Frans Olof

The 33-year-old Swedish-American sea captain received his captain's papers in New York and worked as a skipper in and out of New York. In April 1912, he was first mate on the liner *St. Louis.* When the liner became stranded in Southampton due to a coal strike, the company bought him a first class ticket on the *Titanic*. There is no apparent evidence of Carlson having visited Sweden in 1912, although he had a sister and aunt in Arvika, Värmland.

Carlson wrote a letter from Southampton dated April 8th to his sister and mother saying that the ship owned by his employer had been docked.[435]

---

[433] From Swedish Church records, courtesy Björn-Åke Petersson, Kallinge, Sweden.
[434] www.encyclopedia-titanica.org.
[435] *Hemlandet*, May 14, 1912.

Born September 29, 1878 in Glava parish, Värmland (parish and county), he was the son of the farmer Karl Magnus Nilsson (born in 1835 in Glava parish). Frans Olof had a stepmother by the name of Carolina Magnidotter (born in 1833 in Glava). He lived in Glava until 1899 when he moved to the Seaman House (Sjömanshuset) in Göteborg. Because he had not fulfilled his obligatory Swedish military service, he had to pay a fine. The church records noted that he was a sea captain and that he died April 14 [15], 1912.[436]

The land that he owned in Elmhurst, Long Island, went to his heirs. He had a half sister, Mrs. Caroline Carlson, living in Brooklyn at the time. There is no record of compensation.

Chicago-bound woman struggled in the water

Dahlberg, Gerda Ulrika

Miss Dahlberg, 22, had four sisters. She left her home to join one of her sisters, Signe Dahlberg, residing at Calumet Avenue in Chicago. Signe contacted the White Star offices repeatedly for three days before she received word that dashed her last hope of Gerda being alive. Another sister, Augusta Spetz, lived at 1734 Sedgwick Avenue, Chicago.

Born February 5,1890 in Norrlöt belonging to Näringsberg farm, Västerhaninge parish, Stockholm's län , Gerda was the daughter of the local police constable Karl Magnus Dahlberg (born in 1842 in Muskö, a separate parish in Västerhaninge *pastorat*, Stockholm's län) and his wife Margareta Ulrika Persdotter (born in 1850 in Västerhaninge parish). Gerda Ulrika emigrated March 26, 1912. The church records state that she was lost in the Atlantic Ocean on April 15, 1912.[437]

Gerda sailed on the *Calypso* from Göteborg, April 5, 1912, listed as being from V. Haninge and going to Chicago, Illinois.[438]

While on board the *Titanic*, she became acquainted with Karl Johnsson, who later said that he had recognized her as they both struggled in the water. Karl was saved, but Gerda perished. Her father wrote to the Swedish office for Foreign Affairs asking for assistance, saying that he and his wife were poor.[439]

---

436 From the Swedish Church records, courtesy Björn-Åke Petersson, Kallinge, Sweden. The Titanic sank on the 15h. It is not known when he emigrated. He probably came to England on a merchant ship as a member of the crew.

437 *Ibid.*

438 *Calypso* passenger records.

439 *Hemlandet,* May 14, 1912.

The Mansion House Fund paid 875 crowns to her parents. They also received 911 crowns in damage claims, for a total compensation of $476.00.[440]

Immigrant recruiter buried in Stanton, Iowa

Danbom, Ernst Gilbert Danbom

The American-born 34-year-old farmer and immigrant recruiter, Mr. Danbom, spelled his first name Ernest in the U.S. He received a commission from White Star Line for each immigrant he recruited and brought a substantial sum of cash with him when he left Sweden. He hoped that the money would help the family acquire a fruit farm in Turlock, California. He paid £14 for a family cabin, or about $68.00.

Born October 26, 1877 in Montgomery County, Iowa, he was the son of N. August Danbom, born about 1837 in Sweden and C. Annie Danbom, born about 1837 in Sweden. In 1900, the family lived in Frankfort, Montgomery County, Iowa. Danbom's parents were farmers. They had arrived in the U.S. in 1867. Their children living at home were, Ludvig, born in 1864 in Sweden, G. Andrew, born about 1876 in Iowa, G. Ernest, born in October 1877 in Iowa, N. Henry, born in February 1880 in Iowa, and A. Ada, born in October 1882 in Iowa.[441]

The Danbom family

When Danbom applied for a passport on September 24, 1910, he listed his occupation as laborer. He was 5 foot 9 ½ inches tall, had blue eyes and light hair. He swore that he was born in Montgomery County, Iowa.

On November 30, 1910, he married Anna Sigrid M. Brogren in Chicago (see profile below). Their son, Gilbert, was born in Kisa, Östergötland on November 16, 1911. The Danboms embarked on board the *Calypso* in Göteborg on April 5, 1912 with their residence listed as America and their destination as Aurora, Illinois.

Their traveling companions were their in-laws Alfrida and Anders Andersson, the Andersson children, and Anna Nysten from Kisa. Anna entered a lifeboat. She later said that she had seen all of her travel companions standing on the boat deck.

[440] www.encyclopedia-titanica.org.
[441] 1900 U.S. Census, www.ancestry.com.

The newly-weds went on their honeymoon to Sweden and remained with Mrs. Danbom's mother for about six months. Their son was born in Sweden five months prior to the fateful voyage. The Danboms were on their way home when their lives abruptly ended. Mr. Danbom left an elderly mother, Mrs. Augusta Danbom, and the following siblings: Victor Danbom, Detroit; Alfred Danbom, Stanton, Iowa; Andrew Danbom, Turlock, California and Henry and Augusta Danbom, at home. A half brother, Frank Danbom, reside in Dayton, Iowa. Mrs. Danbom left a sister, Mrs. Zakrison, in Winnipeg, Canada.[442]

The information about the couple varies. *The Manitoba Morning Free Press* wrote that Mr. Danbom was an American citizen who had married his wife in Winnipeg. They were returning to their home in Stanton, Iowa, after an extended honeymoon in Sweden, where a son was born to them.[443]

Mr. Danbom's body was recovered and brought to Halifax before being sent to Stanton, Iowa for burial. He carried $276.00 in cash and $30.00 in gold.

Data from the "Coroner's" files in Halifax, Nova Scotia

The body of Ernst Gilbert Danbom was recovered by the MACKAY-BENNETT as Body No. 197. The Halifax "Coroner's" first printed list has Danbom's personal effects tabulated as:

"CLOTHING - Black overcoat; dark suit; white pleated shirt; black boots. EFFECTS - Wedding ring, marked "S. B. T. E. G. D., June 6, '10"; gold watch and chain; knife; keys; opal and ruby ring; fountain pen; bracelet; ladies watch and chain; knife; 3 memo books; solitaire diamond ring; scissors; U. S. A. naturalization papers; cheque $1,315.79, Security Bank, Sioux City; pocketbook; jewel case; pin; $266.00 in notes; $30.00 in gold."[444]

The inscription on his tombstone reads:

Ernest Danbom
26 Oct 1877~15 Apr 1912
Died 15 Apr 1912, in Titanic Disaster, His Remains Were Recovered From the Ocean. "Nearer My God To Thee."[445]

---

[442] *Hemlandet,* Chicago, April 30, 1912.
[443] Published Saturday, April 20, 1912. *Hemlandet* wrote that they were married in Chicago.
[444] www.encyclopedia-titanica.org
[445] Iowa Cemetery Records, Mamrelund Cemetery, Stanton, Iowa, Grave Records of Montgomery County, Iowa, www.ancestry.com.

Wife and mother lost at sea

Danbom, Anna Sigrid M

Sigrid Danbom, nee Brogren, 28, was the Swedish-American wife of Ernst Gilbert Danbom and the sister of Alfrida Andersson, also onboard the *Titanic* and a victim of the disaster along with her large family. Their son, Gilbert, was born in Sweden, November 16, 1911.

Mrs. Danbom was born March 10, 1884 in Horn parish, Östergötland (county and parish), the daughter of Magnus Peter Constantin Brogren (born 1831 in Horn) and Anna Lena [or Lovisa] Johansdotter (born 1845 in Kisa parish, Östergötland).[446]

She had emigrated in 1905 from Horn parish as Miss Sigrid Brogren, sailing alone from Göteborg July 21 to Chicago. She lived in Canada for several years. The next time she sailed from Sweden, it was as Sigrid Danbom in 1912 with her husband and infant son.

Mr. and Mrs. Danbom boarded the *Calypso* in Göteborg April 5, 1912 with their residence listed as America and their destination as Aurora, Illinois.

They accompanied Anna's sister, Alfrida, and her husband, Anders Andersson, and their children, and the surviving neighbor Anna Nysten.[447]

The Manitoba Morning Free Press wrote that Sigrid had lived with her sister, Mrs. Zachrisson, in Winnipeg for several years and was deeply interested in church work. She was a favorite among the young people, and they waited anxiously to hear she was safe.[448]

The relatives were not considered to be in need of money from the relief fund, but 462 crowns and an 184 crowns in damage claim was paid to her mother, Anna Lovisa Brogren, for the loss of both daughters, Anna and Alfrida, for a total compensation of $172.00.

---

[446] From Swedish Church records courtesy Björn-Åke Petersson, Kallinge, Sweden.
[447] *Ibid.*
[448] Published Saturday, April 20, 1912.

Four-month-old boy was the youngest in the group

Danbom, Gilbert Sigvard E

The 4-month-old infant, born November 16, 1911 in Kisa, Östergötland, was the son of Ernst and Anna Danbom (see profiles above).

Swedish American kissed his wife goodbye

Dyker, Adolf Fredrik Dyker

The 23-year old Swedish American kissed his wife goodbye by Lifeboat 16 and stepped aside. Adolf was educated at a Latin school in Stockholm. He arrived in America on March 6, 1905 at the age of 16. In New Haven, Connecticut, he worked as a tram conductor. He met and married Anna Elisabeth Anderson in 191l, and they were building a house in New Haven. When his father in Sweden had died on December 1, 1911, the young couple went to Sweden to help settle the estate. Their address was 468 Washington Street, New Haven, Connecticut.

Born December 16, 1888, officially in Adolf Fredrik parish, Stockholm (but actually at sea while his parents sailed from New York to Göteborg), he was the son of the merchant and bookkeeper Gustaf Fredrik Dyker (born in 1835 in Stockholm, and Anna Lovisa Andersson (born in 1844 in Löt, Borg parish, Östergötland). In 1890 the family resided in Södertälje and in 1891 in Kungsholm parish, Stockholm. [449]

The paper *Hemlandet*, Chicago, spelled his surname, Düker, and wrote that his father operated a café at Uplandsgatan 11 in Stockholm. The place where Adolf died at sea was not far from the place where he had been born, the paper said.[450]

Dyker and his wife boarded the *Calypso* in Göteborg on April 5, 1912, as residents of America and New York as their destination.

The Mansion House Fund paid 874 crowns ($234.00) to his mother.[451]

---

[449] From the Swedish church records courtesy Björn-Åke Petersson, Kallinge, Sweden.

[450] *Hemlandet*, Chicago, May 21, 1912.

[451] www.encyclopedia-titanica.org.

Farmer's son headed for Joliet, Illinois

Edvardsson, Gustaf Hjalmar

Although Edvardsson was only 18 and too young for military service, he still bought his ticket in Copenhagen, probably because his travel companion, Ernst Aronsson, was of military age and needed permission from the Swedish authorities to leave Sweden.

Gustaf Hjalmar Edvardsson. Photo courtesy Gunter Bäbler, Switzerland

Born December 17, 1893, in Tofta Ljungby parish, Kronoberg's län, Gustaf was the son of farm owner Edvard Johannesson (born September 30, 1856 in Ryssby parish, Kronoberg's län) and stepson of Emma Kristina Andersdotter (born in1864 in Angelstad parish, Kronoberg's län)

Gustaf lived at Tofta, Ljungby with his parents and two sisters, Ellen and Kristina, when he received his emigration certificate in Tofta Ljungby, March 30, 1912. [452]

Edvardsson and Aronsson were headed for the home of a cousin, Claes Bengtsson, 200 Ridgewood Avenue, Joliet, Illinois. Gustaf had a brother, Carl Edvardsson in East Highlands, California. [453]

The Mansion House Fund paid 875 crowns to his parents and 911 crowns to his sisters. On October 5, 1914, his widowed stepmother and the guardian for his underage sisters received 1,663 crowns in damage claims, for a total compensation of $920.00.[454]

16-year old was on his way to Arizona

Eklund, Hans Linus

The 16-year-old emigrant was raised by his grandmother. He was born October 30, 1895 in Kårberg, Snavlunda parish, Örebro län, to Augusta Amalia Albertina Eklund, a single mother, born 1874 in Lerbäck parish, Örebro län. Her parents were Anders August Eklund (born in 1838 in Ljus-

[452] Information courtesy Björn-Åke Petersson, Kallinge, Sweden.
[453] *Hemlandet*, Chicago, May 21, 1912.
[454] www.encyclopedia-titanica.org.

narsberg parish, Örebro län) and Klara Sofia Berggren (born in 1848 in Lerbäck parish). Eklund's death on the *Titanic* was noted in the church register.[455]

Hans Eklund. Photo courtesy Gunter Bäbler, Switzerland

He traveled from Kårberg to Göteborg, where he boarded the *Calypso* on April 5, 1912 listing his residence in Sweden as Snavlunda, Örebro, and his destination as Prescott, Arizona. His brother Bernhard Eklund lived at Jerome Junction, Arizona.

Hans Eklund, a general laborer, probably helped support his mother as the only other known relative was the brother in Arizona.

The Mansion House Fund paid 2,700 crowns to his mother, or about $720.00.[456]

South Dakota Swede brought his elderly father

Ekstrom, John

The 45-year-old Swedish-American was a farmer in New Effington, South Dakota. His earlier name in Sweden was Amandus Johansson. He was on his way from Nennesmo, Reftele to his home in New Effington together with his recently widowed father. His father, Johan Svensson, did not want to leave Sweden and cried when they departed. Both men went down with the ship. [457]

Born July 29, 1866 in Reftele, Jönköping's län, he was the son of Johan Svensson (born May 19, 1837 in Kulltorp parish, Jönköping's län) and Brita Lisa Börjesdotter (born April 11, 1837 in Refteled, and died February 6, 1912). John had two brothers. His brother Janne Leander was born August

---

[455] From the Swedish Church records, courtesy Björn-Åke Peterson, Kallinge, Sweden. Eklund's father was not listed.
[456] www.encyclopedia-titanica.org.
[457] www.ancestry.com and www.encyclopedia-titanica.org. There is no information about compensation to his wife and children.

22, 1870 and moved to Mossebo in 1886. The last record of Janne in Sweden was in 1889 when he reported to the parish that he was moving to Broaryd, but did not register there. He may have left for America. His other brother, Oskar Fridolf, was born September 22, 1882 in Reftele and emigrated November 6, 1902. A married sister, Mrs. John Larson, lived at 165 Chatham St. New Haven, Connecticut. The parents lived on a small rented farm, Normans, belonging to Nennesmo Korsgård farm in Reftele. [458]

Ekstrom farmed in New Effington together with a brother. The 1910 U.S. Census for Hart, Roberts, South Dakota, listed him as John Ekstrom, 43, general farmer, who had arrived in the U.S. in 1889. His wife, Annie, was 35 years old. They had five children. The eldest was 16-year-old Edgar O. The other children were Lilly M., Myrtle, Robert C., Mabel, and Bernard V. Also living in the household was Mary Larson, 77.

The paper *Hemlandet,* Chicago, wrote on May 21, 1912, that Ekstrom had six children, three brothers and one sister, Mrs. A. Larson, New Haven, Connecticut.

Ekstrom boarded the *Calypso* in Göteborg on April 5, 1912, listing his residence as America and his destination as New York.

The editor of a Swedish-language newspaper in Worcester wrote about the Ekstrom connection with New Haven, Connecticut.

Several New Haven Swedes are in mourning due to the awful sea disaster, among them Mrs. John Larson, 165 Chatham Street, whose 75-year-old father and eldest brother were on board. The father's name was John Svenson, and his son .... was John Ekstrom, who together with a brother was a farmer in South Dakota. They had planned to come here to New Haven, where the father was to stay for some time before going to his son's home. Mr. Ekstrom has a wife and six children in South Dakota, who now mourn him as presumed dead. Mrs. Larson's mother died last winter and the old man had no one at home to care for him because all his children are in this country. He was from Refteled parish in Småland. Mrs. Larson almost had a heart attack when she received a letter saying that they were on board the Titanic just after she had read about the disaster in the newspaper. Mrs. Larson is certain that they have perished.[459]

A great niece of John Ekstrom sent information to Dalesburg, South Dakota that included a copy of an old article reprinted in 1999 in a Browns Valley, Minnesota newspaper, which said that Mrs. John Ekstrom, residing on

---

[458] From the Swedish Church records, courtesy Björn-Åke Petersson, Kallinge, Sweden.

[459] *Skandinavia*, Worcester, Mass., April 24, 1912, p. 20. The original text was in Swedish.

a farm near Effington, received a gift of $3,600 from the Red Cross Relief society.

Mrs. Ekstrom's husband had been on a visit to the old country and was one of the victims of the *Titanic* disaster. The money which was sent to the Brown Valley State bank paid for the mortgage on the farm which was for the same amount, the article said. There was no mention of any other compensation.

According the great niece, John had settled on a homestead in Roberts County. His wife, Anna Larson, was born in Minnesota, December 25, 1874 and died March 3, 1948. They were married February 9, 1893. The couple had the following children: Edgar, Lillie, Lulu (died in infancy), Myrtle, Robert, Mabel, and Bernard. Mabel, born March 8, 1908, was the only one who had children: In 1928, she married Carl Hawkinson (1900-1969), and they raised four children: Harlan, who married Betsey, had one daughter; Robert, who married Rita, had one daughter; Janet, who married Chester Adams, and had one son and two grandchildren.[460].

Man from Göteborg traveled as tourist

Enander, Ingvar

The 21-year-old Enander was the fiancé of Dagmar Bryhl. Traveling with them in second class was Dagmar's brother, Kurt Bryhl. Dagmar was the only survivor of the three. Enander paid £13 for his ticket, or about $63.00.

Enander was born December 26, 1890 in Kristine parish, Göteborg, the son of merchant Axel Wilhelm Enander (born in 1858 in Borås, Älvsborg's län) and his wife Hilda Elisabeth Bohle (born in 1858 in the Garrison parish, Göteborg). In 1890, they resided, in Kristine parish, and in 1900 in Gustavi parish, Göteborg. In 1903 the family moved to Masthugget in Oscar Fredrik's parish, and in 1906 they resided in Haga parish before moving back to Masthugget. In 1908, they lived in the newly formed Annedal parish. In 1912, Ingvar was registered in Annedal until April 2. A note in the records said that according to a message from the White Star Line, he had probably perished on the *Titanic*.[461]

Enander left his residence at Olivedalsgatan 1, Göteborg and boarded the *Calypso* in Göteborg on April 5, 1912, together with his fiancée Dagmar Bryhl

---

[460] The letter was written by Corrine Walness, granddaughter of Oscar Svensson, who was John Ekstrom's brother. Information courtesy of Ron Johnson, Dalesburg, S. D.

[461] From the Swedish Church records, courtesy Björn-Åke Petersson, Kallinge, Sweden.

Lustig and her brother, Kurt Bryhl Lustig. Kurt and Dagmar resided in Skara. Their destination was Rockford, Illinois.

The three boarded the *Titanic* as second-class passengers. They planned to visit the Bryhl's uncle, Oskar Lustig, at 511 Pearl St. Rockford, Illinois. Enander's body was never found. His father had written that he wore a blue dress jacket and a gray overcoat, and that he had carried a penknife with a mother-of-pearl handle, a watch with a gold chain, his wallet, tickets, and a box with valuables. He also carried Dagmar's red slippers in a pocket of his overcoat.

The paper *Hemlandet*, Chicago, wrote on May 21, 1912 that Enander had planned to study agriculture while in the United States.

His parents failed to sue the White Star Line until it was too late.[462]

18-year old borrowed money for his ticket

Fischer, Eberhart Thelander

The 18-year-old Fischer was misidentified as Danish or German in several passenger lists, but he was a native of Sweden and so were his parents. He worked in a factory near his home and borrowed money to pay for his ticket. When he left, he said to his nephew, Herman, "When I come back you'll surely be a grown man."

Born June 2, 1893 in Farstorp parish, Kristianstad län, he was the son of Edvard Fischer (born in 1859 in Verum, Kristianstad län) and Johanna Nilsdotter (born in 1865 in Farstorp).

The family lived in Skeinge, Verum parish in 1900. Eberhart is not listed as having emigrated from Verum in 1912.[463]

The problem with the spelling of foreign place names is evident in the White Star Line list where his address is written as "Bjor Kerbergo, Ousby."[464]

The Fischers had six other children. Eberhart travelled with Olof Svensson, 24, also a victim. They bought their tickets in Copenhagen. Eberhart wrote a letter to his home from Southampton.

The Mansion House Fund paid 875 crowns to parents. Damage claims were paid later in the amount of 911 crowns, for a total compensation of $476.00.

---

462 www.encyclopedia-titanica.org.
463 From Swedish Church records, courtesy Björn-Åke Petersson, Kallinge, Sweden.
464 *Ibid.*

Widow's son headed for South Dakota

Gustafsson, Karl Gideon

According to the White Star Line, the 18-year-old emigrant was on his way to his sister, Evelina Johnson, 6 East 64th St., New York, but the *Calypso* passenger embarkation records in Göteborg list his destination as Aberdeen, South Dakota.

Born April 10, 1893 in Skallmeja parish, Skaraborg's län, he was the son of Stina Greta Johansson, apparently a widow as her maiden name was Andersdotter. She was born in 1856 in Skallmeja. In 1900, Gideon lived with his mother in Synnerby parish, Skaraborg's län.[465]

The Mansion House Fund paid his mother 1,057 crowns. Later, she received 1,366 crowns in damage claims for a total amount of $646.00.

Maid from Stockholm buried in Halifax

Henriksson, Jenny Lovisa

Miss Henriksson, 28, had planned her emigration for a long time, and when the Skoog family had decided to return to Iron Mountain, Michigan, she and her friend, Ellen Pettersson, accompanied them. All in the party perished. Jenny's last employment in Sweden was as a maid for C. Påhlman, the senior accountant at a Stockholm bank. Earlier, she had worked as a housekeeper for the Lustig family in Skara and knew the siblings Kurt and Dagmar Bryhl. Her destination was Olaus Rask, 805 East Second St., Iron Mountain, Michigan.

Jenny was born December 21, 1883 in Österplana parish, Skaraborg's län, the daughter of Per Henrik Larsson (born in 1855 in Medelplana, Skaraborg's län) and Emma Christina Pettersdotter (born in 1863 in Västerplana parish, Skaraborg's län). In 1900, the family lived at Härlingstorp, Norra Ving parish, Skaraborg's län. Jenny had moved to Stockholm in 1906.[466].

Listing her residence as Stockholm, Jenny sailed on the *Calypso* from Göteborg together with the Skoog family, all with the destination of Iron Mountain, Michigan

Jenny is buried in the Fairview Lawn Cemetery in Halifax. For many years, her body was unidentified although her clothes were marked with her initials, J. H. She wore a 'cholera belt' because she was afraid of the disease. The belt was impregnated with an ill-smelling fluid that was supposed to keep

---

[465] From Swedish Church records, courtesy, Björn-Åke Petersson, Kallinge, Sweden.
[466] *Ibid.*

the cholera away. It also had pockets for cash. Her recovered clothing included two jackets, one gray and one red, a blue shirt, a blue skirt, black stockings and boots, and gray gloves.

The Mansion House Fund paid 875 crowns to her parents. Her father later received 911 crowns in damage claims. The total amount of compensation was $476.00.[467]

Sea captain hoped to earn good money in New York

Holm, John Fredrik Alexander

The 43-year-old Swedish American was educated at the navigation school in Karlshamn, Blekinge, and worked as a skipper in New York. On his return to Sweden, he became engaged to Emmy Tanngren, the daughter of a ship owner in Karlshamn. Captain Holm decided to return to America to work a while longer at a Yacht Club in Brooklyn, New York, where he had high hopes of making enough money to return to his fiancée in Sweden and start a new life.

Born February 20, 1869 in Tingsryd, Kronoberg's län to a single mother, he was raised by foster parents. His mother, Elsa Nilsson, was born August 6, 1843 in Anderslöv, Malmöhus län. She was registered in Örmo, Södra Sandsjö parish, Kronoberg's län, but may have resided at Klarabergsvägen 69, Stockholm.

In 1879, the ten-year-old John Fredrik moved from Stockholm to live with foster parents in Karlshamn, Blekinge. His foster parents were Charlotta and Nils Peter Johansson (born in 1839 in Asarum, Blekinge) and Charlotta Lovisa Wahlin (born in 1845 in Södra Sandsjö, Kronoberg's län).[468]

The foster parents, residing at Hamngatan 394, Karlshamn, always regarded John as their own son. When the foster father died in 1912, his wife became dependent on John's income. John Holm traveled via Denmark, and probably bought his ticket in Copenhagen, where he met Adelia Landergren and Mauritz Ådahl, also traveling from Karlshamn. After the collision with the iceberg, Holm and Ådahl helped Adelia into lifeboat 13, and stepped back.

---

[467] www.encyclopedia-titanica.org. In 1991, Jenny's clothes finally helped identify her remains.

[468] From Swedish Church records, courtesy Björn-Åke Petersson, Kallinge, Sweden. Holm's mother, supported herself as a maid . She had moved to Stockholm from Västra Skrävlinge, Malmöhus län Nov. 21, 1867. In 1873 she moved to Stockholm from the parsonage in Alsike, Uppsala län, where she had worked as a domestic. In 1875, she moved with her son to Klara parish, Stockholm. In 1879, she moved to Stockholm from Södertälje. She worked for many years in the home of the military physician John Wilhelm von Döbeln.

The Mansion House Fund paid 875 crowns to the mother, Elsa Nilsson, and 911 crowns to the foster mother, Charlotta Johansson. In 1914, Elsa Nilsson received 2,733 crowns in damage claims. The total amount of compensation was $1,205.00.

Smålänning's body buried at sea

Johansson, Erik

The 22-year-old emigrant, headed for St. Paul, Minnesota, probably bought his ticket in Copenhagen to avoid the military authorities in Sweden.

Born October 14, 1889 in Frostensmåla, Vissefjärda parish, Kalmar län, he was the son of farm owner Peter Magnus Johansson (born July 13, 1850 in Långasjö, Kronoberg's län) and Anna Maria Olausdotter (born April 12, 1850 in Vissefjärda).

In 1912, Erik Johansson resided in Frostensmåla and was not listed as having emigrated; however his date of death is noted as April 15, 1912. In *Svenska Centralbyrån's* records, his death is listed with the following notation, "His body found and identified and brought to Halifax to be buried according to report from the White Star Line office in Copenhagen."[469]

Actually, his body was recovered by *MacKay Bennett* and buried at sea April 24. He was dressed in a gray suit and wore no shoes.

The Mansion House Fund paid 875 crowns to his parents. They also received 1,366 crows in damage claims, for a total compensation of $598.00.[470]

Future farmer buried in Halifax

Johansson, Gustaf Joel

The 33-year-old emigrant had planned to become a farmer in North Dakota.

Born March 2, 1879, in Bockby, Åker parish, Jönköping's län, he was the son of farm owner Johan Bengtsson ((born October 11, 1834 in Åker parish) and Anna Johannisdotter (1852-1905 in Åker) The Swedish church records

[469] Information courtesy Björn-Åke Petersson, Kallinge, Sweden. Svenska Central Byrån (SCB) was the Bureau of Swedish Statistics.
[470] www.encyclopedia-titanica.org.

also show that Gustaf emigrated April 2, 1912, and was lost when the steamer *Titanic* sank April 15, 1912.[471]

Gustaf Joel Johansson. Photo courtesy Günter Bäbler, Switzerland

Gustaf boarded the *Calypso* in Göteborg on April 5, 1912, listing his residence as Åker, Jönköping's län and his destination as Eddy, North Dakota.

Traveling with Malkolm Johnson, Gustaf intended to continue to Sheyenne, North Dakota. Malkolm also perished. Johansson's body was recovered and buried in Halifax. Among his effects was a diary with Emil Anderson's name and address in North Dakota. The Consulate in New York wrote to Anderson and asked for details. Anderson answered that he had sent the ticket to Johansson, who had no relatives in the U.S. Anderson was also acquainted with Malkolm Johnson. Johnson's belongings were sent to his father in Sweden. They included $26.00, an empty wallet, and a pocket comb with mirror. Gustaf was buried in the Fairview cemetery, Halifax, Canada.

The Mansion House Fund paid 875 crowns to his father, who also received 1,366 crowns in damage claims for a total of $598.00.[472]

Stucco worker's fiancée safe at home

Johansson, Karl Johan

The 33-year-old Swedish American had emigrated in 1903 and settled in Duluth, Minnesota, where he was employed as a stucco worker and went by the name of Carl Johnson. On his return to Sweden in 1911, he became engaged to his childhood sweetheart, Berta Elisabeth Olsson of Myckleby, and planned to bring her to U.S. in the fall.

Born September 9, 1880 in Gustavi parish, Göteborg, Göteborg's and Bohus län, he was the son of Johan Niclas Olson (born in 1852 in Myckleby,

---

[471] Information courtesy Björn-Åke Petersson, Kallinge, Sweden.
[472] www.encyclopedia-titanica.org.

same county) and Carolina Pehrsdotter (born in 1859 in Bokenäs parish, same county).[473] They had another son named Axel Leonard.

Karl Johan and his fiancée planned to travel together to Duluth in the fall of 1912, but his friends Oscar Olsson (Oscar W. Johansson) and Samuel Niklasson convinced him to leave earlier. Berta was to follow on the *Olympic* later in the year. He may have shared a cabin with Oscar Hedman and Malkolm Johnson.

Karl boarded the *Calypso* in Göteborg, April 5, 1912, as Carl Johnson, residing in America with the destination of Duluth, Minnesota.

Berta later married a widower, and they lived at her parents' home in Hällebord, where she died in 1948. Karl Johan's father, Johan, had pictures of the *Titanic* and the *Olympic* hanging over his bed, and a portrait of his son between them.

The Mansion House Fund paid 875 crowns to Karl Johan's parents, who also received 1,826 crowns in damage claims, for a total compensation of $720.00.[474]

Give my regards to Father and Mother"

Johansson, Nils Johan

The 29-year-old Swedish American had worked as a machine smith for eight years in the U.S. He was engaged to his cousin, Olga Lundin, who also sailed on the *Titanic*.[475]

Following his visit to Sweden, he sailed from Malmö, April 5, 1912, listing his destination as Chicago. Olga went to Meriden, Connecticut, after her rescue. [476]

Born July 4, 1881 in Ulvberga, Hallaryd, Kronoberg's län, Nils was the son of Johannes Carlsson (born in 1845 in Visseltofta, Kristianstad län) and Ingrid (Ingjer) Eriksdotter (born in 1855 in Hallaryd). Nils Johansson emigrated from Kråkeryd Södergård, Svanaryd, Hallaryd in 1903.[477]

---

[473] From the Swedish Church records, courtesy Björn-Åke Petersson, Kallinge, Sweden.

[474] www.encyclopedia-titanica.org.

[475] Nils's mother and Olga's mother, Gustava Eriksdotter, were sisters. Nils, who was related to the Måhlgren family of blacksmiths, was a second cousin of Karl Johnson. Information, Cecilia Månsson, Sweden.

[476] *Emigranten Populär.*

[477] From the Swedish Church records, courtesy Björn-Åke Petersson, Kallinge, Sweden.

One brother, Alfred, born in 1888, had emigrated to Brainerd, Minnesota in 1906, giving his destination as N. Carlson, 1716 Maple Street.[478]

Nils had seven other siblings: Albina (1879-1894), Augusta, born in 1883, Karolina, born in 1884, Edvard, born in 1886 (blacksmith), Olof, born in 1890 (blacksmith), emigrated in 1910, Nelly, (1892-1893) Karl (1895-1896), Ester, born in 1899 (may have emigrated as Ester Carlsson in 1920).[479]

His travel companions were Olga Lundin, Paul Andreasson, Albert Augustsson, all from Hallaryd, and Karl Johnsson from Killeberg. In 1912, Nils listed his final destination as that of this uncle, Oscar Benson at 110 North Ashland, Chicago.

Nils Johansson. Photo courtesy Gunter Bäbler, Switzerland

When Olga could no longer stand the sea in third class, Nils paid the difference in price and procured a place for her in second class. Once separated, they could only communicate from a distance and had to shout to one another.

Olga survived and told her agonizing story of having to part with Nils and her friends when she was put into the lifeboat. Nils's last words to Olga when her lifeboat was lowered were, "Give my regards to father and mother." Except for Karl Johnsson from Killeberg, the men in this group perished.

Johansson had told his parents that he was the co-owner of a factory and property and that he had a life insurance worth $1,000.00. He added that John Hedman, 1716 Maple St. Brainerd, Minnesota, was taking care of the insurance premiums while he was away.[480]

Investigations in 1913 showed that the insurance with "Modern Brotherhood of America" was worthless. There was no property and the

---

[478] This was the address of John Hedman. N. Carlson is apparently identical with Nils Johansson. Information courtesy Cecilia Månsson, Sweden.

[479] Information Cecilia Månsson, Sweden.

[480] Nils may also have lived in Brainerd at one time. His name appears as Nils Carlson in the Minnesota State Census for 1905. Information courtesy Cecilia Månsson, Sweden.

factory in Seattle had gone broke.[481] (See also Olga Lundin in "The Swedish Survivors").

The Mansion House Fund paid 875 crowns to his parents. Later, they received 1,848 crowns in damage claims, for a total compensation of $726.00.

Minnesota Swede carried his money in his socks

Johnson, Malkolm Joakim

The 33-year-old Swedish American had immigrated to Minneapolis in 1902. His surname in Sweden had been Johannesson and his nickname Sever. His last address in America was 814 7th St., Minneapolis. Working as the manager of the concrete surfacing of the city streets, he had saved enough money to buy a farm in Sweden. When the purchase of a farm in Björnaryd did not work out, he decided to return to America. According to his relatives, he was in a bad mood because he had planned to settle in Sweden

Born March 20, 1879 in Klefshult, Åker parish, Jönköping's län, Malkolm was the son of Johannes Nilsson (born July 9, 1836 in Berga, Kronoberg's län) and Anna Katrina Svensdotter (born June 14, 1845 in Byarum, Jönköping's län).

Following the death of Malkolm's father, his mother married Isak Leonard Jonasson, born September 28, 1851 in Byarum. In 1890, the family lived in Björnaryd, Åker parish, Jönköping's län.[482] .

Malkolm boarded the *Calypso* in Göteborg, April 5, 1912, reporting his residence as America and his destination as New York.

He traveled with Gustaf Joel Johansson, but on the *Titanic* he shared a cabin with Oscar Hedman.

According to his brother, Wilhelm Nilsson, Malkolm had sewn $2,150 in dollar bills into his socks. His body was found by *Mackay Bennett* (#37) and taken to Halifax. His brother wrote to *Utrikesdepartementet* (Office for Foreign Affairs) several times, which in turn contacted the Swedish Embassy in New York. According to the list of clothing, Malkolm wore boots but no socks, and was otherwise properly dressed, which made the embassy expect foul play. All in authority denied any knowledge of anything improper, and the mystery of the missing socks was never solved. But together with Malkolm's other belongings sent to Sweden, there was a check in the amount of $1,200.00 and the rest of his cash ($206.00 minus expenses).

---

481 www.encyclopedia-titanica.org. This may or may not be correct. His destination was Chicago and not Seattle.

482 Information courtesy Björn-Åke Petersson, Kallinge, Sweden.

His effects included a gold watch and chain, a diamond set, a diamond solitaire ring, and $165.00 in cash. At *Titanic's* average fare, one writer commented, he could have crossed the Atlantic 30 times using the money he carried."[483]

Malkolm Johnson was buried in the Fairview Cemetery in Halifax. The Mansion House Fund paid 875 crowns to his parents and 456 crowns to his brother. In 1914, a damage claim was paid in the amount of 1,908 crowns. The total amount of compensation was $864.00.

Farmer bought his ticket in Copenhagen

Jönsson, Nils Hilding

According to Swedish church registers, the 27-year-old emigrant leased a farm in Sweden. Rather than continuing the patronymic name tradition, he kept his father's surname of Jönsson. His emigration certificate was dated March 22, 1912. Being of military age, he bought his ticket in Copenhagen, as did his traveling companion Carl Robert Carlsson of Vessingebo, Halland.

Born February 5, 1885 in Tågarp, Vinberg parish, Halland, he was the son of Nils Jönsson (born in 1838 in Grönby, Malmöhus län) and Olivia Kristina Carlsdotter (born in 1850 in Vinberg). He had one brother and four sisters.[484] One brother had emigrated in 1907 and lived in Minnesota.

The County Sheriff wrote that the parents were not in need of aid. They still received 874 crowns from the Mansion House Fund, and in 1914, the father received 455 crowns in damage claims. The total amounted to $354.00.[485]

Inventor planned to register his patents in the U.S.

Karlsson, Julius Konrad Eugen

The 33-year-old Karlsson was a married man. He had invented an automatic shuttle changer for looms and hoped to obtain a patent in the U.S. His wife planned to join him in the fall of 1912. According to one newspaper report, Karlsson had traveled widely and had lived in England. His wife lived in Göteborg. He was described as a self-made man, who, early on, supported himself by working in a factory. By sheer determination, he managed to

[483] Chris Kohl, *Titanic: The Great Lakes Connection*, p. 118.
[484] Swedish Church records courtesy Björn-Åke Petersson, Kallinge, Sweden.
[485] www.encyclopedia-titanica.org.

educate himself and graduate from the Leninska Weaving School in Norrköping.[486]

Born September 29, 1878 in Östra Ny parish, Östergötland's län, he was the son of Anders Samuel Carlsson (born in 1849 in Å parish, Östergötland's län) and Augusta Kristina Andersdotter (born in 1857 in Östra Ny parish). Having lived in Stockholm since 1898, Julius moved to Malmö, Malmöhus län in 1907. In 1908, his parents lived in Barken, Norra Matteus parish, Norrköping, Östergötland's län.[487]

Another source gives the family's address in 1912 as Luntgatan 8, Norrköping. The father was a carpenter, but since the parents did not have the money to fund their son's education, Julius financed it himself. Having developed an interest in looms, he studied in Finland for a few years, and later graduated from a weaving school, after which he obtained employment as a weaving instructor in a textile factory in Vejle, Denmark. In Göteborg he worked for Claes Johansson-Marks, a mechanical workshop. Julius Karlsson was an engineer and inventor.[488]

He resided at Annelund 5, Krokslätt, Göteborg, with his wife, Adelaide Fredrika Karlsson (nee Gran). Although his reason for going to the U.S. was to arrange for patent registrations, he probably planned to settle there, because his wife mentioned that she had intended to join him in the autumn. Julius had a child outside of marriage by the name of Klas Julius Öjvind Hottsberg, who later resided in Oslo. The son was born while Julius lived in Denmark and was the result of a liaison with the shop assistant Alerine Margerethe Sørensen.

He left Malmö April 5, 1912, listed as "vävtagare" (master weaver?). His last residence was listed as St. Johannes Parish, Malmöhus län, and his destination as Chicago.

The Mansion House Fund paid 1,787 crowns to his wife, 875 crowns to his parents and 1,276 crowns to his mother-in-law. In 1914, his wife received 2,733 crowns in damage claims, his father 1,966, and his mother 766 crowns. [His parents were divorced at the time.] The total amount of compensation came to $9,403 crowns or $2,507.00.

---

[486] *Hemlandet,* Chicago, wrote on May 21, 28.
[487] From Swedish Church records, courtesy Björn-Åke Petersson, Kallinge, Sweden.
[488] www.encyclopedia-titanica.org.

Single man planned to settle in Massachusetts

Karlson, Nils August

The 22-year-old single emigrant likely sought to avoid his Swedish military service by going to Copenhagen to buy his ticket. Nils August had one brother and one sister. His last residence was Örebro and his destination Palmer, Massachusetts, where a sister, Mrs. A. Gran, resided.

Born August 14, 1889 in Nicolai parish, Örebro, Örebro län, he was the son of Carl Gustaf Karlsson (born in 1845 in Edsberg, Örebro län) and Leontina Charlotta Lund (born in 1844 in Lerbäck parish, Örebro län). In 1910, Nils August still lived with his parents.[489]

The Mansion House Fund paid 875 crowns to his father. In 1914, his father, who probably depended on his son's earnings, received 1,366 crowns in damage claims, for a total compensation of $598.00.[490]

Los Angeles dressmaker had visited Gotland

Klasén, Hulda Kristina

The 36-year-old widowed Swedish American woman was a dressmaker living in Los Angeles, California. In 1912, she visited Gotland, and on her way back, she brought her niece, Hulda Amanda Adolfina Vestrom, the daughter of Hulda's sister, Emma Josefina Fredrika and Oscar Adolf Westrom (The father lived in the U.S.). Hulda also traveled with the infant girl Gertrude Klasėn living in Fliseryd on the same ticket. Gertrude was the niece of Klas Albin Klasėn, also a *Titanic* victim, and Klas was her brother-in-law.

Born March 18, 1876 in Vänge parish, Gotland's län, Hulda was the daughter of Peter Edvard Löfqvist (born in 1832 in Gammelgarn, Vänge parish) and Johanna Sofia Helena Löfgren (1838-1895 in Vänge). Hulda had four siblings: Wendla Johanna Maria, born in 1865, Ida Olivia Amanda, born in 1868, Emma Josefina Fredrika, born in 1872 (married to Oscar Adolf Weström), and Petter Emil Fredrik, born in 1878. Hulda had immigrated to America already on August 21, 1895. She lived at home from July 27 to October 17, 1902. Hulda's husband may have been Karl Gustaf Klasson, born November 11, 1873 in Grimshult, Fliseryd parish, Kalmar län. He immigrated to Chicago in 1892.[491]

The Klaséns have not been found in the official Swedish departure records. Hulda probably bought the tickets for her niece and the infant girl.

---

[489] From Swedish Church records courtesy Björn-Åke Petersson, Kallinge, Sweden. Not found in any Swedish embarkation records.
[490] www.encyclopedia-titanica.org.
[491] From Swedish Church records, courtesy Judy Baouab of Chicago.

Their destination was Los Angeles, California. On the *Titanic*, Hulda met up with a group of third-class passengers led by Thure Edvin Lundström.

The following obituary appeared in the newspaper *Gotlands Allehanda* in 1912 beside the one for Hulda Amanda Adolfina Veström:

It is my sad duty to announce that my beloved daughter, Hulda Kristina Eugenia Clasėn, nee Lofqvist, perished in the sadly ill-fated Titanic collision in the Atlantic, and is sincerely and deeply mourned by me, siblings, nephews, nieces, parents-in-law, relatives and many friends at an age of 36 years and 27 days. Salmunds in Vänge, April 27, 1912. Petter Löfqvist. She always did her best. [492]

The Mansion House Fund paid 1,787 crowns to her father and 1,276 crowns to her sister, for a total compensation of $817.00. No damage claims were made as her father died before legal processes could begin and the lawyers concluded that nobody else was dependent on her.[493]

Young man emigrated with his infant niece

Klasén, Klas Albin

The 18-year-old Klas Albin emigrated from Fliseryd together with his niece the infant girl, Gertrud Emilia. Their emigration certificates were dated March 22, 1912. The two were accompanied by his Swedish-American sister-in-law Hulda Klasén. All perished. The White Star manifest listed their destination as Los Angeles. Since Klas is not reported as having left from Malmö or Göteborg, he probably bought his tickets in Copenhagen.

Born July 17, 1893 in Grimshult, Fliseryd, Kalmar län, Klas Albin was the son of Klas Viktor Klasson, born Nov. 15, 1851 in Fliseryd, and Johanna Mathilda Jonsdotter, born July 30, 1856 in Mönsterås, Kalmar län. The family had moved from Grimshult 2 to Grimshult 1 in 1888.[494]

The Mansion House Fund paid 1,787 crowns to his parents. In 1914, his father received 1,822 crowns in damage claims, for a total amount of $962.00.[495]

---

[492] *Gotlands Allehanda*, 1912. When translated, the word order was changed for easier reading. From this obituary it is clear that Hulda had been married and that her husband was deceased. www.titanicnorden.com. Courtesy Jonas Söderström.
[493] www.encyclopedia-titanica.org.
[494] Information courtesy Björn-Åke Petersson, Kallinge, Sweden.
[495] www.encyclopedia-titanica.org.

The infant girl was 18-months old

Klasén, Gertrud Emilia

The 18-month-old Gertrud was accompanied by her relative Hulda Klasén and her uncle Klas Klasén. Their destination was Los Angeles. All three perished. Gertrud was listed on the same ticket as Hulda Klasėn (See profile above).

Born July 17 1893 in Fliseryd parish, Kalmar län, Gertrude was the daughter of Alice Ester Amanda Klasson (born August 15, 1890 at Grimshult 2, Fliseryd parish, Kalmar län. Her mother had emigrated March 27, 1911.[496]

Engineer buried in Halifax

Kvillner, Johan Henrik

The 32-year-old engineer had received a government scholarship to study iron construction in the U.S. Financing his own studies, he graduated as an engineer and changed his surname from Johannesson to Kvillner.

He worked for several years for the line construction department of Trollhätte kanalverk (a hydro-electric power station) in Trollhättan, Älvsborg's län.[497]

Kvillner was engaged to Signe Kjellberg, Föreningsgatan 29, Göteborg. He paid £10 for his second-class ticket, or $49.00.

Born April 11, 1881 in Svenneby parish, Göteborg's & Bohus län, he was the son of shoemaker Johannes Olausson (born in 1835 in Bottna in the same county) and Elisabeth Eliasdotter, born in 1845 in Bottna. In 1890 and 1900, the parents lived in Högslätt, Svenneby. In 1900, their son, Johan Henrik, worked as hotel janitor in Göteborg.[498].

---

496 Information courtesy of Björn-Åke Petersson, Kallinge, Sweden.
497 *Hemlandet*, Chicago, May 21, 1912.
498 From Swedish Church records, courtesy of Björn-Åke Petersson, Kallinge, Sweden.

Johan Henrik Kvillner. Photo Courtesy Günter Bäbler, Switzerland.

Kvillner, of military age, has not been found in any official Swedish embarkation records, but is supposed to have sailed from Göteborg. On the *Titanic*, he was a second-class passenger, and his destination was the home of Miss Charlotte Larson, 393 Forest St. Arlington, New Jersey. On the night of the sinking of the Titanic, Kvillner was seen standing on deck with Ingvar Enander and Kurt Bryhl. They had been refused entry to a lifeboat and watched as Kurt's sister Dagmar was rowed away in Lifeboat 12.

Kvillner's body was recovered (body no. 165) and buried in the Fairview Lawn Cemetery in Halifax. His hair was listed as very fair. He wore a blue suit and carried a knife, comb, gold watch and chain, cigarette case, silver name plate, gold ring engraved "Signe 1911, 04 09," letters, passport, a number of coins in a purse, ten crowns, and $89.00 dollars in notes.

On January 23, 1913, the Mansion House Fund paid 1,420 crowns to his fiancée, Elisabeth Olsson, and 874 crowns to his mother, Elisabeth Olsson. She also received 2,918 crown in damages. The total amount of compensation was $1,390.00.[499]

Locksmith on his way to Stamford

Larsson, August Viktor

The 29-year-old married Swedish American had emigrated with the permission of the Swedish King on March 22, 1907. He had worked four years as a locksmith at the Yale and Towne Manufacturing Company in Stamford, Connecticut, while residing with Olaf Blomquist at 25 Division Street in Stamford. Having visited his sick wife, their daughter, and his parents-in-law in Sweden, Viktor was on his way home to Stamford.

Born February 25, 1883 in Eskilstuna parish, Södermanland's län, he was the son of Per August Larsson (born in 1859 in Öja parish, same county) and Sofia Vilhelmina Olsson (born in 1859 in Näshulta parish, same county). The family had resided in both Eskilstuna parish and the city of Eskilstuna. Viktor married Ingrid Elisabet Jonsson in Eskilstuna in 1906. She was born January

---

499 www.encyclopedia-titanica.org.

15, 1885 in Adolf Fredrik parish, Stockholm. They had a daughter, Göta Augusta Fredrika Elisabet (born December 8, 1905).[500]-

Due to Mrs. Larsson's poor health, she and their daughter lived in Eskilstuna, Sweden. Larson boarded the *Calypso* in Göteborg, April 5, 1912, listing his residence as America and his destination as New York.

His wife and daughter received 5,010 crowns ($1,336.00) in damages in 1915. The widow's father, Axel Jonsson, became the guardian of his granddaughter, Augusta, although he claimed that he was only able to support himself.[501]

Hartford-bound man had saved for years for his ticket

Larsson, Bengt Edvin

According to his father, the 29-year-old emigrant was of average height and had an honest and pleasant appearance. Others described Bengt as quiet and tranquil. It had taken him years to save for his ticket (181 crowns). He may have lived at Apelbergsgatan 37 in Stockholm and clerked in a grocery store on Drottninggatan for a short time. Once he was in Southampton, he sent a card to his parents. He was headed for Hartford, Connecticut, but planned to take over the family farm.

Born December 5, 1882 in Tulleru, Norra Vi parish, Östergötland's län, he was the son of Gustaf Edvard Larsson (born in 1839 in Norra Vi), and Hedda Charlotta Petersdotter (born in 1846 in Ekeby parish, Östergötland's län). Bengt Edvin's sister, Gerda Cecilia (born in 1879) resided in America, 1902-1907. On March 12, 1912, Bengt registered his move to Klara parish, Stockholm. He emigrated from there on April 2, 1912.[502]

Bengt boarded the *Calypso* in Göteborg, April 5, 1912, reporting his last residence as Stockholm and his destination as New York. The White Star Line listed his destination as the home of Axel Petersen, 70 Smith Street, Hartford, Connecticut.

The Mansion House Fund paid 875 crowns to his parents. In 1914 they received 911 crowns in damage claims, for a total compensation of $476.00.[503]

---

[500] From Swedish Church records, courtesy Björn-Åke Petersson, Kallinge, Sweden. In 1902, August Viktor moved to the city of Norrtälje, Stockholm's län, and from there he moved to Kristine parish, Göteborg, but the same year, he moved back to Eskilstuna. The permission of the King, e.g. his representative, was needed before emigration for men of military age.

[501] www.encyclopedia-titanica.org.

[502] From Swedish Church records, courtesy Björn-Åke Petersson, Kallinge, Sweden.

[503] *Emigranten Populär* and www.encyclopedia-titanica.org.

Montana Swede heading for home

Larsson, Edvard

In America, the 22-year-old Swedish American changed his name to Edward Rondberg. He lived and worked as a cook in Missoula, Montana. The paper *Hemlandet*, Chicago, wrote on May 21, 1912, that he had been in Sweden since the fall of 1911. The purpose of his visit was to accompany his fiancée, Berta Nilsson, to the U.S. Berta survived, while Edward stayed on the ship and perished.

Born December 2, 1889 in Ransbysäter, Lysvik parish, Värmland (province and county), he was the son of the farmer Lars Persson (born in 1858 in Lysvik) and Maria Nilsdotter (born in 1862 also in Lysvik). Edvard had emigrated April 11, 1908. The church book noted that Larsson perished in the sinking of the *Titanic*.[504]

He boarded the *Calypso* in Göteborg, April 5, 1912 as Edvard Larsson, with his residence listed as America and his destination as Missoula, Montana.

Edvard lived at 533 East Trent St. Missoula, Montana. His brother, Nils Rondberg, resided in Beaver, Montana.

The Mansion House Fund paid 874 crowns to his parents. In 1914, they received 1,366 crowns in damages. The total amount of compensation was $597.00.[505]

New York woman's brother refused to come with her

Lindahl, Agda Torilda Viktoria

The 25-year-old Swedish American Miss Lindahl made a living working as a waitress for a well-to-do family in New York. Except for her youngest brother, her entire family lived in the U.S. Agda was in Sweden to convince her brother to come with her to America. When he refused, she left alone.

Born December 19, 1886 in Jakob & Johannes parish, Stockholm, Uppsala län, Agda was the daughter of tailor Carl Petter Lindahl (born in 1864 in Vissefjärda parish, Kalmar län) and his wife, Johanna Matilda Carlsdotter (born in 1863 in Vissefjärda). The parents were married July 6, 1885, apparently in Stockholm. When Agda was born, they lived at Jacobsbergsgatan 13 A, Sqvalberget 22-23, in Hedvig Elenora parish, Ward 10. Agda had five siblings: Carl Gustaf, born in 1885, who emigrated in 1905,

---

[504] From the Swedish Church records, courtesy Björn-Åke Petersson, Kallinge, Sweden.

[505] www. encyclopedia-titanica.org.

Hugo Vilgot, who emigrated in 1905, Vilma Klotilda Isabella, born in 1890, who emigrated in 1905, *Vera* Lavina Matilda, born in 1895, and Alf Helge Tyko Roland, born in 1903, who stayed in Sweden and died February 13, 1966 in Madesjö parish, Kalmar län.

The records for 1897-1905 show Kajsa Lisa Karlsdotter, born December 24, 1861, also living with the family. Agda's father died of kidney disease at Sabbatsberg Hospital on June 22, 1904.[506]

The mother, Johanna Lindahl, had emigrated from her birth parish, Vissefjärda, Kalmar län, via the port of Malmö, on November 29, 1906 with her daughter Vera. Their destination was New York. She left behind, Helge, her youngest.[507]

Agda's father owned a tailor shop on Kommendörsgatan 16 in Stockholm, but when he died in 1904 his estate indicated that his business was failing. Therefore, the widow (Agda's mother) emigrated with her children, except two-year-old Helge, who was cared for by an aunt in Småland (possibly in Madesjö). In the U.S., the sons Hugo and Gustaf became ill and died at a young age.

Agda's mother, Hanna Lindahl, lived at 20 Woodruff St. Saranac Lake Franklin, New York. In 1912, the purpose of Agda's visit to her uncle, August Lindahl in Stockholm, was to bring Helge to the U.S., but he refused to leave. Agda boarded the *Calypso* in Göteborg, April 5, 1912. Her residence was listed as America and her destination as New York.

The Mansion House Fund paid 875 crowns ($233.00) to her mother. Her brother, Helge, received a small amount. No information about damage claims.

---

[506] From the Swedish Church records, courtesy Bo Björklund, Stockholm.
[507] *Emigranten Populär.* The older children had emigrated in 1905.

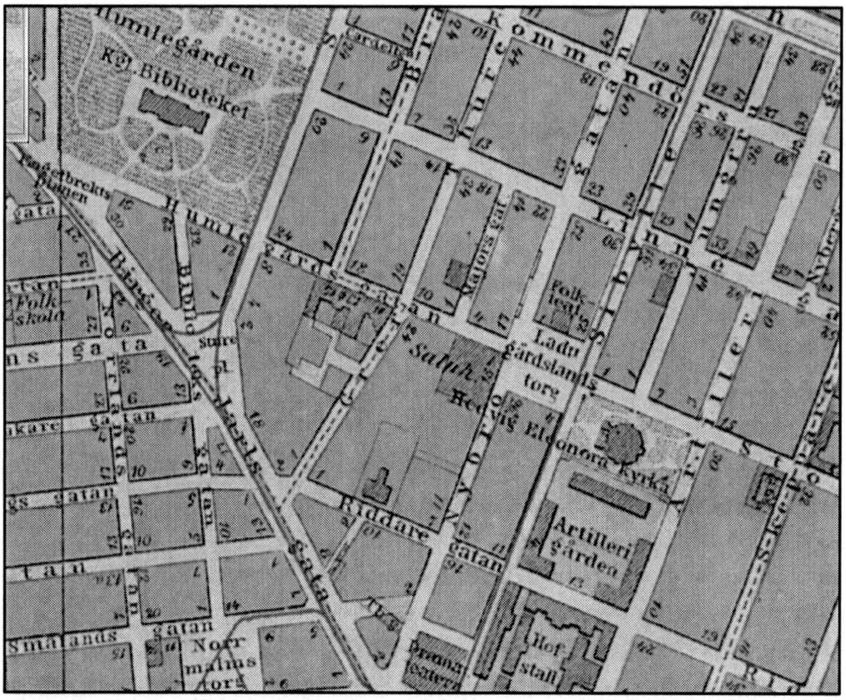

The above map of the area close to the Royal Library (Kungliga Biblioteket) in Humlegården shows Humlegårdsgatan on Östermalm where the family lived 1897-1905[508]

Spinster went to her cabin and locked the door

Lindblom, Augusta Charlotta,

The 45-year-old single emigrant woman had many relatives in America. Her sister, Mrs. John Anderson, Nicholls Avenue in Stratford, Connecticut, had written to her and persuaded her to emigrate.

Augusta was born January 20, 1867 in Kattnäs parish, Södermanland's län, the daughter of Adolf Lindblom (born in 1833 in Nikolai parish, the same county) and Anna Maria Andersdotter (born in 1827 in Björnlunda parish, the same county). Augusta emigrated March 29, 1912 from Lebro 2, Kattnäs to Connecticut. The parish register notes, "Perished in the sinking of the steamer *Titanic* in April, 1912."[509]

---

[508] Map courtesy of Bo Björklund, Stockholm.
[509] From the Swedish Church records and emigration records courtesy Björn-Åke Petersson, Kallinge, Sweden.

Augusta LIndblom sailed on the *Calypso* from Göteborg on April 5, 1912, with her residence listed as Katrinenäs, Södermanland, and her destination as New York.

The surviving passenger, Agnes Sandstrom, had become acquainted with Augusta on board the *Titanic* and learned that she was afraid of vaccinations and "everything." After the collision, she locked herself into her cabin and went to bed.[510]

There is no information about compensation to any of her relatives.

Business man wished to save his estate from creditors

Lindeberg-Lind, Erik

His parents owned the Jordanstorp *herrgård* (landed estate) in Södermanland, but lost it. He was in Sweden to save it, but the rebuilding and repair of the manor and some unsuccessful investments led to the loss of his fortune. To save himself from his debts, he decided to return to the U.S.

E. Lindeberg-Lind. Photo courtesy Günter Bäbler, Switzerland

The 42-year-old former seaman had many names. His birth name in Sweden was Erik Gustaf Åkerlind. He served in the U.S. Navy during the Spanish American War. As a first-class passenger on the *Titanic*, he used the surname Lingrey, but is listed as Lindeberg-Lind.

Born June 18, 1869 in Gryt parish, Södermanland, he was the son of estate owner Per Åkerlind (born 1832 in Gryt) and Eva Tigerschöld (born in 1838 in Gryt). In 1880, they lived at Jordanstorp, Gryt.[511]

He married, but when the marriage ended in divorce, he returned to the Jordanstorp *herrgård* and married Elsa Teresia Karsten, who had one son, Åke Raoul, from an earlier marriage.[512]

One newspaper described Erik Lind as a New York businessman, who had gone to sea at a young age and had for some time worked as a harbor pilot in New York. During the Spanish-American War, he signed on as *matros* (seaman) on an American gunboat and was promoted by the Navy to

---

[510] www.encyclopedia-titanica.org.
[511] From the Swedish Church records courtesy Björn-Åke Peterson, Kallinge, Sweden.
[512] www.encyclopedia-titanica.org.

noncommissioned officer and later to "commander." He served first on a coal steamer and then on the presidential yacht *Mayflower*. After the war ended, he established himself as a coal distributor for the Navy, but after a few years, he returned to Sweden, where he purchased and restored his former home, the Jordanstorp Estate. He continued to work as a businessman in Stockholm, and in 1912, he was on his way to New York on business. His closest survivors were his second wife and his mother.[513]

Erik has not been found under any of his names in the Swedish embarkation records. From Southampton he wrote a loving letter to his wife, Elsa, in which he warned her not to tell anyone on which ship he would be sailing. He described it as a colossal, luxurious ship that could carry 5,000 passengers. (3,500). He hoped to stay healthy so that he would be able to take care of everything. He promised to write to her every day on the ship and mail it when he came ashore. He signed his letter as "Your own lonely, Erik."[514]

Apparently, Erik used the name of Edward Lingrey because he did not want to be recognized by his ex-wife. When damages were claimed, the White Star Line refused the claim because it could not verify that he had been on board. After five years, following assurances from Mauritz Håkan Björnstrom-Steffanson that Lingrey was identical with Lind the damage claims were finally paid.[515]

Emigrant's hair turned gray in a matter of minutes

Lindell, Edvard

The 36-year-old married emigrant's former surname was Bengtsson (son of Bengt). Both he and his wife, Elin Gerda, struggled in the water. Edvard managed to climb into a lifeboat, but his wife was not strong enough. He died shortly after his wife drowned. Witnesses said that his black hair turned grey in minutes. (People who died in the lifeboats were committed to the sea.) Lindell had paid £15 ($78.00) for the tickets for himself and his wife.

Born January 31, 1876 at Mörarp 3, Mörarp parish, Malmöhus län, he was the son of farm worker Bengt Magnus Nilsson (born in 1830 in Hasslöv parish, Malmöhus län), and Botilla Johansdotter, born in 1834 in Mörarp). In 1900, Edvard lived in Helsingborg in the Hannover block and later with his wife and her parents in Gantofta, Kvisttofta parish.[516]

---

[513] *Hemlandet,* May 21, 1912.
[514] www.Titanicnorden.com.
[515] www.encyclopedia-titanica.org. Steffanson said that he had seen Lind jump from the ship and then disappeared.
[516] From Swedish Church records courtesy Björn-Åke Peterson, Kallinge, Sweden.

Edvard Lindell. Photo courtesy Günter Bäbler, Switzerland

For the last four years Lindell had worked at the shoe factory in Ramlösa, Skåne.[517]

He may have lived at Pålstorp No. 5, Skogsgatan 7, Helsingborg. Lindell and his wife are probably identical with the two victims who sailed from Helsingborg.

Their destination was A. Petterson, 10 Smith Street, Hartford, Connecticut. After the *Titanic* collided with the iceberg on April 14, 1912, Lindell and his wife met fellow Swedes August Wennerström and Gunnar Tenglin on the boat deck. As the ship sank, the four of them struggled to walk on the sloping deck until it was too steep. Clasping hands they slid back down.

The Lindell couple ended up in the water and Edvard managed to climb into a lifeboat while Gerda tried to, but was too weak. She was assisted by August Wennerstrom, but he, too, had to give up and try to safe himself. When Gerda let go of the lifeboat, her wedding ring slipped into the boat. It was found after the boat had been recovered. The ring was eventually identified and returned to her relatives.

The life insurance claims filed by his parents-in-law reportedly were $10,000 for life and $250.00 for property. [More likely the claims were for the same amounts in Swedish crowns.][518]

---

517 *Hemlandet*, May 21, 1912.
518 *Ibid.*

Newly-wed's ring found in a lifeboat

Lindell, Elin Gerda

The 30-year-old Gerda and her husband were newly weds. Both died in the sinking. She had married Edvard Lindell January 25, 1912, and they lived at Pålstorp No 5, Skogsgatan 7, Helsingborg, Skåne. They had saved a long time for their immigration to America and left Sweden from Helsingborg. Their destination was Hartford, Connecticut.

Gerda Lindell. Photo courtesy Günter Bäbler, Switzerland

When the *Titanic* sank, Gerda struggled for her life in the water and managed to reach the lifeboat, Collapsible A, but was too weak to hang on. As she let go, her wedding ring slipped off her finger and landed in the boat. The ring was found in the drifting craft by the crew of the *Oceanic* on May 13, 1912. In a long exchange of letters with the Ministry for Foreign Affairs, the Swedish Consulate, and the White Star Line, the ring was identified and sent to her father in Sweden by the White Star Line.

Born August 25, 1881 in Kvistofta parish, Malmöhus län, Gerda was the daughter of Nils Persson (born in 1843 in Raus parish, Malmöhus län), and Johanna Nilsson (born in 1842 in Bårslöv parish, same county). In 1900, Gerda lived with her parents in Kvistofta parish. She had four brothers.[519].

The Mansion House Fund paid 875 crowns (about $233.00) to her parents. In 1914, they received 1,366 crowns (about $364.00) in damage claims.[520].

[519] From Swedish Church records courtesy Björn-Åke Petersson, Kallinge, Sweden.
[520] www.encyclopedia-titanica.org.

Spokane Swede returned to his cabin to die

Lundahl, Johan

Johan S. [Svensson] Lundahl, 51, a naturalized American citizen, had emigrated in the 1880s and settled in Spokane, Washington.[521]

He had left Spokane with his family on May 27, 1910 to visit his former home in Horjemo, Mellangård Ulfö in Kronoberg's län. The Lundahls rented out their home in Spokane for three years and planned to stay in Sweden at least that long. They had bought a nice little farm in Småland, hoping to live out their lives there. But Lundahl longed for his home and Spokane and returned ahead of his family. When he realized that he could not be saved, he bid his travel companions farewell and went to his bunk to wait for the end. [522]

He was born on August 10, 1861 in Västra Torsås, Kronoberg's län, the son of Sven Johansson (born in 1821 in Västra Torsås) and Elin Abramsdotter (born in 1823 in Västra Torsås). The parents lived on a small rented farm at Lilla Näs under Knihult 4 in Härlunda parish, same county. His wife Kristina Svensson, born in 1872 in Västra Torsås, and daughter Mabel Elvira, born in 1899 in Spokane, returned to Spokane in 1913.[523]

The 1900 U.S. Census shows that John Lundahl lived with his family in Ward 3, Spokane, where he owned a home at East Carlisle Avenue. This source says that he had emigrated in 1887 and worked in a saloon. Christine Lundahl had arrived in 1895. Their daughter, Mabel, was 10 months old.

The U.S. Census for 1910 shows the family living in Ward 5, District 201, Addison Street, Spokane. John Lundahl was 48 and worked as laborer for the city. His year of immigration was reported to be 1886 and the year of naturalization, 1894. His wife, Christine, was 37 and born in Sweden. Their daughter, Mable, 10, was born in Washington State.[524]

Lundahl has not been found in the Swedish embarkation records and probably sailed from Denmark.

On June 6, 1913, Christine Lundahl, 40, and her daughter, Mable, 13, (spelling varies) sailed on the *Mauretania* and arrived in New York. Their last

---

[521] He may be identical with Johan Svensson, 23, who emigrated from Härlunda on April 16, 1885. Embarking in Malmö, he gave his occupation as hired man, and his destination as St. Peter, Minn. (*Emigranten Populär*).

[522] *Hemlandet*, Chicago, May 21, 1912. Another source stated that Lundahl had moved to Fyrnan, Urshult parish, Småland, with his wife and daughter on August 21, 1911. August Wennerstrom noted that Lundahl went back to his cabin to die.

[523] From Swedish Church records courtesy Björn-Åke Petersson, Kallinge, Sweden.

[524] The three different years listed in the U.S. Censuses for Lundahl's immigration show that it was not reliable information although it was supposed to be furnished by the resident. Oftentimes, the census taker took the information from anyone answering the door.

residence in Sweden was Västra Torsås and their destination Spokane. Before that, they had sailed together in 1902 on the *Oceanic* when Mable was two years old, arriving in New York August 20. In Spokane, Christine Lundahl applied for a U.S. passport August 3, 1921 so she could visit her mother. Born January 7, 1872 in Sweden, she had become an American citizen when she married on February 8, 1899.[525]

The Mansion House Fund paid 2,699.crowns to Lundahl's wife and daughter. In 1914, they received 5,247crowns in damage claims. The compensation equaled about $2,118.00).[526]

Educated young man was on his way to Chicago

Myhrman, Pehr Fabian Oliver M.

Oliver Myhrman. Photo courtesy Günter Bäbler, Switzerland

The 19-year-old emigrant's last residence was Strömsberg Norra, Kristinehamn, Värmland. His parents had moved from Kristinehamn to Ovanmyra, Rättvik, Dalarna, shortly before their son's departure for America.

Oliver had one sister, Anna Lisa Myhrman. He graduated from *Kristinehamns Praktiska Skola* (Business high school) and worked in the office of Kjellman & Co., Hardware Store in Kristinehamn

Born October 10, 1893 in Sollefteå, Ångermanland, Västernorrland's län, his parents were sergeant, later fanjunkare, Nils Fabian Nilsson (born 1859 in Grava parish, Värmland) and Brita Håhl (born in 1861 in Boda parish, Värmland). Oliver's emigration certificate was dated march 14, 1912.

He sailed on the *Calypso* from Göteborg April 5, 1912 with his residence listed as Kristinehamn and his destination as Chicago. He was on his way to his uncle John Anton Nelson and his wife, residing at 6256 Laflin Street,

---

525 www.ancestry.com. Passenger records and Census and Passport Applications.
526 www.ancestry.com and www.encyclopedia-titanica.org. The paper *Hemlandet* wrote on May 21, 1912 that Lundahl was a tailor.

Ogden Park Station, Chicago. Some newspapers erroneously reported that Myhrman had been saved, but it was later learned that he never entered a lifeboat.

A Swedish newspaper in Dalarna, Sweden, correctly reported that the 18-year-old Oliver Myhrman had perished in the *Titanic* disaster. He was survived by his parents in Solberga, Boda parish.[527] :

From an article in *Chicago Daily News,* we learn that Myhrman's uncle, Anton Nelson of 5256 (or 6256?) Laflin Street met a group of survivors when they stopped in Chicago to change trains. Nelson showed a picture of his nephew to Edvin Lundstrom and asked him if he had seen him. Lundstrom answered that he had seen him many times. "He was a fine boy. We all liked him. He was there on the deck when I jumped," Lundstrom said.[528]

The Mansion House fund paid 875 crowns to his parents and 456 crowns to his sister. Later, his parents received 911 crowns in damages for a total compensation of $598.00.

See more about Myhrman under Lundstrom, Thure Edwin in "The Swedish Survivors."

Farmer's son bid sad farewells

Niklasson, Samuel

The 28-year-old emigrant nicknamed Sandel came from a large family of ten children. His siblings had emigrated one by one, and when it was his turn to leave, he did so reluctantly. He bought his *Titanic* ticket in England.

Born May 15, 1883 in Västra Bogane, Myckleby parish, Göteborg's & Bohus län, Samuel was the son of Niklas Petersson (born in 1832 in Myckleby) and Peggy Charlotta Rasmusdotter (born in 1850 in Forshälla, same county). Samuel lived with his parents in 1900.[529]

His parents were farmers in Västra Bogane, Myckleby, Orust, an island on Sweden's west coast. He had nine siblings: Johan Robert, born in 1867, a sailor; Oskar Pontus, born in 1873, living in the U.S.; Olof Albert, also born in 1873. a sailor, living in the U.S.; Katharina Elisabeth, born in 1878, living in the U.S.; Antoinetta Josefina, born in 1879; Erik Birger, born in 1886, living in the U.S.; Gerda Ottilia, born in 1889, living in the U.S.; Samuel traveled with two other men from Myckleby, Karl Johan Johansson (Carl Johnson) and

---

[527] *Dalpilen*, June 14, 1912, from the Royal Library, Stockholm, digitalized files.
[528] *Chicago Daily News*, April 24, 1912. (See "Titanic news in the American Press," *Chicago Daily News*.
[529] From the Swedish Church records courtesy Björn-Åke Petersson, Kallinge, Sweden.
[530] www.titanicnorden.com

Oscar W. Johansson. Both men had lived in the U.S. and sailed on the *Calypso* from Göteborg, but Niklasson did not accompany them to England and was not be found in any Swedish embarkation records.

He is not listed as a Swedish subject on the White Star Manifest. He mailed a postcard to his parents from Southampton on April 8. It was the last time they heard from their son.

Samuel was described as quiet and unassuming. His brother, Hjalmar, was sickly and remained on the farm. The vice consul in Uddevalla, Charles Thorburn, wrote that he had been visited by an old, poor woman from the area, who told him that her son had perished in the *Titanic* disaster. Samuel's father was described as 80-years-old and his wife about the same age. Samuel supported his parents and was expected to do so to a higher degree from America. The parents were said to have very little, and now that the support from their son was eliminated, their circumstances would become severe.[531]

The Mansion House Fund paid 875 crowns to his parents, and in 1914, they received 1,822 crowns in damage claims, for a total compensation of $719.00.[532]

Man from Skåne wished to settle in St. Paul

Nilsson, August Ferdinand

Since the 21-year-old emigrant was of military age and from Skåne, he most likely bought his ticket in Copenhagen.

Born October 19, 1890 at Årröd 5, Östra Sallerup parish, Malmöhus län, he was the son of Johan Nilsson (a miller, born in 1867 in Västerstad parish, Malmöhus län and died in 1906) and Anna Jönsson (born in 1867 in Östra Sallerup.)[533]

Nilsson's last residence was at Årröd 5, Östra Sallerup. His destination was St. Paul, Minnesota. He travelled with Olof Wendel, also from Östra Sallerup. They are not listed in the Swedish embarkation records.

The Mansion House Fund paid 875 to his widowed mother, and in 1914, she received 1,822 crowns in damages for a total compensation of $719.00.

---

[531] *ibid.* No mention was made of possible support from the other nine children.
[532] www,encyclopedia-titanica.org.
[533] From Swedish church records, courtesy Björn-Åke Petersson, Kallinge, Sweden.

Uncle in Peoria paid for the farm inspector's ticket

Ödahl, Nils Martin

Nils Martin Odahl. Photo courtesy Gunter Bäbler, Switzerland

The 23-year-old emigrant had worked as a farm inspector at Ryds gård, Örsjö, Skåne. He planned to further his education in the U.S. and then return to Sweden. This man is frequently confused with Mauritz Ådahl (See first profile in this section). He has not been found in the Swedish embarkation records and likely bought his ticket in Copenhagen

Born October 22, 1888 in Örsjö parish, Malmöhus län, he was the son of shoemaker Ola Nilsson Ödahl (born in 1865 in Örsjö) and Hanna Nilsson (born in 1863 in Villie parish, Malmöhus län). The couple had six other children. In 1900, the family lived in Örsjö, No. 14. [534]

He had attended agricultural schools in Denmark. His uncle, Mr. N.O. Nelson 725 Warner Ave. Peoria, Illinois, had sent him the ticket.[535]

He left from Malmö on April 5, 1912 with his destination listed as Peoria, Illinois.[536]

The Mansion House Fund paid 875 crowns to his parents and 912 crowns to his siblings. In 1915, 954 crowns were paid in damage claims, for a total compensation of $731.00.).

Engaged woman perished after entering a lifeboat

Olsson, Elida

The 31-year-old Miss Olsson Elida worked as a maid in Malmö (Malmöhus län), 1909-1911. She intended to seek employment in St. Paul, Minnesota, where her brother, Olof Olsson, a master builder, resided. Together with

534 From Swedish church records, information courtesy Björn-Åke Petersson, Kallinge, Sweden.
535 *Hemlandet*, Chicago, May 21, 1912.
536 *Emigranten Populär.*

her fiancé, Thure Edvin Lundström, Elida traveled via Copenhagen and is not listed in the Swedish embarkation records. The surviving Lundstrom said that he had seen to that his fiancé was placed in a lifeboat. (See Lundstrom in "The Swedish Survivors.")[537]

Born January 26, 1881 in Östra Nöbbelöv parish, Kristianstad län, the daughter of fisherman Ola Olsson (born in 1845 in Östra Nöbbelöv) and Kjersti Håkansdotter (born in 1844 in Östra Nöbbelöv). She had a brother by the name of Olof, born May 21, 1886 in Östra Nöbbelöv. In 1890 the family lived at Södra Brantevik 34 in Östra Nöbbelöv. Elida is not listed as having emigrated from the parish in 1912. [538].

The Mansion Fund paid 875 crowns to her father. In 1914, he received 911 crowns in damages for a total amount $476.00.

Blacksmith bought his ticket in Copenhagen

Olsson, Nils Johan

The 28-year-old emigrant had also used the surname of Göransson in Sweden. Being of military age, he most likely bought his ticket in Copenhagen.

Born May 13, 1883 in Västra Sallerup parish, Malmöhus län, he was the son of Olof Göransson (born in 1844 in Gudmundstorp parish, Malmöhus län) and Sissa Nilsdotter (born in 1842 in Hammarlunda parish, Malmöhus län.) In 1900, they lived in Eslöv, block 77, Eslöv, Västra Sallerud parish.[539]

Nils Johan worked as a blacksmith, and his father worked in a brewery. When the father injured one of his hands, he became dependent on his son's income.

The Mansion House Fund paid 875 crowns to his parents. In 1914, they received 2,282 crowns in damage claims, for a total compensation of $842.00.

16-year old wished to support his parents

Osén, Olof Elon

The 16-year- old young emigrant had promised to support his parents once he was in the U.S.

His father was the signee for a loan of 500 crowns to pay for young Elon's ticket and other expenses. His ticket cost about 162 crowns (about $43.00).

---

[537] www.encyclopedia-titanica.org.
[538] From Swedish Church records, courtesy Björn-Åke Petersson, Kallinge, Sweden.
[539] *Ibid.*

His father, a laborer, had a stroke in November of 1912, which limited his ability to work by 50 percent. In 1914, another child, Rut, was born to the family.

Born September 24, 1895 in Nora, Vestmanland's län, Elon was the son of Erik Osén (born in 1867 in Hedesunda, Gävleborg's län) and Erika Didia Andersdotter (born in 1871 in Nora parish). In 1900, the family lived at Ön, Hedesunda parish.[540]

Elon boarded the *Calypso* in Göteborg, April 5, 1912, as Elon Olsén from Hedesunda, Gävleborg's län, headed for Mitchell, South Dakota.

Elon's siblings were Erik, Berta, Olof, Einar, Addie, Judit, Östen, and Elvin. The White Star Line reported that Elon's destination was Nils Tilberg, Ethan, South Dakota, located just to the south of the city of Mitchell.

The Mansion House Fund paid 875 crowns to the parents, and in 1914, 1,366 crowns in damage claims, for a total compensation of $598.00.

Mother of four identified and buried in Halifax

Pålsson, Alma Cornelia

Mrs. Pålsson, nee Berglund, 29, was the wife of Nils Paulson, who lived in Chicago and had sent for his family. On board the *Titanic,* Alma became acquainted with August Wennerström, and when she finally came up on deck with her children, she asked him to hold on to two of them. He did so until the water became too high and he lost his grip and both children disappeared. Wennerstrom survived, while Alma and her children perished.

Alma Pålsson

The inscription on Alma's tombstone at the Fairfax Lawn Cemetery in Halifax reads:

ALMA PAULSON LOST WITH FOUR CHILDREN
APRIL 15, 1912
WIFE OF NILS PAULSON *IN THE "TITANIC"*
TORBURG DARNIA AGED 8,
PAUL FOLKE, AGED 6,
STINA VIOLA AGED 4
GOSTA LEONARD, AGED 2
206 [Grave number]

---

[540] *Ibid.*

Born on August 3, 1882 in Välinge, Malmöhus län, Alma was the daughter of Anders Berglund (former *husar* and later coalminer, born in 1852 in Fleninge parish, Mamöhus län) and Maria Nilsson (born in 1859 in Fleninge parish). Alma had four brothers: Oskar Albert, Hilding Waldemar, Axel Ferdinand, and Gustav Gabriel Berglund. She was married to Nils Pålsson, born November 8, 1890 in Farhult parish, Malmöhus län, the son of shoemaker Pål Jönsson (born in 1837 in Farhult) and Christina Svensson (born in 1841 in Välinge). Nils worked as a coalminer in Gruvan, Bjuv.[541]

Following a general strike in Sweden in 1909, Nils quit mining. [He may have been blacklisted and unable to find another job.] The only jobs available in Bjuv were said to be miner, brick worker, and farm hand.

Nils Paulson

In 1910, Nils decided to emigrate and received his papers on June 10. His destination was Chicago, where he was employed as tram conductor and changed the spelling of his surname to Paulson. Having saved enough money to bring his family over, he sent for them in the spring of 1912. His place of residence in Chicago was 938 Townsend Street. Alma's brothers: Olof (Oskar?) Berglund lived at 2304 North Spring St. and Axel Berglund at 1725 Kimball Avenue. Alma and her children were not found in the Swedish embarkation records and may have had prepaid tickets from Copenhagen.[542]

After the tragedy, Nils clung to the hope that stories about a rescued boy might refer to one of his children. He spent much money and time looking for the boy until the Chicago office of the White Star line told him that his entire family was missing. A heart-wrenching story about his search for the family is published online with no reference to the source.

According to the online story, Paulson looked pale and ill when he leaned hungry-eyed over the desk and asked in broken English if there was an accounting for his wife and children. Chief Clerk Ivar Holmstrom scanned his list of saved third-class passengers, but failed to find their names. Paulson answered hopefully that perhaps they did not sail. Having found them on the list of those who sailed on the *Titanic*, he realized what had happened.

---

[541] Oskar (?Olof) Albert Berglund (born 18 January 1881 in Velinge, Sweden)
Hilding Waldemar Berglund (born 2 March 1884 in Velinge, Sweden)
Axel Ferdinand Berglund (born 15 March 1886 in Velinge, Sweden)
Gustav Gabriel Berglund (born 8 February 1898 in Bjuv, Sweden).

[542] It can be assumed that Alma's husband, who lived in Chicago, had sent her the tickets, possibly issued for travel from Copenhagen.

Paulsson was then assisted to a seat where he fainted. The face and hands of the unconscious man were dabbed with cold water. A friend, Gust Johnson, arrived and assisted the grief-stricken Paulson out of the building. His entire family had been wiped out.[543]

An article in *Chicago American*, Chicago, April 21, 1912, said Paulson was prostrated with grief and was placed in the care of a physician.

Alma's body, number 206, was recovered by the *Mackay-Bennett* and buried in the Fairfax Lawn Cemetery in Halifax. Her tombstone gives her name as Alma Paulson. An unknown child buried in the next plot was long thought to be the body of her child, Gösta, but later DNA tests show that he was an English boy. The bodies of Alma's children were not found.

Described as having fair hair, Alma was dressed in a brown coat, a green cardigan, dark shirt, brown skirt, boots, but with no stockings. Her effects were listed as a wedding ring; brass keeper; mouth organ; purse and two coins; a letter; 65 *kronor*; a letter from husband, Neil Paulsson (Nils) 94 Townsend St, Chicago.

The Mansion House Fund paid 875 crowns to Alma's mother. In 1914, she received 1,366 crowns in damage claims, for a total compensation of $598.00. There is no record of Nils having received any money. He remained in the U.S and died in 1962.[544]

---

[543] www.encyclopedia-titanica.org.

[544] Maria Berglund (née Nilsson) was born on 22 December 1859 in Fleninge, Sweden. Anders Berglund (born 7 August 1852 also in Fleninge).
Oskar (?Olof) Albert Berglund (18 January 1881 in Velinge, Sweden)
Hilding Waldemar Berglund (born 2 March 1884 in Velinge, Sweden)
Axel Ferdinand Berglund (born 15 March 1886 in Velinge, Sweden)
Gustav Gabriel Berglund (born 8 February 1898 in Bjuv, Sweden). In America Nils changed his name to Nels Paulsson.

Eight-year-old girl lost to the sea

Pålsson, Torborg Danira

Torborg was the 8-year-old daughter of Nils and Alma Pålsson. She was born December 19, 1903 in Bjuv, Malmöhus län.

Six-year-old boy lost to the sea

Pålsson, Paul Folke

Paul was the 6-year-old son of Nils and Alma Pålsson. He was born April 14, 1906 in Bjuv, Malmöhus län.

Three-year-old girl lost to the sea

Pålsson, Stina Viola

Stina was the 3-year-old daughter of Nils and Alma Pålsson. She was born June 19, 1908 in Bjuv, Malmöhus län.

Two-year-old boy lost to the sea

Pålsson, Gösta Leonard

Gösta was the 2-year-old son of Nils and Alma Pålsson. He was born January 3, 1910 in Bjuv, Malmöhus län. For a long time, it was thought that he was the "Unknown Child" buried near his mother, Alma, in the Fairfax Lawn Cemetery in Halifax. But later DNA evidence, proved he was an English boy.

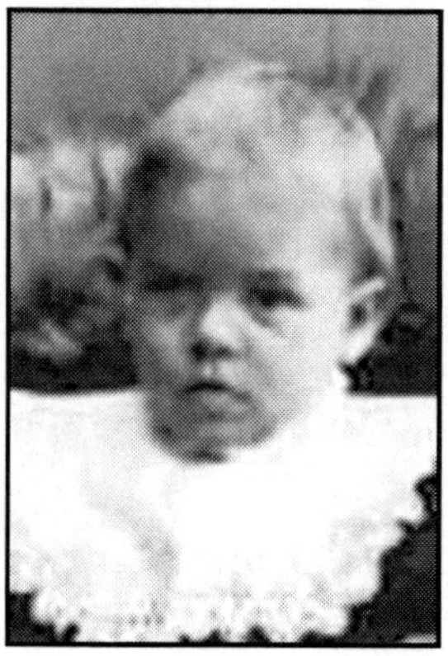

Gösta Pålsson

Young woman headed for mining town

Pettersson, Ellen Natalia

Ellen, 18, was a cousin of Jenny Henriksson and related to Wilhelm Skoog and his family. Ellen and Jenny had planned to emigrate, and when their Skoog relatives were returning to the U.S., the girls saw the opportunity to travel with them.

Born July 19, 1893 in Österplana parish, Skaraborg's län, Ellen was the daughter of Gustaf Petterson (born in 1865 in Österplana) and Anna Natalia Andersdotter (born in 1870 in Forshem parish, Skaraborg's län). The family lived in Hällekis, Mederplana parish, Skaraborg's län when Ellen moved to Stockholm December 30, 1910.[545]

She may have lived with relatives in Stockholm. Ellen's destination was Olaus Rask, 805 East 2nd Street, Iron Mountain, Michigan. She boarded the *Calypso* in Göteborg, on April 5, 1912 together with the Skoog family and Jenny Henriksson, all headed for Iron Mountain, Michigan. Ellen was listed as being from Stockholm.

The Mansion House Fund paid 874 crowns to her parents, and in 1915, they received 455 crowns in damages, for a total compensation of $354.00

Emigrant traveled with his Minnesota sister

Pettersson, Johan Emil

The 25-year-old emigrant was accompanied by his married sister, Johanna Persdotter Ahlin, who lived in Akely, Minnesota.

Pettersson boarded the *Calypso* in Göteborg, on April 5, 1912. His last residence in Sweden is listed as Västermo, Södermanland, and his destination as Chicago. His specific destination was 4947 Lincoln Avenue, Chicago. His sister also perished.

Born November 19, 1886 in Västermo parish, Södermanland's län, he was the son of Per Larsson (born in 1839 in Västermo) and Anna Stina Larsdotter (born in 1842 in Arboga.) Johan Emil lived with his parents in Närlunda, belonging to Norr Åby in Västermo, until he emigrated. His certificate is dated March 18, 1912. The church records state, "Perished along with 1600 fellow passengers when the steamer *Titanic* foundered in the Atlantic, April 15, 1912."[546]

---

[545] From Swedish Church records, courtesy Björn-Åke Petersson, Kallinge, Sweden.
[546] From the Swedish Church records, courtesy Björn-Åke Petersson, Kallinge, Sweden.

His life insurance paid 1,000 crowns ($267.00) to his father. The Mansion House Fund paid 874 crowns ($233.00) to his parents. In 1914, they received 1,366 crowns ($365.00) in damage claims.

Horticulture student on his way to Red Wing

Salander, Karl Johan

The 24-year-old emigrant had studied horticulture in England and Germany and practiced his trade in Stjärnarp, Halland.

He sailed from Malmö as Karl J. Selander, giving his residence as Tjärby and his destination as Red Wing, Minnesota.[547]

Karl had received his ticket from his brother, Gustaf Salander in Red Wing, Minnesota.[548]

Salander was born July 27, 1887 in Eldsberga parish, Halland (province and county) to master gardener Jöns Nilsson (born in 1846 in Brömmestad parish, Kristianstad län) and Kerstin Persson (born in 1855 in Vellinge, Malmöhus län). They lived in Vellinge, near Falsterbo, and in 1900 in Tjärby parish, Halland.[549]

He gave his destination as that of his brother Ernest Gustaf Salander, 1906 West Main St. Red Wing, Minnesota. In 1912, Karl's mother, Kerstin Salander, was a widow living at Daggarp, Genevad, Tjärby, Halland.

A short notice in *Red Wing Daily Republican* said that Carl Salander, nephew of Mrs. Gustaf Holmer, may have been a passenger of the ill-fated steamer *Titanic*, but that this had not been confirmed.[550]

The Mansion House Fund paid 874 crowns to his mother, and in 1914, she received 1,366 in damages and an additional 48 crowns from another fund, for a total compensation of $610.00.

---

[547] *Emigranten Populär.*

[548] *Hemlandet*, Chicago, April 30, 1912.

[549] From the Swedish Church records, courtesy Björn-Åke Petersson, Kallinge, Sweden.

[550] "Local News," April 17, p. 5. No follow-up news about him was found.

Mining engineer's career ended abruptly

Sjöstedt, Ernst Adolf

Traveling in second class, the 59-year-old married Swedish-Canadian inventor and family man was employed as a mining engineer in Sault Ste Marie, Ontario. Having earned his degree from the Stockholm School of Mining, he apprenticed with the Creusot [?] Iron Works in France before emigrating in 1878 (or 1880). In the U.S. he gained employment at Bethlehem Steel in Pennsylvania. He was on his way home to Canada.

Ernst Adolf Sjöstedt, photo courtesy Günter Bäbler, Switzerland

In 1890, Sjostedt moved to Canada to join the Nova Scotia Steel Company in Bridgeville, Nova Scotia. There, he met and married Kathleen Winslow of Nova Scotia. They had two daughters.

In 1904, he was hired by the Lake Superior Steel Company and moved to Sault Ste. Marie, Ontario. He was the inventor of the Sjostedt Sulphur Roaster and the Sjostedt Electric smelting furnace. The Canadian Department of Mining had sent him to Sweden to study methods of extracting copper-sulphide ore, as well as electric iron melting.

Upon his graduation from the School of Mining in Stockholm in 1976, he went to France. From France, he went to Bethlehem Steel Company in South Bethlehem, Pennsylvania, where he worked as assistant chemist. After that he experimented with the rusting of iron ore in Katahdin [?], Maine, and then worked for five years as the boss for the charcoal mines in Shelby, Alabama, and Cherocee [?], Georgia. He returned to Katahdin to work as superintendent for five years. He organized the Picton Charcoal Company in Nova Scotia and was the company's managing director for six years. In 1897, he established himself in Montreal as consultant engineer, and two years later he became the chief metallurgist for the Consolidated in Sault St. Marie, Ontario. Sjöstedt was an avid contributor to technical magazines, among them the *Iron Age*. He is credited with important patents for his inventions. He was a member of the American Electrochemical Society and the Swedish Engineer Society in Chicago.[551]

Born September 9, 1852 in Hjo *landsförsamling* (country parish), Skaraborg's län, he was the son of merchant Anders Gustaf Sjöstedt (born in 1822 in Skara, Skaraborg's län) and Emma Gustafva Forssell (born in 1829 in Hjo parish). Ernst Adolf emigrated December 15, 1880 from the Hjo city parish.[552] His two brothers, Professor Yngve Sjöstedt and *Direktör* Sten Sjöstedt, both lived in Sweden. Ernst Sjöstedt's name cannot be found among those who embarked from Göteborg. There is no information about claims paid.

Machinist and his entire family lost to the sea

Skoog, William

The 40-year-old married Swedish American and his wife had moved from Iron Mountain, Michigan, to Sweden in November of 1910 to establish a home, but regretted the move and decided to return to Iron Mountain. He and his wife and their four children all perished.

William and Anna Skoog (standing) with three of their four four children, Thorsten, Harald, and Mabel. Margit not included.

Skoog was related to Ellen Petterson and Jenny Henriksson. Both girls were interested in emigrating, and they appreciated the opportunity to travel with the Skoog family. Mr. Skoog paid £28 for the tickets for himself and his family, or about $136.00.

Born April 6, 1872 in Forshem, Skaraborg's län, he was the son of Anders Johan Johansson (born in 1844 in Fullösa parish, Skaraborg's län) and Kristina Svensdotter (born in 1843 in Österplana parish, Skaraborg's län). Wilhelm moved to Österplana, Skaraborg's län in 1898. On June 5, 1898, he married Anna Bernhardina Karlsdotter, born November 13, 1866 in

---

551 *Hemlandet*, Chicago, May 21, 1912.
552 From the Swedish Church records, courtesy Björn-Åke Petersson, Kallinge, Sweden.

Kinne-Vedum, Skaraborg's län, and they emigrated from Österplana on April 25, 1900.[553]

In 1900, Skoog and his wife settled in Iron Mountain, Michigan, where he worked as a machinist at the Pewabic Copper Mine and became a U.S. Citizen in 1905. William and Anna had four children, Harald, Karl, Mabel, and Margit.

The 1910 U.S. Census lists the family as follows in Ward 5, Dickinson, Iron Mountain: Skoog, William, 38, year of immigration 1900, naturalized, fireman in the mine. Wife Anna, 43, year of immigration 1900, son Carl T., 9, Mable C. 7, Harald V., 3, Margaret E, less than a month old. All the children were born in Michigan.[554]

The Skoog family had been in Sweden since November 1910 and planned to stay there, but Mr. Skoog changed his mind and they were all on their way back to Iron Mountain when they perished.[555]

The family sailed on The *Calypso* from Göteborg on April 5, 1912, listing everyone's residence as America and their destination as Iron Mountain, Michigan.

The Mansion House Fund paid 875 crowns to William Skoog's parents. In 1917 they received 911 crowns in damage claims, plus 350 crowns in 1917. The total compensation came to $570.00. William's father was not satisfied with the damage claims paid by White Star, and with the help of an American lawyer he filed a suit against the company, but refused to pay the lawyer.

Mother of four lost to the sea

Skoog, Anna

Mrs. Skoog, 43, was the wife of William Skoog and the mother of their four children. She and her husband had emigrated in 1900. The family was on the way to their hometown of Iron Mountain, Michigan. Anna was born November 13, 1868 in Hällekis, Österplana parish, Skaraborg's län. Her siblings were Eva, Hedda, Kristina, and Ludvig.

---

553 From the Swedish Church records, courtesy Björn-Åke Petersson, Kallinge, Sweden.

554 www.ancestry.com. *Hemlandet,* May 21, 1912, says that he worked as a machinist.

555 *Hemlandet*, Chicago, May 21, 1912.

Eleven-year-old boy lost to the sea

Skoog, Karl Thorsten

According to a magazine article, Karl had lost a leg in an accident when he visited the mine to bring food to his father and to watch the trains. His left leg and the toes on his right foot were crushed. He was born July 13, 1900 in Iron Mountain, Michigan, the son of William and Alma Skoog.[556]

Nine-year-old girl lost to the sea

Skoog, Mabel C.

Mabel was born July 22, 1902 in Iron Mountain, Michigan, the daughter of William and Alma Skoog.

Five-year-old-boy lost to the sea

Skoog, Harold

Harold was born August 22, 1906 in Iron Mountain, Michigan, the son of William and Alma Skoog.

Two-year-old girl lost to the sea

Skoog, Margit Elizabeth

Margit was born April 14, 1910 in Iron Mountain, Michigan, the daughter of William and Alma Skoog.

---

[556] "The Skoog Girls: Unraveling a Titanic Mystery," *The Titanic Commutator*, Volume 34, Number 189, 2010. The article is illustrated with a lovely photograph of Mabel, 9, and Margit, 2.

Husband waited for her in Indiana Harbor

Strom, Elna Matilda

The 29-year-old Mrs. Strom, nee Persson, was on the way home to her husband and their home at 3905 Grapevine Street, Indiana Harbor, Indiana. She had visited her parents in Julita with her 2-year-old daughter, Telma, but postponed her return because she had scorched her hand on hot water. The delay put her on the *Titanic.* She was accompanied by Selma's brother, Ernst Persson, who survived.

Elna Ström, right, with her sister, Alfrida. Photo courtesy of Mike Pearson

Born August 3, 1882, Elna was the daughter of Per Ulrik and Kristina Persson, Julita farm, Södermanland. Elna and her daughter sailed with her brother, Ernst Persson, on the *Calypso* from Göteborg, April 5, 1912. She was listed as Lena, residing in America. Her destination was Chicago.

On the *Titanic*, Elna and her daughter shared a cabin with Agnes Sandström and her children. (See "The Swedish Survivors.") Elna had to visit a nurse every day to have her injury checked and bandage changed. After the collision with the iceberg, the Sandströms and the Ströms lost contact on the way to the boat deck. Ernst tried to keep as close to his sister as he could, but they came too late to the lifeboats. At 2.15 a.m. when they were on the poop deck, the ship made a lurch and Ernst lost the grip of them and never saw them again.

The following describes the shock that Wilhelm Ström experienced when he received the sad news:

A wife, 20 years of age and daughter of 3 returning from a visit to relatives, were drowned. They were accompanied by her brother, who was saved. The husband, employed in a steel mill in Indiana, was terribly shocked and distressed by his loss. He spent his savings in coming to New York to search for his wife, and in assisting his brother-in-law who did not immediately secure work.... He suffered a severe injury and required hospital treatment for several weeks.[557]

Elna's husband, Wilhelm, travelled to New York to try to identify his daughter among the children who had survived, but did not find her. Some years later, he married Alma Karlsson, born July 25, 1888, originally from Trollhättan, Sweden. She worked in the home of a wealthy family on Chicago's East Side.

Wilhelm had three children with his second, wife, Anna. The eldest named Helen was born August 9, 1923. Elsie and Fred were born later. When Helen was about 6-years old, she came down with pneumonia and almost died. She later said that she could never understand why her father was so upset and protective of her. Eventually, he was blessed with seven grandchildren and nine great children. Alma passed away on July 10, 1989. Wilhelm died October 9, 1964. He had been employed as an iron worker for nearly 50 years.

The Mansion House Fund paid 874 crowns to Elna's parents on January 23, 1913. In 1914, her parents received 455 crowns in damage claims for a total compensation of about $354.00. Financial relief was also forthcoming from the American Red Cross: The amount of damage claims, if any, paid to Wilhelm Ström is not known.

Two-year-old girl lost to the sea

Strom, Telma Matilda

Her birth record as listed in Chicago, Cook County, reads Thelma Mathilda Wilhelmina Strom, born December 15, 1909 to William O. Strom and Elinor M. Peterson. Should be Elna Matilda, whose maiden name was Persson.

Elderly man did not want to go to America

Svensson, Johan

Johan lived on a small rented farm, Normans, belonging to Nennesmo Korsgård, Reftele. His wife, Brita Lisa Börjesdotter, had died February 2, 1912.[558]

---

[557] Source unknown.

Johan Svensson. Photo courtesy Gunter Bäbler, Switzerland

He was born May 17, 1837 in Kulltorp parish, Jönköping's län. His wife, Brita Lisa Börjesdotter, was born April 11, 1837 in Reftele parish, Jönköping's län. His son, Amandus (John Ekström, see profile above), was born July 29, 1866 in Reftele. Johan had two other sons, Janne Leander, born in 1870, who moved away from home in 1888, and Oskar Fritiof, who was born in 1882 and emigrated in 1902.

His son, John Ekstrom, also perished. Johan had one daughter in New Haven, Connecticut, and two sons in South Dakota. [559]

The daughter in New Haven was Mrs. John A. Larson, 165 Chatam Street.[560]

Together with his son, John Ekstrom, Johan boarded the *Calypso* in Göteborg, April 5, 1912, listing his residence as Reftele, Jönköping's län, and his destination as New York.

The Swedish-language newspaper, *Skandinavia*, Worcester, reported that Johan had planned to stay with his daughter in New Haven for a while before going to his son's home in South Dakota. (See profile for John Ekstrom.)

A song was written about this emigrant

Svensson, Olof

The words to a song about Olof and his travel companion, Eberhart Fischer, said that both worked in Skeinge and that Olof had sent a letter from Southampton on April 9. It was the last anyone heard from him.

The 24-year-old emigrant was born May 30, 1887 in Osby, Kristianstad län, the son of the hired man Sven Persson (born in 1856 in Osby) and Hanna Persdotter (also born in 1856 in Osby). In 1900, Olof lived with his

---

[558] From the Swedish Church records, courtesy Björn-Åke Petersson, Kallinge, Sweden.
[559] www.encyclopedia-titanica.org.
[560] *Hemlandet*, Chicago, April, 30, 1912.

parents in Verum parish, Kristianstad län, but is not listed as having emigrated from there in 1912.[561]

His father had died in 1902. Olof has not been found in the Swedish embarkation records, and likely bought his ticket in Copenhagen together with Eberhard Fischer, who was from the same area. Their destination is unknown. Eberhard also perished.

The Mansion House Fund paid 874 crowns to Olof's mother, and in 1913, she received 1,822 crows in damage claims, for a total compensation of $719.00.

Grave in the Atlantic replaced life in St. Paul

Vendel, Olof Edvin

The 29-year-old emigrant was not listed in the Swedish embarkation records and probably bought his ticket in Copenhagen in the company of his travel companion August Nilsson, also from Östra Sallerup, Skåne.

Born May 1, 1891 at Pårup 2, Östra Sallerup parish, Malmöhus län, he was the son of bricklayer Per Olsson Wendel, born in 1858 in Vittskövle, Kristianstad län, and Karna Jönsdotter, born in 1855 in Skurup parish, Malmöhus län.[562]

Olof had five siblings. His last residence was Östra Sallerup, Skåne and his destination St. Paul, Minnesota. Both men perished.

The Mansion House Fund paid 418 crowns to Olof's parents. Later, they received 1,366 crowns in damage claims, and an additional 350 crowns, for a total compensation of $569.00.

14-year-old girl's father lived in America

Veström, Hulda Amanda A.

The 14-year-old Hulda traveled with her Swedish-American aunt, Hulda Klasén. Born July 11, 1897 in Vänge parish, Gotland's län, she was the daughter of Oscar Adolf Weström [spelling varies] and Emma Josefina Löfqvist (born in 1872 in Vänge parish, Gotland's län, the sister of Hulda Klasén).

---

[561] From Swedish Church records courtesy Björn-Åke Petersson, Kallinge, Sweden.
[562] *Ibid.*

Notation in the parish records: "Perished along with some 1,200 to 1,500 people, among them Hulda Clasėn, nee Löfqvist, when the giant steamer *Titanic* collided with an iceberg south of Newfoundland."[563]

Hulda Amanda had at least two sisters, one of them named Johanna Maria. Their father lived in America. She traveled on the same ticket as her aunt, Hulda Klasén, nee Löfqvist. Their destination was Los Angeles. They were not found in the Swedish embarkation records and likely bought their tickets in Copenhagen.

The Mansion House Fund paid 875 crowns to the mother, and later 455 crowns in damages, for a total compensation of $355.00.

Sailor had his home on Long Island

Widegren, Carl/Charles Peter

Widegren, 51, a former sailor and Swedish American, lived in New York and was on his way home. He was married to Edit, nee Söderlund, his second wife. He traveled from Öland, where he had visited his son, Carl Edvard Widegren, a minor living in Algutsrum with Fredrik and Emma Carlsson. The son was born in North Sheath, England, and grew up to become a carpenter. According to a letter from the consulate to the ministry of foreign affairs, Widegren owned a house in Algutsrum.

Carl Widegren was born in 1861 in Sörby, Högsrum parish, Kalmar län, Öland, but had moved to Hönstorp, Algutsrum, on the island of Öland. He was the son of Johan Gustaf Widergren of Algutsrum (1830-1880) and Ingeborg Elisabeth Jeansdotter (born November 24, 1828 in Algutsrum, and also died there.) Carl Peter was married to Paulina Gustava Olsdotter, Algutsrum (1856-1889). It was noted in the church records that Carl Peter had been married in a civil ceremony in England and that his wife lived in America. It also said that he and his wife had a son.[564]

Widegren boarded the *Calypso* in Göteborg on April 5, 1912, as Charles Widegren, residing in America and returning to New York. His destination address was c/o Mrs. Ericson, Garfield Avenue, Jamaica South, Long Island, New York).

The Mansion House Fund paid 1,329 crowns to his son. In 1914 his son received 3,188 crowns, supposedly from the White Stare Line, to be held in trust by his guardian A. F. Carlsson, for a total compensation of $1,205.00.

---

[563] Her father resided in the U.S. From Swedish Church records courtesy Björn-Åke Petersson, Kallinge, Sweden.

[564] From the Swedish Church records courtesy Björn-Åke Petersson, Kallinge, Sweden.

A few caveats

There are many "what ifs" when it comes to the *Titanic.*

1. What **if** the wireless message received at 9:40 p.m. with the warning about heavy ice and bergs in the path of the *Titanic* had been delivered to the bridge? Would that have changed the outcome?

A surviving officer deemed it fatal that the captain did not get that message. The wireless operator working at the time did not survive.

2. What **if** the lookouts had had the benefit of binoculars? Would that have changed the outcome?

The binoculars were bad according to lookout Fredrick Fleet, who testified at the Senate Hearing. Officer Murdoch on the bridge, who had binoculars, saw the berg himself and immediately ordered the officer at the wheel to change course, but it was too late. Murdoch had the lives of more than 2,000 people to consider and had to act in a split second. He perished.

3. What **if** the rivets that held the *Titanic's* plates together had been stronger? Would that have prevented the sinking?

Perhaps it could have delayed the sinking, but good steel was in short supply at the time the *Titanic* was built. The builder chose to use steel rivets for the hull of the ship and iron rivets for the rest. The iceberg hit the side of the bow.

4. What **if** the captain on a nearby ship, the *Californian*, had responded to the rockets sent up by the *Titanic*? Would that have saved lives?

The *Californian* reported that it was stuck in ice and unable to move. There are those who say that the *Californian* could have made it in time to save all the people who were not in the lifeboats.

The general opinion was, and is, that Captain Lord should at least have tried. It took the *Californian* two hours to arrive at the scene in the morning. Covering the same distance at night surrounded by ice would have taken longer.

5. What **if** there had been lifeboats for all on board? Would that have made a difference?

Since the *Titanic* sank in less than 2 ½ hour, there would not have been time to launch more lifeboats. The last boat floated off the deck by itself when the water engulfed the ship. Some of the boats were not filled because the women were reluctant to come forward. They were afraid of descending 70 feet onto the dark water and felt safer on the ship. They were unaware of how fast the ship was sinking and that it was a matter of life and death.

Current historians place the blame on Captain Smith for not saving more people in the available boats:

"If Smith had not failed in his duty, all these lifeboats could have been loaded to their stated capacity in time, or even with many more, for the numbered capacity reflected shipyard workers, not women and children and, in the flat calm conditions that night, the first boat to leave *Titanic's* side, with a capacity of 40, contained just 12 people"[565]

[565] Paul Louden-Brown, Edward Kamuda and Karen Kamuda in "Titanic Myths."

The 2012 Anniversary

Poem by Dick Stahl[566]

The target date is April 15, 2012, arriving
at the exact spot
deep in the North Atlantic
where the unsinkable White Star Liner Titanic
sank.

I hope Frederick Fleet, standing high
in the crow's nest, has found
a pair of binoculars
by this time and sees the berg dead ahead earlier
than before

and calls down
to the bridge so the great ship can turn
safely. I hope Captain John Edward Smith slows the ship
down this time so as not
to make the racy New York headlines.

I hope the other steerage passengers
with me will be welcome
on the top deck the moment the deck ice
rains down

like little stars so we can climb up
to the millionaires before
going down
two and half miles

as the musicians bravely play on
as the last lifeboat
splashes down.

---

566 Published by permission from Dick Stahl.

Bbliography

Books:

Beavis, Debbie. *Who Sailed On Titanic? The Definitive Passenger Lists.* Ian Allan Publishing, Hersham, Surrey, UK, 2002.

Barratt, Nick. Lost Voices from the Titanic. Palgrave Macmillan, New York, New York, 2010.

Denny, Ron. *Shadow of the Titanic: A Survivor's Story.* The Biography of Eva Hart, MBE, JP as told by Ron Denney with a Foreword by Peter Bottomley, MP. Chadwell Press, Sevenoaks, Kent, UK. 2nd ed., 2000. (Greenwich University Press, 1994).

Eaton, John P. and Haas, Charles A. *Titanic: A Journey Through Time.* W-W. Norton & Company, New York and London, 1999.

Geller, Judith B. Titanic: *The Artifact Exhibition.* RMS Titanic, Inc. Atlanta, GA 2009.

Hustak, Allan. *Titanic: The Canadian Story.* Vėhicule Press, Montreal, Quebec, Canada, 1998.

Kohl, Chris. *Titanic: The Great Lakes Connections.* Seawolf Communications, Inc. West Chicago, Ill., 2000.

Lord, Walter. *A Night to Remember: The Classic Account of the Final Hours of the Titanic.* 2nd ed., Henry Holf & Company, LLC, New York, NY, 2006. (Holt, Rinehart & Winston, 1955.)

Merideth, Lee W. *Titanic: A Complete List of the Passengers and Crew.* Rocklin Press, Sunnyvale, Cal., 2002.

Molony, Senan. *The Irish Aboard Titanic.* Wolfhound Press, Ltd, Dublin, Ireland, 2000.

Sebak, Per Kristian. *Titanic: 31 Norwegian Destinies.* Genesis, Oslo, Norway, 1998.

The story of the Titanic as told by its survivors. Jack Winocour, ed. Dover Publications, New York, 1960.

This book contains reprints of the following survivor accounts:

Beesley, Lawrence. *The Loss of the S.S. Titanic: Its Story and Its Lessons.* Copyright 1912 by Lawrence Beesley.

Gracie, Archibald, Colonel. *The Truth About the Titanic.* Copyright 1913 by Mitchell Kennerley.

Lightoller, Commander. *Titanic.* This section originally appeared as Chapters 30-35 in the book *Titanic and Other Ships.* Ivor Nicholson and Watson, 1935.

Bride, Harold. "Thrilling Tale by Titanic's Surviving Wireless man." As told in *New York Times*, April 28, 1912.

Titanic: An Illustrated History. Text by Don Lynch. Paintings by Ken Marschall. Madison Press Books, Toronto, Ontario, Canada, 1998.

The Titanic Disaster hearings: The Official Transcripts of the 1912 Senate Investigation. Tom Kuntz, editor. Pocket Books, 1998,

Wetterholm, Claes-Göran. *Letters from the Titanic.* Postal Museum Publication No. 48, Stockholm, Sweden, 2000.

Articles:

Wetterholm, Claes-Göran. "Titanic International mourns Beatrice Sandström: Swedish Titanic survivor passes away at age 85." In *Voyage*, Summer/Autumn, 1995, p. 45.

"The Last American Survivor of the Titanic Disaster: October 21, 1906- May 6, 2006." The Editors. In *The Titanic Commutator*, Volume 30, Number 173, 1906. Indian Orchard, Mass.

"Voices Cast Upon the Sea: Minnesota's Titanic Passengers." In *Minnesota History: The Quarterly of the Minnesota Historical Society.* 60/7 Fall 2007.

Microfilms:

Swedish Church records (birth, re-location, and household records) researched by genealogists in Sweden.

Swedish-American Church records. Swenson Swedish Immigration Research Center, Augustana College, Rock Island, Illinois.

Swedish-American Newspapers, Swenson Swedish Immigration Research Center, Augustana College, Rock Island, Illinois.

The New York Times, New York, April 1912. Augustana College Library, Rock Island, Illinois.

Data bases:

Emigranten Popular, CD containing Swedish embarkation records for the cities of Gothenburg and Malmo, produced by the Swedish Emigrant Institute, Växjö, Sweden.

The *Calypso* manifest of passengers traveling from Gothenburg to Hull, England, April 5, 1912. Swenson Swedish Immigration Research Center, Augustana College, Rock Island, Illinois.

Online records:

Swedish digitalized newspapers.

American digitalized newspapers

Web sites:

www.encyclopedia-titanica.org

www.ancestry.com

www.titanicnorden.com

www.findagrave.com

About the author

Lilly Setterdahl is a native of Sweden. For some thirty years she assisted her husband, Lennart, in his research about the Swedish immigrants in the United States, Canada, and lastly in Australia. She began her writing career in the 1970s by writing research articles and books about the Swedes in America, their settlements, and their accomplishments. This volume is her fourteenth nonfiction book. She has also written two historical novels: *Maiden of the Titanic* (2007) and *Hero of the Titanic* (2011).

Lilly has received many awards for her research and writing.

Cross references

Åkerlind, Erik Gustaf, see Lindeberg-Lind
Anderson, Anna Elisabeth, see Dyker, Elisabeth
Andersson, August Edvard, see Wennerstrom, August
Bengtsson, Agnes Charlotta, see Sandstrom, Agnes
Berggren, Carolina, see Byström, Karolina
Bjorklund, Vilhelm Henry, see Tornquist, William Henry
Brogren, Alfrida, see Andersson, Alfrida Konstantia
Brogren, Anna Sigrid, see Danbom, Anna Sigrid
Carlson, Einar, see Karlsson, Einar
Christensen, Bertha, see Nilsson, Berta
Forsander, Vivian, see Ohman, Velin
Göransson, Nils Johan, see Olsson, Nils Johan
Gustafson, Anna, see Nysten, Anna
Johannesson, Johan Henrik, see Kvillner, Johan Henrik
Johanson, Oscar W., see Olsson/Johansson, Oscar W.
Johansson, Amandus, see Ekstrom, John
Johnson, Adelia, see Landergren, Adelia
Johnson, Carl Olof, see Jansson, Carl Olof
Johnson, Charlie, see Johnsson, Karl
Johnson, John Cervin, See Svensson, Johan Cervin
Jonsson, Karolina, see Bystrom, Karolina
Larson, Hilda, see Hellstrom, Hilda
Lind, Erik Gustaf, see Lindeberg-Lind
Linder, Helmina, see Nilsson, Helmina
Lingrey, Edward, see Lindeberg-Lind
Lofquist, Hulda Kristina, see Klasén, Hulda Kristina
Lustig, Dagmar, see Bryhl, Dagmar
Lustig, Kurt, see Bryhl, Kurt
Olsson, Oscar W., see Johansson, Oscar W.
Olsén, Olof Elon, see Osén, Olof Elon
Påhlsson, see Pålsson
Palmquist, Oscar, see Johansson, Oscar Leander
Paulson, see Pålsson
Persdotter, Johanna, see Ahlin, Johanna
Rondberg, Edward, see Larsson Rondberg
Shuman, Eleanor, see Johnson, Eleanor
Svensson, Johan, see Lundahl, Johan
Turnquist, see Tornquist

Name Index for Swedish Passengers

A

Ådahl, Mauritz · 210
Ahlin, Johanna Persdotter · 211
Andersson, Alfrida Konstantia · 214
Andersson, Anders Johan · 212
Andersson, Ebba Iris Alfrida · 215
Andersson, Ellis Anna Maria · 216
Andersson, Ida Augusta M · 216
Andersson, Ingeborg Constantia · 215
Andersson, Johan Samuel · 217
Andersson, Sigrid Elisabeth · 215
Andersson, Sigvard Harald Elias · 215
Andreasson, Paul Edvin · 217
Aronsson, Ernst Axel A · 218
Asplund, Carl Edgar · 222
Asplund, Carl Oscar · 219
Asplund, Clarence Gustaf Hugo · 222
Asplund, Felix · 111
Asplund, Filip Oscar · 222
Asplund, Johan Charles · 104
Asplund, Lillian Gertrud · 111
Asplund, Selma · 106
Augustsson, Albert · 222

B

Bengtsson, Jon Viktor · 223
Björklund, Ernst Herbert · 224
Björnstrom-Steffanson, Mauritz Håkan · 114
Braf, Elin Ester Maria · 225
Brobeck, Karl Rudolf · 226
Bryhl, Dagmar Lustig · 118
Bryhl, Kurt Arnold Gottfrid Lustig · 227
Bystrom, Karolina · 121

C

Carlsson, August Sigfrid · 228
Carlsson, Carl Robert · 229
Carlsson, Frans Olof · 229

D

Dahlberg, Gerda Ulrika, · 230
Danbom, Anna Sigrid M · 233
Danbom, Ernst Gilbert Danbom · 231
Danbom, Gilbert Sigvard E · 234
Dyker, Adolf Fredrik Dyker · 234
Dyker, Anna Elisabeth Judit · 123

E

Edvardsson, Gustaf Hjalmar · 235
Eklund, Hans Linus · 235
Ekstrom, John · 236
Enander, Ingvar · 238

F

Fischer, Eberhart Thelander · 239

G

Gustafsson, Karl Gideon · 240

H

Hedman, Oscar · 125
Hellström, Hilda Maria · 131
Henriksson, Jenny Lovisa · 240
Holm, John Fredrik Alexander · 241

J

Jansson, Carl Olof · 134
Johansson, Erik · 242
Johansson, Gustaf Joel · 242
Johansson, Karl Johan · 243
Johansson, Nils Johan · 244

Johansson, Oscar Leander · 140
Johansson, Oscar W. Olsson · 142
Johnson, Eleanor Ileen · 147
Johnson, Elisabeth (Alice) · 144
Johnson, Harold T · 146
Johnson, Malkolm Joakim · 246
Johnsson, Karl · 147
Jönsson, Nils Hilding · 247

K

Karlson, Nils August · 249
Karlsson, Einar Gervasius · 153
Karlsson, Julius Konrad Eugen · 247
Klasen, Gertrud Emilia · 251
Klasen, Hulda Kristina · 249
Klasen, Klas Albin · 250
Kvillner, Johan Henrik · 251

L

Landergren, Aurora Adelia · 155
Larsson, August Viktor · 252
Larsson, Bengt Edvin, · 253
Larsson, Edvard · 254
Lindahl, Agda Torilda Viktoria · 254
Lindblom, Augusta Charlotta, · 256
Lindeberg-Lind, Erik · 257
Lindell, Edvard · 258
Lindell, Elin Gerda · 260
Lindström, Sigrid Posse · 156
Lundahl, Johan · 261
Lundin, Olga Elida · 156
Lundström, Thure Edvin · 160

M

Myhrman, Pehr Fabian Oliver M · 262

N

Niklasson, Samuel · 263
Nilsson, August Ferdinand · 264
Nilsson, Berta Olivia · 163
Nilsson, Helmina Josefina · 165
Nysten, Anna · 166

O

Ödahl, Nils Martin · 265
Öhman, Velin · 170
Olsson, Elida · 265
Olsson, Nils Johan · 266
Osén, Olof Elon · 266

P

Pålsson, Alma Cornelia · 267
Pålsson, Gösta Leonard · 270
Pålsson, Paul Folke · 270
Pålsson, Stina Viola · 270
Pålsson, Torborg Danira · 270
Persson, Ernst Ulrik · 172
Pettersson, Ellen Natalia · 271
Pettersson, Johan Emil · 271

S

Salander, Karl Johan · 272
Sandstrom, Agnes Charlotta · 183
Sandstrom, Beatrice Iren · 184
Sandstrom, Marguerite Rut · 184
Sjöstedt, Ernst Adolf · 273
Skoog, Anna · 275
Skoog, Harold · 276
Skoog, Karl Thorsten · 276
Skoog, Mabel C. · 276
Skoog, Margit Elizabeth · 276
Skoog, William · 274
Strom, Elna Matilda · 277
Strom, Telma Matilda · 278
Svensson, Johan · 278
Svensson, Johan Cervin · 185
Svensson, Olof · 279

T

Tenglin, Gunnar Isidor · 191
Tornquist, William Henry · 195

V

Vendel, Olof Edvin · 280
Veström, Hulda Amanda A. · 280

W

Wennerström August Edvard · 197
Widegren, Carl/Charles Peter · 281

CPSIA information can be obtained at www.ICGtesting.com
Printed in the USA
BVOW06s1214070913

330577BV00005B/17/P